THE CORPORATION THAT CHANGED THE WORLD

THE CORPORATION THAT CHANGED THE WORLD

How the East India Company Shaped the Modern Multinational

NICK ROBINS

Orient Longman

ORIENT LONGMAN PRIVATE LIMITED

Registered Office
3 6 752 Himayatnagar, Hyderabad 500 029 (A.P.), India
Email: cogeneral@orientlongman.com

Other Offices
Bangalore, Bhopal, Bhubaneshwar, Chennai
Ernakulam, Guwahati, Hyderabad, Jaipur
Kolkata, Lucknow, New Delhi, Patna

This book was originally published by Pluto Press
Pluto Press, 345 Archway Road,
London N6 5AA, United Kingdom

First Published in India by Orient Longman 2006

ISBN 81 250 3022 0

Printed at
Pragati Offset Pvt. Ltd., Hyderabad 500 004

Published by
Orient Longman Private Limited
3 6 752, Himayatnagar
Hyderabad 500 029
Email: hyd2_ollhyd@sancharnet.in

The coastline and external boundary of India as depicted in the maps in this book are neither correct nor authentic.

For our parents and our children

Contents

Lists of Tables, Figures, Maps and Illustrations	viii
Acknowledgements	ix
Introduction	x
Chronology	xiv
1 The Hidden Wound	1
2 This Imperious Company	19
3 Out of the Shadows	39
4 The Bengal Revolution	58
5 The Great East Indian Crash	81
6 Regulating the Company	99
7 Justice Will be Done	117
8 A Mercantile Sovereign	141
9 Unfinished Business	168
Notes	191
Select Bibliography	205
Index	210

Lists of Tables, Figures, Maps and Illustrations

TABLES

1.1 The changing share of world GDP 1600–1870 7
2.1 Corporate governance compared 31
3.1 Dutch and English East India Company exports from Asia 1688–1780 55
8.1 The opium trade with China 1800–1879 152

FIGURES

2.1 The Company's share price 1693–1874 26
5.1 The Company's share price 1757–1784 88

MAPS

1 The Company's world xvi
2 India in the late 1760s 62
3 The Company's London 171

ILLUSTRATIONS

1.1 Spiridione Roma, *The East Offering Her Riches to Britannia*, 1778 2
2.1 William Daniell, *East India Docks*, 1808 21
7.1 Unknown, *East India House*, late eighteenth century 131
8.1 *Punch, Execution of 'John Company'*, 1857 165
9.1 Statue of Robert Clive, London 169

Acknowledgements

This book started with a walk, and I'd like to express my appreciation to all those who came all or part of way with me. None of this would have happened without my wife, Ritu, who was not just the inspiration for the book, but its sustainer – providing the patience and encouragement that brought the journey to an end.

I'd also like to express my gratitude to Jane Trowell of Platform in London who co-hosted the East India Company walks, which have been such great sources of ideas and insights into the corporation's London presence: see <www.platformlondon.org> for details of future walks and the wider Museum of the Corporation project.

Numerous others read through drafts and provided indispensable feedback, notably Huw Bowen, Peter Kinder, James Marriott, Prasannan Parthasarathi, Rajiv Sinha, John Sabapathy, Andrew Simms and Jonathon Sinclair-Wilson. The Delhi seminar that Anu Bhasin and Ranjan Pal organised proved extremely valuable in testing some of the emerging themes of the book. I'd like to thank Huw Bowen for graciously allowing me to read the pre-publication proofs of his work, *The Business of Empire*, and Jack Greene for allowing me to quote from his *Arenas of Asiatic Plunder*.

I am indebted to the Al-Furqan Islamic Heritage Foundation based at Eagle House in Wimbledon for allowing me to use its library during the summers of 2004 and 2005 to write the book.

Satish Kumar first published my initial thoughts on the Company in the pages of *Resurgence* magazine, and Mari Thekekara first suggested that it should be turned into a book. Jem Bendell, Sushil Chaudhury, Kate Crowe, Ram Gidoomal, Caspar Henderson, Hameeda Hossain, Leslie Katz, Malcolm McIntosh, Derek Morris, Steven Pincus, Munro Price, John Robins, Richard Sandbrook, David Somerset and Halina Ward all helped in their different ways with the research process.

For me, this book is an attempt to grapple with the shared past of Britain and Asia, confronting the Company's legacy so that future interactions can be based on principles of justice. This book is therefore dedicated to our parents and to our children: Elizabeth and John, Pushpa and Sushil, and Oliver, Joshua and Meera.

The author and publisher would like to thank the following individuals and institutions for their kind permission to use their images in this book: Illustration 1.1: the British Library; Illustration 2.1: Museum of London; Illustration 8.1: Punch Ltd; Illustration 9.1: Andrew Simms. The maps were drawn by The Argument by Design. The Agha Shahid Ali verse on page 78 is reproduced by permission of Wesleyan University Press.

Wimbledon, January 2006

Introduction

The year 2000 was the 400th anniversary of the founding of the English East India Company. It was also the year that I came to work in the City of London, where the Company had been headquartered throughout its 275-year existence. Then and now, the City forms one of the major hubs of international finance. As the new millennium opened, market euphoria was still in the air, though with hindsight the crazed dot.com bubble had already peaked on the last day of 1999. I was entering the world of socially responsible investment as this speculative surge started to implode, revealing malpractice on a scale not seen since 1929. Once started, the slide in share values kept going for three full years until prices had halved. Momentarily, there were signs of humility on the trading floors. Across the world, inquiries got under way to discover if it was just a few 'bad apples' at Enron, Worldcom and Tyco who were to blame, or whether the entire 'barrel' of corporate capitalism was at fault.

Seeking relief from the red trading screens that spelled continued market decline, I explored the historic streets of the Square Mile, past the Royal Exchange and the Bank of England, down Exchange Alley where jobbers had first gathered in the coffee houses to swap rumour and trade shares. One day, I walked further east, heading along Leadenhall Street, aiming to visit the site of the East India Company's headquarters and then head back to work. I was in for a surprise. When I reached the corner of Leadenhall and Lime Street, where East India House had stood for over two hundred years, there was nothing – no sign, no plaque, nothing to mark the fact that this was the location where the world's most powerful corporation had once been based. In a country that is drenched in the culture of heritage, this absence puzzled me: why had this historic Company been so completely erased from the face of London?

This book is an attempt to answer this question and, more importantly, to re-examine the meaning of the Company's legacy for the global economy of the twenty-first century. As I delved deeper into this corporation from the Age of Enlightenment, it became clear that this was not just a thing of the past, but an institution whose practices were strikingly familiar. The Company had pioneered the shareholder model of corporate ownership and built the foundations for modern business administration. With a single-minded pursuit of personal and corporate gain, the Company and its executives eventually achieved market dominance in Asia, ruling over large swathes of India for a profit. But the Company also shocked its age with the scale of its executive malpractice, stock market excess and human oppression. For me, the parallels with today's corporate leviathans soon became overpowering, with the Company outstripping Wal-Mart in terms of market power, Enron for corruption and Union Carbide for human devastation.

There are countless histories of the East India Company, yet none address its social record as a corporation. This is a gap that this book seeks to fill, recovering a sense of the ferocious struggles over corporate accountability that the Company generated in the eighteenth century. Importantly, this is not an exercise in applying twenty-first-century values to an earlier age. Leading lights of its own times examined its practices and found them wanting. Adam Smith, Edmund Burke and Karl Marx were all united in their critique – for quite different reasons – of this domineering, overbearing corporation. From the right to the left of the political spectrum, those who lived with the Company saw the corporation as a fundamentally problematic institution. For Smith, the corporation was one of the great enemies of the open market, while for Burke it posed a revolutionary threat to the established order in Britain and India. It also exhibited ethical failings of a structural nature. 'Every rupee of profit made by an Englishman', Burke told Parliament, 'is lost forever to India.'[1] And for Marx, writing 70 years later as the Company was on its last legs, it was the standard-bearer of Britain's 'moneyocracy', a more terrible creation than 'any of the divine monsters startling us in the Temple of Salsette' near Mumbai.[2] Yet, what makes the Company's story so inspirational is the way that its bid for unbounded economic power was repeatedly met by individuals such as these struggling to make it accountable. As a result, the Company provides timeless lessons on how (and how not) to confront corporate excess through reform, protest, litigation, regulation, and, ultimately, through corporate redesign.

To recover a sense of the Company's physical presence, I decided to take the investigation out of academia and encounter the Company's heartlands in Britain and India. By revisiting its headquarters and its warehouses, its mansions and its docks, I hoped to gain a much fuller understanding of the Company's character. The book has a narrative structure, but moves between past and present. To aid the reader, a chronology of milestones in the Company history is provided. The first chapter then delves deeper into its contested legacy, and explores the very different ways it is remembered in Europe and Asia. This is followed in Chapter 2 by an analysis of the Company's metabolism, examining its systems of governance and finance, as well as the inherent tensions that led to its downfall. Its initial trajectory as a seventeenth-century 'spice trader' is laid out in Chapter 3, along with the catastrophic consequences of its first bid for market supremacy in the 1690s. Eventually, the Company managed to engineer the takeover of Bengal in the middle of the eighteenth century: the causes and consequences of this momentous event are discussed in Chapter 4.

But like so many corporations in the 1990s, the East India Company over-reached itself. Chapter 5 describes how incompetence and negligence combined to produce a stock market crash and one of India's worst famines. Many in Britain feared that the Company would use its new-found wealth to end England's hard-won liberties. Chapter 6 reviews Adam Smith's ferocious critique of the corporation and places it in the context of the wider movement of public protest, parliamentary activism and outright rebellion that sought to end the Company's abuses in the 1770s. Yet, justice was still not done, and Chapter 7 examines how Edmund Burke tried to place responsibility at the heart of the Company's charter. But the imperatives of empire and not ethics won the day. Chapter 8 explores how the British state successfully transformed the Company so that it progressively shed its commercial functions and became the profit-making agent of the British Crown in India. Rebellion in 1857 signalled the end of the Company's anachronistic position, placing it in a twilight zone before it was wound up in June 1874. Finally, Chapter 9 looks at how a more honest encounter with the Company's legacy can be achieved, and what lessons can be drawn for today's encounter with the global corporation.

A peculiar amnesia continues to hang over the role that corporations such as the East India Company had in the creation of the modern world. My hope is that this book will go some way to revealing how much just one company shaped the global past, and how we can use this knowledge to make today's corporate sector more fully accountable in the present.

A NOTE ON THE TEXT

As the spelling of Indian place names has changed over time, the wording used in the past is generally preferred in historical contexts (thus Calcutta), and current spelling applied for references to the present (thus Kolkata).

To give the Company's affairs greater immediacy, I have also converted some of the key financial statistics into current values. For this, I have used the online service provided by Economic History Resources, <www.eh.net>.

Chronology

1498	Portuguese fleet led by Vasco da Gama arrives off the Malabar coast
1595	Dutch Compagnie Van Verre established to take the ocean route to the East
1600	31 December: English East India Company (EIC) established
1602	Formation of the Dutch Verenigde Oostindische Compagnie (VOC)
1618	English Company negotiates first trade agreement with the Mughal Empire
1623	EIC merchants executed at Amboina (Indonesia) by VOC forces
1639	Fort St George at Madras established by the English Company
1648	The EIC moves headquarters to East India House at Leadenhall Street
1657	The EIC becomes a permanent joint stock corporation
1668	Bombay transferred to the EIC by King Charles II
1681	Josiah Child first elected as EIC governor (chairman)
1686–89	Child launches war with Mughal Empire
1690	Company establishes new base in Bengal at Calcutta
1695	First parliamentary investigation into Company corruption
1698	Parliament awards monopoly of Asia trade to the New Company
1709	Merger of New and Old Companies finalised
1717	Company receives comprehensive trade privileges (*firman*) in Mughal India
1721	Bubble in South Sea Company shareprices implodes
1729	Qing Empire bans import of opium except for medicinal purposes
1751–52	Robert Clive wins siege of Arcot
1756	Calcutta captured by Nawab of Bengal and 'black hole' incident
1757	February: Recapture of Calcutta by EIC 23 June: EIC troops under Clive defeat the Nawab at Plassey
1764	EIC defeats an alliance of Mughals, Bengal and Awadh at Buxar

1765	Clive acquires the management of the Bengal treasury (*diwani*) for the EIC
1769	Peak of 'Bengal Bubble' in the Company's shares
1770	Bengal Famine: between 1 and 10 million die of starvation
1772	Company appeals to government for financial assistance
1773	Regulating Act passed to reform EIC governance, and Warren Hastings becomes first Governor-General of India. Tea Act passed to encourage sale of EIC tea in the Americas; in December, American patriots dump EIC tea in Boston harbour
1776	Publication of Adam Smith's *Wealth of Nations*
1778	Spiridione Roma's *Offering* installed at East India House
1780	Duel between Philip Francis and Warren Hastings in Calcutta
1781	Hastings sends shipments of opium to China
1783	Failure of Charles James Fox and Edmund Burke's East India Bill
1784	William Pitt's India Act passed, increasing state powers over the EIC
1788	Start of impeachment trial of Warren Hastings in the House of Lords
1793	'Permanent Settlement' of Bengal's finances and new Charter Act, breaching Company trade monopoly for first time
1795	Warren Hastings acquitted at impeachment trial
1799	Dissolution of Dutch VOC, and conquest of Mysore by EIC
1806	Opening of new East India Dock
1813	Company loses monopoly of trade with India
1833	Parliament ends the Company's commercial operations; remains as territorial administrator in India
1839–42	First Opium War between Britain and China
1856–60	Second Opium War, resulting in legalisation of opium in China
1857	Outbreak of Indian Mutiny or First War of Independence in northern India
1858	Parliament replaces Company with direct British rule in India
1861	East India House demolished
1874	1 June: Dissolution of English East India Company

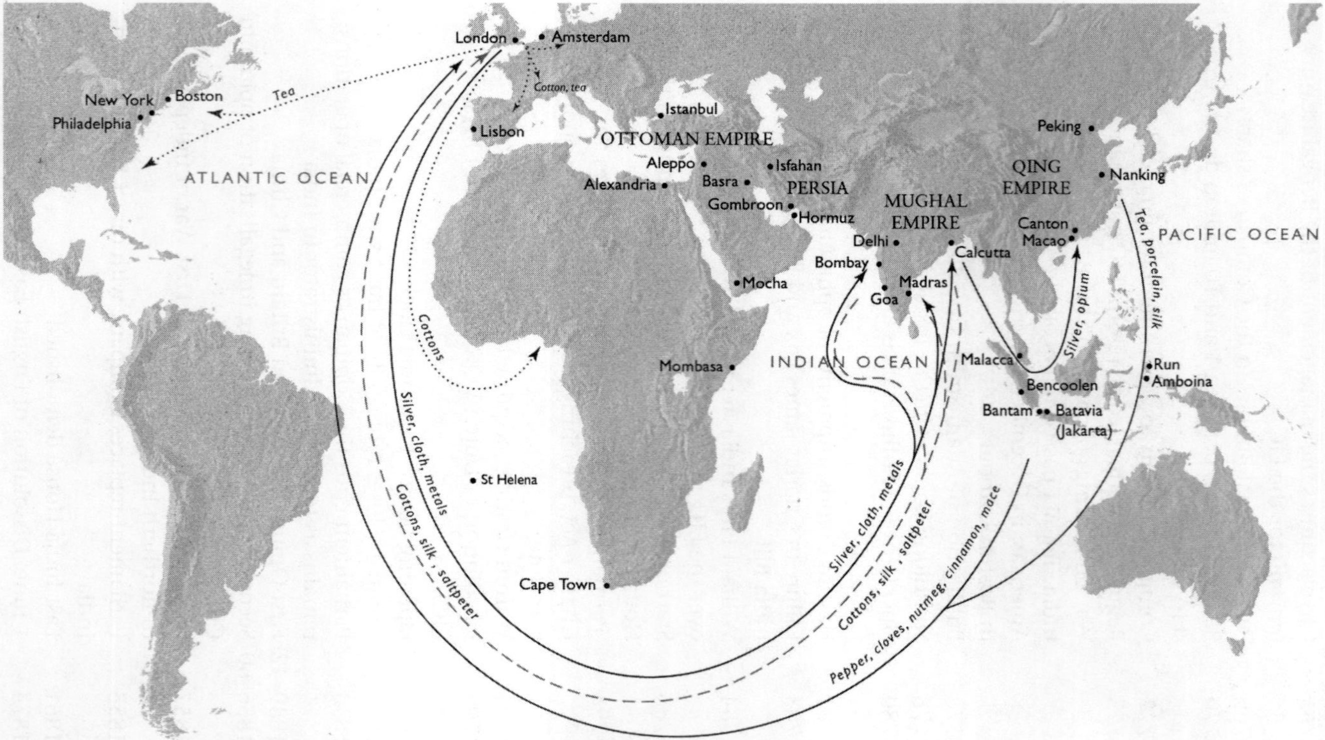

Map 1 The Company's world

1
The Hidden Wound

THE OFFERING

In 1778, the directors of the Honourable East India Company installed an extravagant new painting in their London headquarters, East India House. Like much corporate art before and since, the quality of the painting was generally regarded as poor, with one commentator describing it as 'a work too feeble to confer any credit either on the artist or his employers'.[1] But the directors were not seeking applause for the artistic merit of their commission. Ten feet across and over eight feet high, Spiridione Roma's giant allegory of *The East Offering Her Riches to Britannia* was designed to impress (see Illustration 1.1). Fixed to the ceiling of the Company's revenue committee room, where the directors monitored the flow of profit and loss, the purpose of *The Offering* was simple: to convey the commercial domination that the Company had now achieved in Asia.

At the heart of the painting is the relationship of three women, each representing their country. The scene is an Asian shoreline. Sitting high on a rock high to the left, a fair Britannia looks down on a kneeling India who offers her crown surrounded by rubies and pearls. Beside her, China presents her own tribute of porcelain and tea. From a grove of palms trees to the right comes a convoy of labourers carrying bales of cloth, along with an elephant and a camel, all directed westward by a stern Mercury, the classical god of commerce. The British lion sits at Britannia's feet, as does Old Father Thames, a sign that it was to London that much of this wealth would flow.[2] Far off, beyond the figures, one of the Company's famous merchant ships sails into the distance, laden with the treasure of the East, its striped ensign fluttering in the wind.

For *The Offering*, Spiridione drew on a long line of similar depictions of European trading supremacy. The early success of the Honourable Company's main rival, the Dutch United East India Company (Verenigde Oostindische Compagnie – VOC), had provided Pieter Isaacsz with the inspiration he needed for his 1606 painting symbolising Amsterdam as the centre of world trade.[3] In Isaacsz's allegory, Amsterdam holds a horn of plenty in her right hand, and

Illustration 1.1 Spiridione Roma, *The East Offering Her Riches to Britannia*, 1778

with her left controls the globe. Servants offer her pearls, while three VOC ships command the centre of the painting. A century later, in 1729, the English Company had enlisted the fashionable Dutch sculptor Michael Rysbrack to create a grand marble chimney piece for its new headquarters. On the left of the carving sits Britannia, receiving a treasure chest from a woman representing Asia, escorted by two other women, one leading a camel, the other a lion; two Company ships frame the piece on the right. Importantly, Britannia and Asia look each other in the eye, as if to symbolise that this was still an age when the Company based its wealth on exchange. The English Company had certainly gained ground, but still lagged its Dutch rival, and was also starting to face tough competition from new French Compagnie des Indes.

By 1778, however, there was little doubt that 'John Company', as it has become known, had replaced 'Jan Compagnie' as master of Europe's trade with Asia. Years of argument over trading rights with local rulers in India had culminated two decades earlier in the takeover of Bengal in 1757. Combining economic muscle with its small but effective private army, the Company's forces under Robert

Clive had defeated the Nawab of Bengal at Plassey (Palashi), 90 miles north of its trading base of Calcutta (Kolkata). The Company quickly installed Mir Jafar – a general who had betrayed the defeated Nawab – as the first of a series of puppet rulers of Bengal. More of a commercial transaction than a real battle, Plassey was followed by the systematic looting of Bengal's treasury. In a powerful symbol of the transfer of wealth that had begun, the Company loaded the treasury's gold and silver onto a fleet of over a hundred boats and sent them downriver to Calcutta. In one stroke, Clive had netted £2.5 million for the Company and £234,000 for himself.[4] Today this would be equivalent to a £232 million corporate windfall and a cool £22 million success fee for Clive. Historical convention views Plassey as the first step in the creation of the British Empire in India. It is perhaps better understood as the East India Company's most successful business deal.

In the decade that followed, the Company used its dominant position to monopolise the foreign and internal trade of Bengal, driving out Asian, Dutch and French merchants in the process. In August 1765, the Company's supremacy was formally recognised by the impoverished Mughal Emperor Shah Alam II with the grant of Bengal's *diwani*. This office of state gave the Company control over tax collection for more than 10 million people. For a stock market-listed company with profit as its primary motive, this acquisition of a country's public finances was truly revolutionary. Not surprisingly, the Company's share price boomed when news of the acquisition reached London's financial markets in April 1766.

Just as Spiridione portrayed, the wealth of the East began to pour into England. This represented an extraordinary turnaround. Before Plassey, the 'balance of trade was against all nations in favour of Bengal', wrote Alexander Dow in his 1773 *History of Hindostan*.[5] Bengal had been 'the sink where gold and silver disappeared without the least prospect of return'. Now that flow was reversed. Monopoly power and windfall revenues combined to create unrivalled purchasing power that bought ever-increasing quantities of Eastern goods to European markets. In spite of tough trade barriers against cheap Indian calicoes, Bengal's textiles, notably the soft Dhaka muslins, were still an essential fashion item for Britain's female elite. Indeed, Spiridione's Britannia seems swathed in muslin. But tea was now the Company's prize commodity, and the riches of Bengal helped to boost shipments from the Company's Chinese subsidiary in Canton (Guangzhou) three-fold in the five years following 1768. The annual consumption of tea rose to some one pound for each man, woman and child in England. On the streets of London, the Company also made its presence felt, not least at its imposing headquarters on Leadenhall Street, the huge dock complex in Blackwall and the fine merchant houses around Stepney Green. For a Parliamentary Select Committee investigating the Company's affairs five years later, 1778 – the year of Spiridione's triumphal portrayal of commercial success – would be seen as 'the high flood tide' of its exports from Asia.[6]

MISSING ELEMENTS

The East Offering Her Riches to Britannia provides us with a fascinating window onto the ways in which the Company wished to see itself – and be seen – at the peak of its commercial powers. Its mix of classical imagery and oriental exoticism – Mercury in a palm grove – captures well the sense of unlimited opulence that the Company's success in the East had made possible.

Yet much is missing from this vast tableau. Like so many high-profile corporate ventures since, the takeover of Bengal proved to be an acquisition too far for the East India Company. Initial stock market euphoria quickly gave way to excess, mismanagement and collapse. As the Company transformed itself from a modest trading venture into a powerful corporate machine, its systems of governance completely failed to cope with the new responsibilities it faced. Oppression of local weavers and peasants became the norm. Military spending spiralled out of control as adventurers took over from traders. Corruption assumed epidemic proportions and speculation overtook its shares, stoked up by Clive and others. Then, in 1769, conflict in south India rattled nervy investors, sending its share price into free fall. Financial crisis stalked Europe and the Company faced bankruptcy. Across the world in Bengal, drought turned to famine as Company executives profiteered from rising grain prices. Plays, pamphlets and poems poured from the presses back in Britain to pillory the Company and its executives. Company executives became caricatured as grasping Nabobs (or Nobs), the Yuppies of Georgian England. Like many of his contemporaries, the Glasgow Professor of Moral Philosophy, Adam Smith, was horrified at the way that the Company 'oppresses and domineers' in the East Indies.[7] Parliament was forced to intervene, while over the Atlantic in Britain's American colonies, patriots focused on the Company's tea as a symbol of oppression. For one 'Mechanic' appealing to the tradesmen of Pennsylvania, America was faced with 'the most powerful Trading Company in the Universe', an institution 'well-versed in tyranny, plunder, oppression and bloodshed'.[8] On the night of 16 December 1773, patriots dressed as 'Indians' dumped East India Company tea into Boston harbour, the symbolic start to the American War of Independence.

War still raged in the Americas when *The Offering* was first unveiled in the Company's headquarters. In London, the Company's share price continued to languish at half the level it had reached during the 1760s. To the east in India, the Company's most senior executive, Governor-General Warren Hastings, had taken a succession of desperate measures to restore the Company's financial health. Looking back on this era as Parliament once more sought to bring the Company to account in the early 1780s, the philosopher/politician Edmund Burke was savage in his criticism. For him, India had been 'radically and irretrievably ruined' through the Company's 'continual Drain' of wealth – a phrase that would haunt the next 150 years of British presence in India.[9]

Yet, none of this – the speculation, wars and corruption – could be allowed to disturb the expression of supreme corporate confidence that the Company's 24 directors had commissioned Spiridione Roma to portray. Then, as now, some things are always hidden.

A STRANGE INVISIBILITY

Established on a cold New Year's Eve, 1600, England's East India Company is the mother of the modern corporation. In its more than two and a half centuries of existence, it bridged the mercantilist world of chartered monopolies and the industrial age of corporations accountable solely to shareholders. The Company's establishment by royal charter, its monopoly of all trade between Britain and Asia and its semi-sovereign privileges to rule territories and raise armies certainly mark it out as a corporate institution from another time. Yet in its financing, structures of governance and business dynamics the Company are undeniably modern. It may have referred to its staff as servants rather than executives, and communicated by quill pen rather than email, but the key features of the shareholder-owned corporation are there for all to see.

Beyond its status as a corporate pioneer, the sheer size of its operations makes the Company historically significant on a global scale. At its height, the Company's empire of commerce stretched from Britain across the Atlantic and around the Cape to the Gulf and on to India. Trading posts were established at St Helena in the mid-Atlantic, where Napoleon drank Company coffee in exile; 'factories' were also established at Basra and Gombroon (Bandar Abbas) in the Middle East. But it was in India that the Company's impacts were most profound. Some of the country's major cities grew on the back of the Company's trade, not least Bombay (Mumbai), Calcutta (Kolkata) and Madras (Chennai). Beyond these coastal ports, the Company established a huge land empire, first as an opportunistic quest for extra revenues and later as an end in itself, eventually ruling most of the subcontinent. Yet, the Company's footprint did not stop there, but stretched to South-East Asia and beyond to China and Japan. Penang and Singapore were both ports purchased by the Company in an age when territories could be bought and sold like commodities. And if India was the site of the Company's first commercial triumphs, it was in China that it made its second fortune. The Company's 'factory' at Canton was the funnel through which millions of pounds of Bohea, Congo, Souchon and Pekoe teas flowed west to Britain and beyond. In the other direction came first silver and later a flood of Patna opium, smuggled in chests proudly bearing the Company *chop* (or logo).

Throughout its existence the Company was in a state of almost constant metamorphosis. Its end would come following the uprising against Company rule in 1857–58, a contest generally known as the Indian Mutiny in Britain and the First War of Independence in India. By then, the Company had lost almost all connection with the band of merchants who set out in four tiny ships to break into the Indonesian pepper market at the beginning of the seventeenth century. It no longer traded, and it administered its conquests in India as a licensed agent on behalf of the British Crown. But one abiding link remained: its ultimate purpose as a profit-making agency, always with an eye to its shareholders and the annual dividend. Following the suppression of the great rebellion, there was a fierce public backlash against the Company's anachronistic status. In the India Act of 1858, the Company was effectively nationalised, with all its rights and responsibilities taken over by the British state; the British Raj had begun. Yet, the Company lingered on, 'a shadow of a shade', according to one observer. It may have lost its purpose, but its directors were insistent that its capital should be protected for the remaining years of its last charter. Eventually, time ran out, its shares were exchanged for government bonds, and on 1 June 1874, the Company ceased to exist.

Colonial rule was certainly the final outcome of the Company's adventurism in Asia. But it was the hunt for personal and corporate profit that had drawn the Company inexorably on. The results of this enduring dynamic were world-shattering. By the time of its demise, the Company had changed the course of economic history, reversing the centuries' old flow of wealth from west to east. From Roman times, Europe had always been Asia's commercial supplicant, shipping out gold and silver in return for spices, textiles and other luxury goods. European traders were attracted to the East for its wealth and sophistication at a time when the western economy was a fraction the size of Asia's. And for its first 150 years, the Company had to repeat this practice, as there was almost nothing that England could export that the East wanted to buy. Then first in Bengal in the decades that followed Plassey, and then in China through the opium trade, the Company broke this longstanding pattern of trade and wealth. By the time of its demise, Europe's economy was double the size of those of China and India, a complete reversal of the situation in 1600 (see Table 1.1). There are many elements in this turnaround, but the East India Company was certainly one of the chief agents that engineered the great switch in global development that marked the birth of the modern age.

Table 1.1 The changing share of world GDP 1600–1870 (in million 1990 international $)

	1600	% of total	1700	% of total	1870	% of total
Britain	6 007	1.80	10 709	2.88	100 179	9.10
Western Europe	65 955	20.02	83 395	22.46	370 223	33.61
China	96 000	29.14	82 800	22.30	189 740	17.23
India	74 250	22.54	90 750	24.44	134 882	12.25
World	329 417		371 369		1 101 369	

Source: Angus Maddison, *The World Economy*, Paris: OECD, 2001, p. 261, Table B-18.

Yet, if you walk to the site of East India House as I did, you will see that nothing marks the tumultuous impact of this once mighty corporation. Today Richard Rogers's glass and steel Lloyds Building stands in its place. It was here that the Company's board of directors guided its global operations, and where its famous quarterly auctions were held. Sometimes lasting for days, such was the ferment generated by these auctions that the noise of 'howling and yelling' from the Sale Room could be heard through the thick stone walls on the street outside. Lawrence Norfolk's wonderful 1991 novel

Lemprière's Dictionary captures some of these passions, with his tale of how a secret society manipulates the Company from caverns deep beneath the streets of London. As the hero approaches East India House, he finds 'a stone hulk stretched down Leadenhall Street like a petrified carcass'.[10]

Leadenhall Street was not the Company's first headquarters. When it was newly established by Elizabeth I as 'The Governor and Company of Merchants of London Trading to the East Indies', its business was done at the City mansion of its first Governor (or Chairman), Sir Thomas Smythe. His house was situated on the narrow lane of Philpot Lane, where an echo remains in the appropriately named 'Spice Trader' curry restaurant. The Company then shifted a few hundred yards to the north and occupied Crosby Hall. Long after the Company had moved on, this magnificent Jacobean structure remained in the financial heart of London. When property developers threatened it with demolition at the turn of the twentieth century, a public campaign paid for it to be dismantled and re-erected brick by brick on the riverfront at Chelsea. The hall remained in public use as a college until it was sold off by Mrs Thatcher after her abolition of the Greater London Council in 1986. It was then purchased by a financier who had recently left the insurance giant, Lloyds – itself the site for the next phase of the Honourable Company's rise.

First occupied by the Company in 1648, East India House went through numerous incarnations during its 200-year life. In the 1690s it was known as 'the house belonging to the East India Company which are a corporation of men with long heads and deep purposes'.[11] By the early eighteenth century, it had become one of the landmarks of the City of London, and along with the South Sea Company and the Bank of England formed the corporate trinity of the age. Topped with a statue of a sailor and two dolphins, East India House had a distinctly maritime feel to it, and conveyed its importance to the passer-by in having both the royal and its own corporate crests emblazoned on its façade. With the collapse of the South Sea Company following its infamous bubble in 1721, the Company and its headquarters achieved a new ascendancy in Walpole's England. Rebuilt in 1729, the new East India House conveyed its global reach to visitors in a series of oil paintings depicting its key trading posts from the Atlantic (St Helena) to Africa (Cape Town) to the west coast of India (Bombay and Tellicherry) and round to Madras and Calcutta.

After Plassey, these emblems of commercial prowess were joined by statues of the Company's military heroes, first Clive and Stringer

Lawrence, and then the Marquis of Cornwallis and Arthur Wellesley, the 'sepoy general', who would later become the Duke of Wellington. But as the Company's power grew, so the solid building of the 1720s no longer matched the grandeur of its global operations. James Noorthouck in his *New History of London*, published in 1773, observed that 'the appearance of the building is nowise suited to the opulence of the Company, whose servants exercise sovereign authority in the Indian territories'.[12] So, between 1796 and 1799, an immense 200-foot long classical building was constructed. Above the six-columned portico, the triangular tympanum displayed George III defending the commerce of the East, once again with three allegorical ladies: Britannia on a lion, Europe riding a horse and Asia following on a camel.

Behind this imposing edifice sat the scores of Company clerks, many of whom live on in Britain's cultural memory, not for their corporate careers, but for their literary connections. Author of the *Essays of Elia* and friend of Romantic poets, Charles Lamb worked in the Company's accounts department from 1792. Samuel Taylor Coleridge dedicated his 1797 poem, 'This Lime Tree Bower', to 'my gentle-hearted Charles', 'who had "pined and hunger'd after Nature, many a year, in the great City pent!"' For 33 years Lamb would alternately bless the steady income that his job provided and curse the boredom of office life. 'Confusion blast all mercantile transactions, all traffick, exchange of commodities, intercourse between nations...' he wrote to his friend William Wordsworth in 1815.[13] Wordsworth's own brother, John, would die in the wreck of the Company's ship, the *Earl of Abergavenny*, in February 1805. In 1819, Lamb was joined at East India House by the gothic novelist Thomas Love Peacock, who took up the position as one of three assistant examiners. Amused by Peacock's new job, Leigh Hunt wrote to the poet Percy Bysshe Shelley that 'we joke upon his oriental grandeur, his Brahminical learning and his inevitable tendencies to become one of the corrupt'.[14] The utilitarian activist James Mill entered the Company's service in the same year, and was joined in 1823 by his son, John Stuart, and in 1835 by another son, James Bentham (who took up a position in Bengal). After the father's death, George Grote Mill would follow in his footsteps, becoming a clerk in 1844. One way or another, whether through direct employment, family connections or the consumption of its products, almost everyone in eighteenth- and nineteenth-century England was connected to the East India Company.

This third and final incarnation of East India House is now long gone, torn down in 1861, just three years after the Company's possessions had been absorbed into Queen Victoria's empire. Spiridione's allegory of Britannia was one of the many objects that made the short but symbolic journey across London from the commercial east to the political west. Many of the Company's artefacts now fill the Victoria and Albert Musuem, most memorably the clockwork tiger of Tipu Sahib, Sultan of Mysore. *The Offering*, however, was used to decorate first the India Office, and then its successor, the Foreign and Commonwealth Office in Whitehall, where it still stands above the Gurkha staircase. Elsewhere in London, the rest of the Company's physical legacy is scant, but, this being Britain, there is a pub – the East India Arms on Fenchurch Street – a mere fragment of a huge warehouse complex that stretched towards Aldgate.

The City of London is full of monuments, but none record the existence of the East India Company. This absence is particularly strange given the fact that the Company was a London institution *par excellence*, its charter explicitly excluding merchants from other ports from trading with Asia. It is not as if London does not choose to remember some of its past. At the site of East India House, for example, a plaque commemorates the founding of the London Penny Post by William Dockwood in 1680. But there is nothing to mark the fact that the East India Company was headquartered here for more than two hundred years.[15] Many institutions have justifiably disappeared into the anonymity of history. But the erasure of the East India Company is highly suspicious.

Explaining this absence goes to the heart of the contested position that the Company holds in history. Outside the world's universities, its legacy is still a living part of collective memories across the world, a legacy that is constantly being evoked and re-evoked through publications, exhibitions and documentaries. The recall is uneven, however, with deeply clashing perspectives in Europe and Asia – none more so than in India, where the Company retains a powerful symbolic force in contemporary culture.

CONFRONTING THE SYNDROME

From the ruins of the Company's fort at the pepper port of Tellicherrry on the west coast to the grandeur of Chennai's Fort St George on the east, the Company's physical presence in India continues to impress. The mark is greatest in Kolkata, a 'company town' of immense proportions. Some of the British street-names have been changed, but the weight of the Company's imprint on the city is unmistakable. Recent excavations by the Archaeological Survey of India have shown that the area around what subsequently became Kolkata had been a thriving commercial centre centuries before Job Charnock claimed it for the Company in August 1690. Known throughout the East as a 'Paradise on Earth' for its wealth and prosperity, Bengal attracted waves of European merchants for the quality of its textiles. Portuguese traders were first to establish a presence in 1535, only to be replaced by the Dutch a century later. The English Company came relatively late to Bengal, but the new base at Calcutta grew quickly. The first battlements of what became Fort William were erected in 1696, and two years later, the Company acquired lordship (*zamindari*) rights over the three adjacent villages of Sutanuti, Govindpore and Kolikata. By the 1720s Bengal was contributing over half of the Company's entire imports from Asia, most of this coming via Calcutta. Many Indians were attracted by the prosperity the city offered, and by the middle of the eighteenth century, Calcutta had over 120,000 inhabitants, of which just 250 were Company officials.

Two hundred years on, Fort William still sits squat by the river Hugli, a mile south of the original site. The original Fort had been besieged and captured by the Bengali army in June 1756. Following the recapture of Calcutta and the victory at Plassey, Clive relocated it in a more strategic position. Its impregnable defensive walls have never been tested, and the Fort continues its military traditions as the base for Eastern Command of the Indian Army. Nearby, the white-marble Victoria Memorial displays a remarkably balanced exhibition on Calcutta's history and the Company's formative role in the city's rise. To the north, the Company-era Government House maintains a continuity of occupation as Raj Bhavan, the residence of the Governor of Bengal. Construction of this huge building began almost as soon as the fifth Governor-General of Bengal, Richard Wellesley, had arrived in India in 1798. Not to be outdone by the grandeur of the new East India House, which was nearing completion back in London, Wellesley modelled his future residence on Kedleston Hall, a country mansion in Derbyshire. Eager to get even with his employers, whom he dismissively referred to as 'the cheesemongers of Leadenhall Street', Wellesley spared no expense in this monument to vainglory. Close by stands the Writer's Building named after the Company's clerks, who once filled this administrative hub; it still houses the civil servants of the West Bengal government.

These tangible representations of the deep entanglement between the Company and Calcutta are accentuated by questions of identity that generate conflict centuries on. Only recently, for example, local families successfully challenged the claim that Job Charnock was the official 'founder' of Calcutta, arguing that there were numerous Indian settlements in the area long before the Company arrived. Plassey also continues to evoke strong emotions among ordinary Bengalis. Mir Jafar, the general who sided with Clive in order to seize the throne, remains a popular symbol of betrayal. More broadly in India, the East India Company continues to be an icon of the potential dangers of foreign corporations that 'come to trade but stay to rule'. This perspective has deep roots in India's independence movement, which eventually expelled the British in 1947. In his *Economic History of India under British Rule* (1908), Romesh Chunder Dutt revived and redirected Burke's earlier critique of the East India Company so that it served his cause of root-and-branch reform. 'A change came over India under the rule of the East India Company', concluded Dutt, arguing that the Company simply 'considered India as a vast estate or plantation, the profits of which were to be withdrawn from India and deposited in Europe'.[16] Through Dutt's works, the 'drain' became a powerful symbol of the British exploitation of India, first by the Company and then by the Raj.

Forty years later, the Company's role in India's oppression was taken up by Jawaharlal Nehru as part of his campaign for full independence from Britain. In the summer of 1944, India's future prime minister was once again behind bars. Locked away in Ahmadnagar Fort, Nehru was serving his ninth – and final – term of imprisonment from the British authorities, this time following the Congress Party's 'Quit India' campaign of 1942. As in previous spells in gaol, Nehru turned his attention to writing in order to make sense of his predicament. In the space of just five months, he had filled a thousand pages, only stopping, he said, because he almost ran out of paper. The result was *The Discovery of India*, the final and perhaps most profound of his 'prison trilogy'. In it, Nehru presents his vision of how India's rich and complex past related to its struggle for independence. For him, the writing of history was not a remote, academic exercise but intimately bound up with taking action to change the present.

Running through the book is Nehru's conviction that the two centuries of British rule had imposed a terrible burden on India that needed urgent removal. But it is when he describes the English East

India Company and its plunder of Bengal following Clive's victory at Plassey that this cool voice of humanist reason boils over in anger. 'The corruption, venality, nepotism, violence and greed of money of these early generations of British rule in India', he thunders, 'is something which passes comprehension.' To underline his distaste at the Company's practices, he then adds, 'it is significant that one of the Hindustani words which has become part of the English language is "loot"'.[17]

Today, after a decade of economic liberalisation in India, this critical analysis of the Company's role in Indian history has come to the surface once more. For many Indians – particularly in Bengal – the Company's story has two profound morals: first that multinational companies want not just trade, but power; and second that division and betrayal among Indians enables foreign rule. 'Every child knows the perfidious story of how Bengal was lost at Plassey,' writes Gurcharan Das, adding, 'is it surprising that we are suspicious of merchants and foreign companies?'[18] The human rights abuses and corruption associated with the Enron power project at Dabhol brought these fears to a head in the late 1990s. 'It's the second coming of the East India Company,' argued Justice Daud, a retired judge of the Mumbai High Court, who led a fact-finding team following a series of violent incidents at Dabhol in March 1997.[19] For many, what made Enron's practices at Dabhol so unacceptable was the way in which the company had flagrantly manipulated the permit process. The result was a contract with the Maharashtra State that is regarded as 'the most massive fraud in the country's history', according to Arundhati Roy.[20] Enron achieved this, she argues, by deploying a 'time-tested strategy' first used by the East India Company, of corrupting decision-making and dividing the community.[21] Again and again, 'the return of the East India Company' is used as a catch-phrase to describe the recent influx of multinationals into India, whether global mining corporations or business more generally.[22]

For some, this focus on the 'creeping acquisition of effective control and wealth' by foreign interests amounts to a full-blown 'East India Company Syndrome'.[23] In a wide-ranging review of the lessons learned from economic reform, Arvind Virmanji identifies a generational divide between those brought up before independence and those born afterwards. 'The most important cultural memory of the former was about being ruled by the British government for a century and (most galling) by the British East India Company for a century before that.' This translated into a fear of foreign capitalists and, in its most extreme form, this syndrome 'encompassed a lack of confidence in one's abilities relative to white foreigners'.[24] A reaction against this 'syndrome' is now in motion, with observers arguing that it is time for India to 'get over' the East India Company. A new sense of national assertiveness also informs real decisions about India's future economic path, whether the issue is tightening patent rules for pharmaceuticals or opening up the retail sector to foreign companies.[25] It also influences the popular media, most strikingly in the TV advertisement for Rajnigandha *pan masala*. Set in London, the advert shows an Indian tycoon stopping his car in front of the East India Company's headquarters and telling his secretary that he wants to buy the firm: 'they ruled us for 200 years, and now it's our turn to rule'.

A NEW ROMANTICISM

If India can sometimes seem to be remembering the East India Company too much, then Britain can be easily accused of not remembering its lessons at all. The Company's physical disappearance from the streets of London has been matched until recently by a blank in the country's cultural memory. For most of the 60 years since Britain left India, John Company was regarded as something that could be consigned to the history books, its deeds to be squabbled over by competing academics. The onset of globalisation changed all this, prompting a resurgence of interest in the Company's contribution to earlier eras of world trade. Indeed, for an organisation that has been defunct for more than a century, 'John Company' is undergoing something of a comeback. Exhibitions at the British Library and the Victoria and Albert Museum along with a string of popular histories have revived the Honourable Company's reputation. Its founders are hailed as swashbuckling adventurers crossing the globe in search of spices and its executives profiled as multicultural 'white mughals'.

In the business community, the attraction of the Company lies in its commercial success, a model for today's global economy. Standard Chartered Bank, for example, was one of the sponsors of the British Library's 2002 'Trading Places' exhibition on the East India Company. Its then chief executive drew clear conclusions from its history, arguing that the challenge is now to 'build on the courageous, creative and truly international legacy of the East India Company'.[26] Rod Eddington, one-time chief executive of British

Airways, took similar encouragement from the Company's record, seeing it as a case study in how corporations succeed 'by dint of hard work, shrewdness and charm'.[27] A dot.com entrepreneur even relaunched the East India Company as a web-based 'virtual factory' offering a range of branded products. According to the site, using the Company's name 'gives credibility to virtually any product or service', combining 'the great strengths of British brands – tradition, old-fashioned luxury, impeccable class – with the general appeal of exotic countries, seafaring, travel and adventure'.[28] Interestingly, this upbeat vision of the East India Company is not confined to British firms. In Malaysia, the Metrojaya department store has its own East India Company range of clothes, which seeks 'to capture and celebrate' the spirit of the British, Dutch and French Companies all competing for 'supremacy in reaping the rewards of trade in the bounty of the region'.[29]

Others in Britain are drawn to the Company's cultural legacy, arguing that its encounter with India generated a fusion of lifestyles, with English merchants adopting local clothes, and some even embracing Hindu and Muslim religion. William Dalrymple in particular has praised what he sees as 'the vibrant multiculturalism of the East India Company'.[30] Through the tale of an eighteenth-century love affair between a Company official and a Hyderabadi noblewoman, Dalrymple's *White Mughals* projects a world where English traders not only fell for the women of India, but its culture as well. His message for the present day is that this demonstrates a 'clash of civilisations' is not inevitable, that 'East and West are not irreconcilable'.[31] Similarly, a major TV documentary series in Britain during 2001, *An Indian Affair*, set out to challenge the received wisdom about the British–Indian encounter, portraying the Company's 'live and let live' relationship with India as mutually beneficial – before being perverted by imperialists in the early nineteenth century.[32]

Yet both of these romantic reinterpretations – the entrepreneurial and the cultural – fail to confront the costs associated with the Company's business practices. Then, as now, trade can generate real wealth, but it can equally create misery and devastation. In their rush to focus on the twin themes of celebrity and consumption in the Company's story, the new imperial romantics often portray a very limited and rose-tinted picture of the Company. In particular, by looking at the Company through the lens of culture, the underlying purpose of its presence in India is forgotten. Even the British Library appeared to fall in this trap when it hosted the

'Trading Places' exhibition in 2002. Bringing together a wealth of artefacts, the exhibition focused on the Company's role in the birth of the modern consumer society, exploring how Britain 'became a nation of tea drinkers' and how 'words like shampoo, rice and bungalow became part of the English language'. The exhibition acknowledged the seamier side of the Company's activities, stating that in the years after 1757 became 'notorious for the plunder of India as Company employees amassed personal wealth', describing this as the 'bleeding of Bengal'. These admissions were, however, largely buried among a glorification of the consumption patterns that the Company pioneered. The exhibition was certainly keen to draw out the contemporary resonance of commodities the Company traded. But it shied away from making equally powerful linkages between the issues of corporate power, fair trade and human rights that affected eighteenth-century merchants as much as twenty-first-century multinationals.

More serious still, the initial plans for the exhibition had failed to consider how its vision of the Company would be received across Britain's diverse communities. When the Chinese community in the UK heard of the preparations, the reaction was one of horror. A campaigning website, The Truth About Trading Places, was established to highlight the human suffering caused by the import into China of opium grown under first Company and later British imperial monopoly.[33] The campaign proved successful and an additional panel was added to the exhibition, stating that 'free trade in Asia came to mean the lucrative and immoral freedom to deliver cargoes of opium'. The Company is long dead, but its battles live on.

RECKONING WITH JOHN COMPANY

The East India Company deserves to be looked at as it was – a profit-making company that generated great wealth, but one that also contributed to immense suffering. The Company's contemporaries from its early days as a spice trader through to its time as a licensed administrator of India were deeply conscious of this duality. People in both Britain and Asia were drawn by its unparalleled economic capacities – whether Indian weavers seeking steady employment or British entrepreneurs looking for a prosperous career in the East. Equally, however, its role and conduct were continually contested by merchants excluded from the Asia trade, by Indian rulers uneasy about its ultimate intentions and by parliamentarians critical of its overseas conduct.

Often the same person would carry within them both admiring and hostile perceptions of the Company. The *Gentleman's Magazine*, one of the leading English journals of the eighteenth century, exemplifies the way the Company could stimulate both fear and admiration. In March 1767, a year after the news of Company's capture of the *diwani* had reached London, the *Magazine* was proclaiming that 'the prodigious value of these new acquisitions may open to this nation such a mine of wealth as not only in a few years to pay off the national debt, to take off the land tax, and ease the poor of burdensome taxes; but to add to the dividends upon the Company's stock such a proportion of the increased revenue as will astonish Europe and exceed the most sanguine expectations'.[34] Only a month later, however, the same magazine was warning of the potentially disastrous consequences of a commercial body gaining such riches, arguing that the Company could soon 'repeat the same cruelties in this island which have disgraced humanity and deluged with native and innocent blood the plains of India'. For the writer of this article, the only solution was to cut the Company down to size, rallying his readers with a concluding slogan, 'down with that rump of unconstitutional power, the East India Company!'[35]

This duality extended to the Company's own executives, who were equally able to show great sensitivity to Indian culture in their private lives while carrying out acts of terrible exploitation on their employer's behalf. The career of Warren Hastings, who became the Company's first Governor-General of India in 1773, highlights this conflict between the cultural and the commercial. Fluent in local languages, he was a great philanthropist, sponsoring the first English translation of the Hindu *Bhagavad Gita*, supporting a new madrasa for Muslim students in Calcutta and ordering the construction of a Buddhist temple on the banks of the Hugli. Nehru himself argued that 'India owes a deep debt of gratitude' to Company executives such as Hastings and William Jones for helping to rediscover India's heritage.[36] Yet, these cultural interventions were always secondary to Hastings's primary role of generating wealth for the Company and its shareholders. This was the man who monopolised Bengal's salt and opium production for corporate benefit, and ordered the first mission to smuggle opium into China in deliberate defiance of the longstanding import ban. And, in spite of well-founded charges of extortion, bribery and corruption, Hastings would be declared innocent at a marathon impeachment trial by a grateful British House of Lords.

Just as corporations today should be judged by the impacts of their core business rather than their often peripheral donations to cultural events, so the East India Company has to be assessed on the basis of its underlying activities rather than the occasional philanthropy of its executives. The continuing reluctance to examine the full scope of the East India Company's impacts is part of a more general amnesia about the historical role of business. It remains an oddity that although companies are among the most powerful institutions of the modern age, our histories still focus on the actions of states and individuals, on politics and culture, rather than on corporations, their executives and their impacts. If we are to fully understand our corporate present, then we must understand our corporate past – and this means grappling with the legacy of John Company. Indeed, some of its most vocal critics expected future generations to take just such a hard look at the Company's performance as a corporation. 'Historians of other nations (if not our own)', wrote Richard Clarke in 1773, 'will do justice to the oppressed of India and will hand down the Memory of the Oppressors to the latest Posterity.' In the introduction to his long satirical poem entitled 'The Nabob, or Asiatic Plunders', Clarke urged on his fellow countrymen 'to perpetuate an honest indignation against these enemies of mankind'.[37]

Far from being a dusty relic, the Company exemplifies the constant battle within corporations between the logic of exchange and the desire for domination. Two centuries on, it demonstrates that the quest for corporate accountability is a perpetual exercise in directing the energies of merchants and entrepreneurs so that their private passions do not undermine the public interest. And as we approach the 250th anniversary of the battle of Plassey, the continuing clash of perceptions between corporate activists in India and imperial romantics in Britain underlines the need for some 'honest indignation' once more to comprehend the scale of the Company's impacts. To borrow a couplet from the nineteenth-century Urdu poet Asadullah Khan Ghalib, *zakhm gardab gaya, lahu na thama*, 'though the wound is hidden, the blood does not cease to flow'.

2
This Imperious Company

For hundreds of years, commodities, peoples and ideas have washed in and out of London's docks. In its time, the East India Company was one of the primary engines of this interchange. The docks were the place where the Company's commercial supremacy was felt most tangibly, and if you want to assess the Company's former greatness, London's docks are a good place to start.

Heading east from London's financial district lies Poplar, and on its High Street stands St Matthias Church. Erected by the East India Company as its chapel in 1654, this was where the Company's directors, workers and sailors went to care for their souls. Nondescript, even ugly on the outside following nineteenth-century renovations, the church is airy and cool within. Eight columns, seven of oak and one of stone, define the central space, and high up on the ceiling the Company's crest – or logo – stands out, a shield with three merchant ships sailing East. Now deconsecrated, the church buildings are run in trust for the diverse communities of the area – indigenous English and immigrant Bangladeshi, Caribbean and Chinese. Outside, St Matthias stands in the shadow of the new financial centre of Canary Wharf, whose huge towers carry the logos of some of today's corporate giants, Barclays, Citigroup and HSBC.

Less than a mile east of St Matthias is the site of the Company's docks at Blackwall (see Illustration 2.1). The original one and a half acre plot was first constructed in 1612, and soon became a thriving commercial area. By 1620, the Company was managing a fleet of 10,000 tonnes, operated by over 2,500 sailors and maintained by 500 ships' carpenters. It was here that the oceangoing 'East Indiamen' ships were built and fitted out. After 1637, the Company stopped building and owning its own ships, and leased them from a variety of ships' masters. Once completed, the Company's ships would sail down past Deptford, turn into the Channel and head for Asia. If successful, the ship would be back in London two or more years later. On their return, the ships were unloaded in Blackwall Reach, and their cargoes taken upriver to the Legal Quays, where they would be unloaded and carted through the streets to the Company's nearby warehouses. But as the ships increased in size during the eighteenth century, they had to anchor in deeper water at Blackwall.

To cope with their ever-increasing volumes of commodities, the Brunswick Basin was constructed in 1789, covering a full eight acres. All around lay a vast industrial complex, supplying the ships from nearby timber yards, foundries, rope works, bakeries and gunpowder mills. The centrepiece was the 120 foot-high Mast House, regarded as one of the technological marvels of the day, where the tall masts for the Company's ships were pieced together. Nearby were the pubs and tenements that served the Company's workforce, along with the Poplar chapel and the Company's almshouse to care for poor sailors. Unlike East India House, many of whose inhabitants, such as Charles Lamb and John Stuart Mill, still retain their identity, the thousands of Company employees who operated the East India Docks are for the most part anonymous.

This is particularly true of the Indian sailors, or *lascars*, who by 1700 made up about a quarter of the crews sailing the East Indiamen to and from Asia. All sailors of the time faced appalling conditions on board ship, enduring rotten food, disease and brutal punishments. But the *lascars* suffered additionally. Once landed in London, they were often abandoned by their ships' masters and left to roam destitute through the streets. By the 1780s, many in London were outraged by *lascar* misery, calling it a 'disgrace to humanity' and 'the utmost discredit to a country universally distinguished for its humanity'.[1] One of those affected was John Lemon, a 29-year-old hairdresser and cook from Bengal who married an Englishwoman, Elizabeth. As the numbers of poor *lascars* grew, the authorities hatched a plan to resettle them in Sierra Leone along with African-American loyalists from the American War of Independence. We know that Lemon and his wife survived the voyage out, and were alive a year later, but after that they are lost to history. *Lascars* continued to live in the East End, however, confined to unwholesome barracks in Shoreditch and Shadwell. Today, a third of the population of the Docklands area of Tower Hamlets is of Bangladeshi origin, the result of late twentieth-century immigration from the subcontinent. But through the *lascars* that sailed the Company's ships, Bengal's links with London extend far deeper into Britain's past.

As is so often the case with monumental architecture, the East India Docks reached their most perfect expression just as the Company's commercial rationale was coming to an end. Following in the wake of the ambitious West India Dock project, the triumphal East India

Illustration 2.1 William Daniell, *East India Docks*, 1808

Dock was opened in August 1806, with a massive new 16-acre Import Dock, which could hold over eighty 800-tonne ships. The dock was built like a fortress, with 20-foot high perimeter walls, some of which still stand, along with a prison inside for 'thieves, radicals and French agents', according to a panel at the nearby Museum in Docklands. The East India Company also paid for the construction of a new highway – the Commercial Road – to take its imports into the heart of the City. Soon afterwards, however, the first blow against the Company's monopoly was struck, with the removal of the Company's exclusive trading rights with India in 1813.

Twenty years later, in 1833, its treasured monopoly over the tea trade with China was also eliminated. The docks were sold, but continued in use under different ownership until 1943, when the Import Dock was pumped dry and filled with bomb rubble to act as a base for building the Mulberry Harbours used in the D-Day landings. After the war, the Export Dock was finally closed to traffic in 1967. Decades later, the East India complex has now become part of the resurgent Docklands, covered with apartment buildings and office blocks. The names of the new streets that run on top of the old docks – Clove Crescent and Nutmeg Lane – reveal something of its former purpose. Part of the outer basin still contains water, and has been reconstituted as a bird sanctuary where cormorants lazily dry their wings. A few dejected signs give descriptions of the size of the dock's lock-gates: 'four foot longer than any other lock on the Thames'. But nothing tells the story of the millions of tonnes of produce that passed through these gates, the wealth that was generated and the exploitation that so often accompanied it.

A MODEL CORPORATION

The Company that built these docks was the model for the multinational enterprise – 'the greatest corporation in the world', according to Victorian historian, poet and Indian administrator, Thomas Babington Macaulay.[2] Throughout its long life as a trading concern, it confronted and overcame many of the timeless questions facing business enterprise: how to keep employees motivated, customers satisfied, shareholders happy and society content. For K.N. Chaudhuri, one of its most insightful historians, 'the East India Company was the direct ancestor of the modern giant business firm, handling a multitude of trading products and operating in an international setting'.[3]

The East India Company was one of a number of companies granted a royal charter by the British state to take advantage of the opportunities opened up by the age of European expansion and exploration. Some of these directed their attentions eastwards, such as the Muscovy (1555) and Levant (1581) Companies. A succession of companies – including the Company of Royal Adventurers (1663) and the Royal African Company (1672) – were also founded to exploit the slave trade. Others focused on settlement and commerce in the New World, notably the Virginia (1606) and Hudson Bay (1670) Companies. Most of these were wound up centuries ago, but the Hudson Bay Company lives on as one of Canada's largest department stores.

Unlike the pioneers of the Asia trade, the Portuguese, who adopted a wholly state-led strategy. or the Dutch, who introduced a mixed public–private model, the English pushed forward a private sector strategy for tapping the wealth of the East. What makes the English East India Company special is the way it bridged the medieval concept of the corporation as an essentially public body with the industrial model of an enterprise acting primarily in the interests of its shareholders. In the rising commercial world of sixteenth-century England, the chartered company brought together a number of institutional ingredients. The Crown had a long tradition of setting up corporations as independent bodies to manage public services, such as municipalities and universities, like Oxford and Cambridge. Indeed, the local government of London's financial district is still managed by the Corporation of London, whose electors include businesses as well as citizens. From Italy came the invention of the *compagnia*, a name deriving from the Latin phrase for the act of sharing bread, *cum panis*. This was essentially a family firm, where fathers, brothers, sons and other relatives would pool their labour and capital.[4]

In England, the first generation of chartered companies brought together a band of merchants who would then buy and sell goods under a common umbrella. These regulated companies operated more akin to a guild, setting standards for a chosen field of endeavour, and collecting fees for shared services, such as docks and warehouses. Where the East India Company differed was in its fusion of the institutional structure of the public corporation with the financial mechanism of joint stock ownership.[5] Unlike earlier regulated companies, the East India Company was established as 'one body corporate and politick'. This brought a whole series of financial and organisational benefits, which were especially valuable for the long-distance trade to the East Indies. Capital costs were high in terms of both shipping and the bullion required to buy homebound goods. In addition, risks were extreme, both natural and political, with a high likelihood of the loss of some or all of the investment.

The joint stock mechanism provided a solution to this challenge. First, it enabled a separation of investors and managers, thus broadening the pool of capital that could be tapped to include both City merchants as well as passive investors from elsewhere in the moneyed elite. Second, risks were shared widely: if profits were made, then dividends could be disbursed, but if losses were incurred, investors would only be liable up to the nominal value of their paid-in capital. This limited liability endowed the Company with a special dynamism, substantially reducing the risks for investors compared with the usual partnership model of ownership. Third, trading was conducted by the joint stock company on its own account, rather than by the members themselves. This gave the Company a separate identity and its own legal personality – one that could conduct business strategies that went beyond the interests of individual merchants. It also gave it a unique institutional structure when confronting the merchant partnerships and states of Asia.

The Company's basic joint stock model evolved in significant ways over successive decades. Initially, the Company constructed separate joint stocks for each voyage, whereby investors would decide to allocate capital on a case-by-case basis. Only in 1657 did the Company become a permanent joint stock corporation, a 'continuous unlimited investment taking place without reference to individual voyages'.[6] This provided the basis for shares in the Company to be valued and exchanged at its headquarters in Leadenhall Street. Later, trading in India stock moved to the courtyard of London's Royal Exchange. When this proved too cramped, dealing shifted across Cornhill to the coffee houses of the Exchange or 'Change Alley until the formal establishment of the London Stock Exchange in 1773.

Like the modern corporation, the Company's share price was its heart-beat, communicating to the world the market's estimates of its future prospects. For the jobbers clustered around Exchange Alley, the Company's stock – along with its bonds and annuities – became the bellwether for the market as a whole. From the 1690s, its share price graph for the next 180 years would be dominated by a series of peaks and troughs, reflecting both the state of its commerce and the health of its relations with governments at home and abroad. Looking at the graph today (Figure 2.1), what is striking is how it starts out with a significant drop in value. Following the Glorious Revolution of 1688, the 1690s was a period of ferocious speculation. For the Company, its share price peaked in 1693, and then fell for the next five years as successive parliamentary inquiries exposed corruption and proposed potentially disastrous remedies. The low point was in 1698 when a rival company was established, sending the Company's shares with a nominal value of £100 down to a mere £39. By the turn of the century, the threat had been seen off, and prices had returned to well over £100 once more, rising to over £200 in 1717.

Along with the rest of the market, the Company's shares then became caught up in the market mania that followed the end of war in 1713 and subsequently came to be known as the South Sea Bubble. The price of Company stock doubled from £200 at the end of 1719 to £420 in June 1720, before collapsing to £150 in the following summer. Yet while this spike was extreme, the underlying vitality of the East India Company can be seen in the way that its share price continued a slow, but steady climb once the South Sea crisis had abated. But the next surge was all its own making. From 1757 to 1769, its shares more than doubled to reach £276. But in a crisis that almost cost it its independence, the Company's share price continued on a downward path for the next 15 years, ultimately halving in value.

The big fear that drove markets was that parliament would take a savage revenge on the Company, even removing the board of directors and replacing it with its own appointees. As we shall see in Chapter 7, when this threat was removed in 1784, the Company's financial fortunes recovered, and its shares began to rise once more. Deepening state intervention into the Company's affairs also brought some surprising benefits for the Company's shareholders, with the government increasingly guaranteeing a high level of dividends, making the stock a truly attractive investment after the mayhem of the 1760s. Buoyed by the surge in share prices that followed the end of the Napoleonic War in 1815, the Company's shares reached a third peak of £298 in April 1824. From this point on, the value of the Company's stock rarely slipped below £200, the generous level at which the government had agreed to buy out Company stock. Finally, on 30 April 1874, the stock was liquidated and Company's financial heart stopped beating.

A WORLD OF DIFFERENCE

Such characteristics make the Company immediately recognisable as a close relative of the modern multinational. Yet it is also important

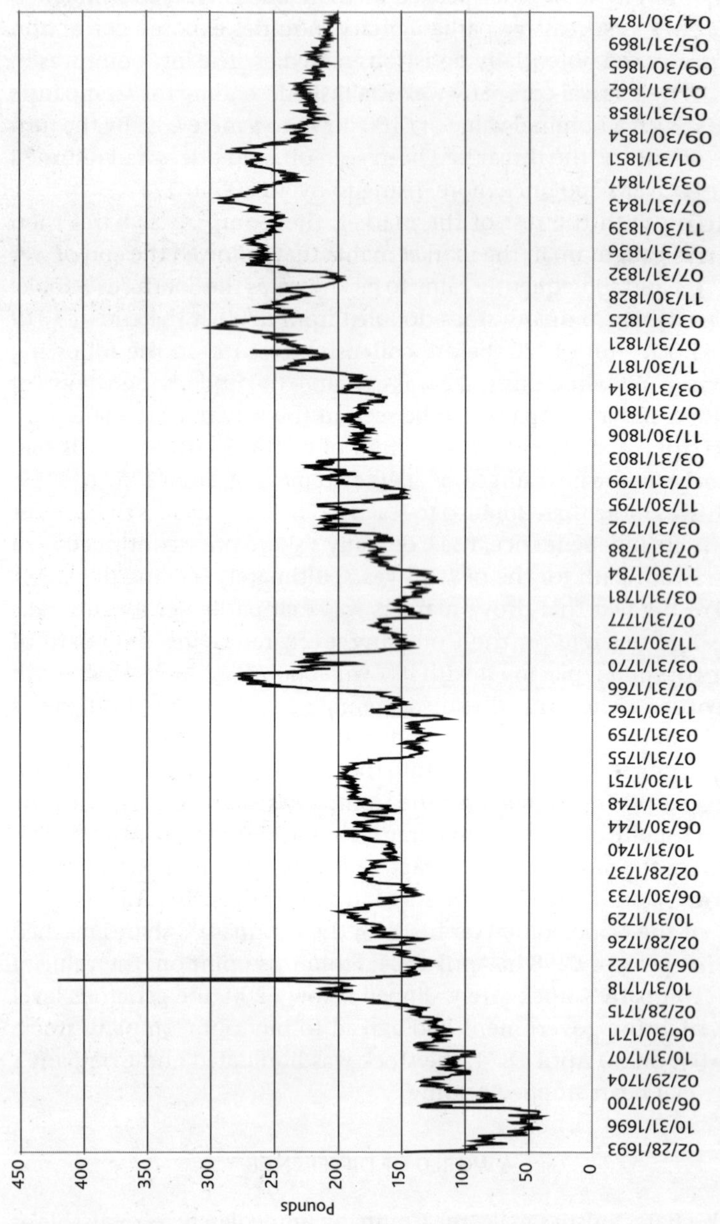

Figure 2.1 The Company's share price 1693–1874

to recognise the considerable differences that separate its world from ours, extending from often mundane matters to fundamental structural factors. Unlike today's globalised world of air freight and instantaneous communication, for the Company a round trip from London to India and back could take up to two years. Not only was considerable capital locked up in the voyages of these 'East Indiamen', but the exchange of information was also woefully slow, making planning and management exceptionally tough. The risks the Company faced were equally acute, not just from shipwrecks and pirates, but also from disease. Over half of its employees posted to Asia died while in service.

A more structural difference was the Company's status as a state-chartered enterprise. Today, people regard the ability to establish a company as a basic right in democratic market economies. In the Company's time, however, this was a special privilege granted by the Crown (and later Parliament). Charters would generally be awarded only for ventures that mixed private interest with a broader public purpose – which in the Company's case was to ensure that England gained a slice of the lucrative Asia trade. As one commentator put it in 1767, the Company was a 'national object' and 'the members of it bound to attend to the interest of the public as well as their own'.[7] This bargain with the state also had a limited life, and the Company's charter had to be renewed at regular, usually 20-year intervals. The Crown retained the right to revoke the charter if it judged that the Company had broken its terms and conditions. One of the few surviving examples of this model of the chartered corporation is the British Broadcasting Corporation (BBC), whose charter comes up for renewal in 2007. Unlike today's technically immortal multinationals, the East India Company was on constant life support, repeatedly having to justify its existence to the state, pointing to the healthy customs revenues it earned and the plump presents it could provide.

As part of its charter, the Company gained a whole series of special rights, most valuable of which was the monopoly awarded to this London-based corporation of all trade between England and the lands beyond the Cape of Good Hope. This gave the Company's investors extra confidence by creating a captive home market for its products. In the real-world conditions of global competition, of course, the Company was for many years just one player among many, striving against the Portuguese, the Dutch and the French. It also faced home-grown challenges from so-called interlopers who sought to break its exclusivity, along with the more informal bands of smugglers. Nevertheless, its monopoly powers were real, keeping prices high and ensuring substantial profits for shareholders.

For the Company, achieving a favourable relationship with the state was therefore essential. At home, the English Crown and then Parliament possessed the power of corporate life and death. The state not only set the boundaries of its commercial operations, but laid down the fiscal bargain that would govern the distribution of the Company's surplus. Overseas, the Company had to establish first the right to trade and then extract favourable terms of trade. Like today's multinationals, the Company often succeeded in winning sizeable tax breaks, placing it at a distinct advantage compared with local traders. Not surprisingly, in both cases, the Company was a constant target for state action to divert some of its booty into public coffers. The Company's history reveals an ever-shifting balance of power between the Company, the British Crown and Asian states.

The Company's great strength lay in its ability to generate extra revenues for the low-income states of the pre-industrial world. Sizeable loans to the British Crown and large-scale bullion imports into Mughal India made the Company indispensable. For the merchants who managed the Company, the arrangement of royal charters at home and imperial decrees *(firmans)* abroad was all part of the wider business of buying and selling. These were financial transactions that established contractual rights that could not be infringed. What the Company sought was a zone of commercial sovereignty that ensured it free rein to operate as it wished. Giving presents to princes and paying bribes to parliamentarians were simply part of the fundamental costs of business.

Allied with the state-backed nature of its charter were a number of semi-sovereign privileges. These included the right to mint coin in its overseas subsidiaries, to exercise justice in its settlements and, crucially, the right to wage war. From the beginning, armed force was essential for the Company's ability to gain and sustain access to Asian markets. It was the Company's demonstration of naval superiority over the Portuguese off Surat in 1612 that paved the way for its first trade concessions from the Mughal Emperor Jahangir, and its military weakness against the Dutch that forced it from Indonesia's spice islands ten years later. Throughout its existence, the Company's directors maintained an ambivalent attitude to the role of military might. A tight concern for limiting overheads meant the directors were continually nervous of military expense, particularly on land, fearing the sunk costs of forts and castles. But the Company also appreciated the value of conducting 'commerce with sword in your hands', in the words of the Company's Governor of Bombay, Gerald Aungier, in 1677. The direct application of violence by today's corporations is thankfully rare. But the links between successful trade and military force remain as powerful as ever. As Thomas Friedman, the *New York Times*'s ebullient promoter of globalisation, explains, the 'hidden hand of the market will never work without a hidden fist'. In simple terms, 'McDonald's cannot flourish without McDonnell Douglas, the designer of F-15s'.[8]

A final distinction between today's giant firms and the East India Company is also derived from the chartering process. In the Company's age, the reliance on state approval for specific commercial privileges meant that it was among a rare breed of corporations, usually numbering fewer than twenty in all of England. A rush of speculative ventures towards the end of the seventeenth century resulted in over 140 joint stock companies by 1695. But most failed to survive, and by 1719, there were only 21 left. The explosion in stock market listings during the first six months of 1720 brought another 174 companies to market. The subsequent failure of the South Sea Company prompted the introduction of the Bubble Act, which forbade formation of further joint stock companies without explicit approval of Parliament, a ban that would remain in force for the next 105 years. This exclusivity made the Company all the more notable in the Georgian economy of the eighteenth century. The Company was a corporate colossus, alone accounting for between 13 and 15 per cent of all Britain's imports between 1699 and 1774.[9] Every seventh pound of goods brought into Britain would be carried on Company ships, unloaded at Company docks and sold in Company auctions, a phenomenal presence in the Enlightenment economy. Today, the corporation is the dominant economic form, a pervasive feature across the globe. But few, if any, can match the individual might of the East India Company.

GOVERNING THE COMPANY

These differences are significant, but they should not obscure other traces that show a profound link with the modern corporation, most notably in the area of governance and business administration. The Company's joint stock identity merely provided a platform for commercial operations, but gave no guarantee of success. What made the Company's fortune was its management framework, which had achieved a distinctive shape by the early eighteenth century.

The English Company shared many structural features with its Dutch rival, the VOC. Both had strictly hierarchical systems of administration, supported by a small army of clerks – known as writers in England, a term borrowed from the Dutch *shcruyvers*. Both were publicly held and publicly traded, with the VOC usually offering the more attractive investment through the seventeenth century. But in their governance the two companies differed markedly. The VOC's directors were chosen by its six provincial chambers – Amsterdam, Middelburg, Hoorn, Enkhuizen, Delft and Rotterdam; in Amsterdam's case, their representatives on the board were nominated by the burgomasters and appointed for life. The directors had to hold a substantial portion of VOC stock, but there the link with the shareholding base ended. The VOC's shareholders provided the capital, but had no say either in the choice of those who would manage their investment or in the direction of policy. The VOC might well have been a mighty company, but it was not a corporation.

The public origins of the English company's corporate form gave its shareholders not only a financial stake, but the franchise, making them almost like constituents of an eighteenth-century parliamentary borough. Like the England that gave it birth, the Company operated as a limited, property-based democracy, one that was run by and for its shareholders. Just as the right to vote in Georgian England was restricted to those with property, so the Company's shareholders had to have £500 of nominal stock before they could vote either in the quarterly meetings of the Court of Proprietors held in March, June, September and December, or at the annual meeting in April. This was the high point of the Company's calendar when over a thousand shareholders would gather to elect a slate of 24 directors. No matter how large a shareholding, each individual with more than £500 in stock only had one vote, a surprising expression of financial egalitarianism. In turn, only shareholders with over £2,000 in stock – the mercantile aristocracy – could put themselves forward as candidates to be a director. This directorial elite would then choose from among their number a chairman and deputy chairman. Until 1709, the chairman went by the name of governor and directors were known as committees.

Power was controlled within a relatively narrow group of affluent merchants on the Court of Directors. But shareholders had the right to override executive decisions taken by the directors up until

1784. Not for nothing were the annual meetings of the shareholders described as 'little parliaments' by William Pitt the Elder.[10] Meeting quarterly to hear the directors' reports and vote on corporate policy, the shareholders were particularly vigilant in sustaining high rates of dividend payments. In 1733, the Court of Proprietors rebelled when the directors proposed a cut in the dividend from 8 to 6 per cent in response to poor trading conditions. Shareholders voted this down and instead agreed their own payment of 7 per cent, an ominous sign for the future. Alongside the dividend, shareholding also gave investors access to the Company's vast network of economic opportunities, notably jobs. The 24 directors controlled the Company's system of patronage, enabling them to place friends, relatives and business partners in key positions, a gift that became increasingly valuable in the second half of the eighteenth century.

Compared with the modern company in the UK, the East India Company's structures of governance gave shareholders considerably greater powers (see Table 2.1). The entire Court of Directors was elected on an annual basis, and the successful directors then guided the business for the year ahead. There was no chief executive – although there were a company secretary, accountant and auditor – and today's distinction between executive and non-executive directors did not yet exist. In essence, all directors became executive upon election.

Table 2.1 Corporate governance compared

	East India Company, c. 1709	Modern UK company, c. 2005
Formation	Crown charter, for limited period	General incorporation, unlimited life
Voting rights	'One shareholder, one vote'	'One share, one vote'
Number of directors	24	10–20
Election of directors	Annual elections of entire board	Staggered elections
Director qualifications	More than £2,000 in shares	No shareholding qualification
Election of chairman	Indirect election, chosen by directors	Elected directly by shareholders
Board composition	All part-time executives	Majority non-executive, plus executive directors
Board limitations	Maximum four consecutive years; return after one year out	Three-year term, usually two terms

Note: Data for modern company taken from practices of the largest five companies on the London Stock Exchange in 2005.

The Court of Directors oversaw the operations of a rigorously hierarchical administrative system. At the pinnacle sat the chairman, who ran the weekly board meetings of the 24 directors, which took place each Wednesday. Each director was assigned to one of ten committees that looked after different dimensions of the Company's operations. Among these, three committees were regarded as supreme: Correspondence, which handled all the communications with the Company's far-flung subsidiaries; Treasury, which managed relations with financial markets, buying bullion and paying dividends; and Accounts, which aimed to maintain financial discipline. In addition, there were committees for buying commodities, warehousing, shipping, managing East India House, regulating (and preventing) private trade and lawsuits. Alongside these was the all-powerful Secret Committee, which defined the Company's political and military strategy in times of war.

From East India House, the directors would send precise orders to their overseas subsidiaries covering the quantity, quality and price of goods to be purchased. In the case of textiles, this could cover details such as the type of thread, weave, colour, pattern, stiffness and packing. These orders were implemented by a system of autonomous presidencies, headed by a president (or governor), who controlled the operations of his particular port or factory, as well as smaller outposts in his zone of operations. Although East India House laid down clear parameters on the content of its commerce, it gave considerable freedom to local management to determine how these goals were to be achieved, including in their relations with host governments. As the fortunes of trade fluctuated, so different presidencies took the lead. The Mughal Empire's port of Surat on the west coast of India and Bantam in the Spice Islands (now Indonesia) were the first to be established. As these declined in importance, so Bombay, Madras and Calcutta grew in the latter part of the seventeenth century. In 1773, the Bengal Presidency, with its capital at Calcutta, was made pre-eminent.

Below the president lay another hierarchy, with promotion strictly by seniority. New recruits would enter the Company's service as 'writers', where they would stay for five years before progressing to the rank of 'factor' for a further three years. This would be followed by promotion to junior and then senior merchant, and thereafter possible selection for their presidency's council, and even governor. The expectations of employment were clearly set out for all employees in a covenant, backed by a bond and the threat of dismissal for malpractice. This was strengthened in 1764, when the Company introduced a ban on the receipt of gifts above a certain level, one of the first corporate codes of ethics.

In return, the Company's overseas staff received a minimal salary and the right to conduct private trade on their own account within Asia. This maintained the Company's monopoly over exports to Europe, while giving employees a strong incentive to stay and make their fortune in India.[11] For its executives, the purpose of a career with the Company was to achieve a 'competence', making enough money to be able to retire and adopt the conspicuous consumption patterns of the British landed gentry. This could not be achieved by saving from the salaries received from the Company, which barely covered living expenses. As a result, the ambitious Company man had to use his position as a platform for patronage and private trade. It was the hunger for perquisites (or perks) that drove the Company's executives to adventurism when opportunity allowed. The privilege of private trade also exacerbated the inherent tension between corporation and employee, making staff both executives and entrepreneurs in their own right. Entirely understandable in the context it operated in, this system of private trade created a second tier of divided loyalties, which would ultimately spawn an army of cuckoo businesses operating in the heart of the corporate machine.

For the most part, however, the Company's managerial structures and human resources were utilised to drive a highly focused business model. The East India Company was essentially a trading enterprise in the import–export business. Compared with Dutch VOC, the English Company proved more adept at moving into new markets, shifting from pepper to textiles and then to tea. From time immemorial, merchants had wished to 'buy cheap and sell dear', in the words of St Augustine. This was a strategy that the East India Company sought to apply by minimising the amount of goods – notably bullion – sent to the East, keeping the costs of supply as low as possible, and then maximising the price of goods sold at auction back in England. The Company outsourced as much as it could, not least the manufacture of goods in the East, its shipping, as well as the ultimate retailing of its products. The value it added to the process was in the selection of goods and the efficiency of delivery. In a situation characterised by extremely poor information, the Company's strength lay in its ability to achieve an equilibrium between supply and demand on opposite sides of the planet.[12]

A BUNDLE OF TENSIONS

Just as the Company pioneered the organisational structures of the modern multinational, it also contained the same bundle of tensions that are inherent in the corporate form. As a corporation, the Company lay at the centre of a web of relationships. Internally, the interactions between owners, executives and employees defined the fundamental direction and dynamic of the business. Externally, fiscal and regulatory relations with states at home and abroad defined the Company's scope for action, while in the marketplace, its standing with customers, competitors and suppliers determined its chances of success. Ultimately, however, it was the Company's ability to maintain a basis of trust with society at home and abroad that decided its fate – and once this trust was broken, protest, rebellion and, ultimately, removal would follow.

Then and now, it is important to recognise that the corporation is not a neutral force. In the words of Timothy Alborn, an expert on nineteenth-century business, the corporation 'employs a balance of political and economic means to achieve economic ends'.[13] As well as a constant jostling for a share of the commercial rewards of the Company's operations, a more fundamental struggle was always underway to determine positions of power and pre-eminence. For much of the first half of its corporate career, the Company was bringing steady profits for its shareholders, cheap imports for its customers, good prices for its Indian textile suppliers as well as substantial customs revenues for both the British and Asian exchequers.

But this web of relationships also contained the potential for open conflict. In the Company's case, something went radically awry in the 1750s, leading to the violent takeover of Bengal. Its shareholders certainly benefited, but only temporarily. Suppliers were squeezed as the Company exerted a new-found market power, and the struggle with the regulatory authority of host states erupted into open warfare.

Seeking to explain this extraordinary turnaround, many analysts have focused on circumstantial factors, notably the constraints the Company faced in enforcing its will in India owing to the combination of distance and ineffective means of communication. Others highlight the moral failings of key executives. Critics then and now have been united in their condemnation of the greed and rapacity demonstrated by Clive and the new class of nabobs that came to control the Company's operations in India.

More structural factors were at work, however. Adam Smith's *Inquiry into the Nature and Causes of the Wealth of Nations* is well-known for its championing of the free market. But it also contains one of the most thoroughgoing investigations into the corporate metabolism. Written in the wake of the Company's conquest of Bengal, Smith dissected the corporation as an institution and evaluated the factors that led to the East India Company's own particular crisis. Uniquely, Smith was emphatic in downplaying the actions of individuals as the root cause of the problems. 'I mean not to throw any odious imputation upon the general character of the servants of the East India Company,' he wrote, stressing that 'it is the system of government, the situation in which they are placed, that I mean to censure.'[14] The problem for Smith was one of corporate design. Across 400 years of modern corporate history, three design flaws in particular unite the Company with the global corporations of the twenty-first century: the drive for monopoly control, the speculative temptations of executives and investors, and the absence of automatic remedy for corporate abuse.

THE MONOPOLISING SPIRIT OF MERCHANTS[15]

One of the main prizes that the Company sought from the British state was a market monopoly over trade with the East. Like many modern multinationals, the Company was eager to avoid the mere interplay of supply and demand. The Company jealously guarded its exclusive rights over imports from Asia, lobbying and bribing the authorities to retain the barriers to entry that defined its charter. It also wanted to eliminate competition in Asia so that it could force down the costs of supply. By controlling both ends of the chain, the Company could guarantee high profits for its shareholders. Negotiation was the preferred method of achieving market dominion. But, if required, it would use both force and fraud.

Outside the state sector, few companies today have similar monopoly privileges, except those managing infrastructure utilities, such as energy, telecoms, transport and water. But two decades of global deregulation has resulted in economically damaging and politically dangerous levels of corporate concentration. Over 60 per cent of international commerce now takes place within corporations rather than in the open marketplace, making it idle to talk of free markets.

Emblematic of this new age of monopoly is the US-based giant Wal-Mart. With over $300 billion in annual sales, Wal-Mart is now the world's largest corporation measured in terms of revenue and accounts for 2.5 per cent of US gross domestic product. Just as the East India Company once dominated Britain's patterns of trade with Asia, so Wal-Mart is America's largest single importer of goods from China. Indeed, if Wal-Mart was a country, it would be China's eighth largest trading partner, outstripping the UK. But in its stated quest for 'everyday low prices', Wal-Mart has come to represent 'the lowest common denominator in the treatment of working people'.[16] It faces America's largest sex discrimination case, affecting 1.6 million current and former women employees, and has been the subject of over a hundred charges of unfair labour practices in recent years. Human rights organisations have also exposed poor labour standards in its Asian supply chain, while communities across America have opposed Wal-Mart for the impact that its Big-Box formula has on local choice and economic vitality.[17]

For all the efforts to liberalise the world economy, the current pattern of global commerce is better described as one of corporate trade – a situation with great similarities to the Company's own day. In such situations, there is often no need for the formal grant of monopoly, which the East India Company fought so strenuously to secure.

IMMEDIATE AND EXCESSIVE RETURNS

What distinguishes the corporation from other commercial institutions is its separation of owners and managers. This structure has a number of strengths, notably the ability to source capital from a wide pool of investors, and the possibility of replacing hereditary owners with effective professional executives. But it also holds the potential for a double negligence. Limited liability frees shareholders from the full consequences of careless investments, while the separation of ownership and control creates the context for executive malpractice, as executives exploit the corporation for their own ends. In the jargon of modern corporate governance, what the corporation creates is a fundamental 'agency problem'. This problem is not fatal, but needs to be consciously and continuously scrutinised to ensure that the corporation does not become the plaything of shareholders and executives.

It was the speculative behaviour of corporate insiders and short-term investors that emerged as the most powerful factor in the Company's spectacular fall from grace in the middle of the eighteenth-century. Financial engineering, flimsy managerial controls and inadequate regulation all played their part – just as they did in the late 1990s.[18]

In the wake of Enron's collapse in November 2001, the Company's much earlier boom-and-bust cycle becomes eerily familiar – the same passion for aggressive acquisitions, the same obsession with exclusive perks for corporate insiders, and the same focus on executive self-preservation as ordinary shareholders started to suffer the consequences of excess. Standards of corporate governance may well have been transformed over the past two centuries and systems of private trade eliminated. But some of the underlying driving forces behind corporate action remain largely intact.

SETTING JUSTICE AT DEFIANCE[19]

Perhaps what infuriated the Company's contemporaries most through the seventeenth, eighteenth and nineteenth centuries was its impunity, its ability to shrug off the consequences of its actions. For an insidious corollary to the Company's speculative drive for market dominion was its willingness to engage in immense crimes, safe in the knowledge that domestic and international remedies were not in place. A large part of the problem lay in the legal void at the time, with courts in both Europe and Asia wholly ill-equipped to bring corporations and their executives to account. This – as we shall see – did not stop the Company's contemporaries from trying.

Today, the globalisation of markets has still not been matched by an equivalent globalisation of justice. Compared with the immense political capital that has been expended in recent decades to liberalise international trade, precious little has been done to ensure that common human rights are respected and enforced. Special tribunals have been established to judge some of the more outrageous instances of crimes against humanity. Sadly, the courageous initiative to end the global impunity of individuals through an international criminal court has been hampered by the unilateral opposition of the USA. And in the corporate sphere, Union Carbide has yet to be held to account for the 1984 toxic release at its Bhopal facility in India, which has killed 22,000 and resulted in around 100,000 people still suffering chronic and debilitating illnesses. More than 20 years on, United Carbide – along with the governments of India and the United States – have failed to comply with their obligations to bring the perpetrators to justice or provide adequate compensation to the victims.[20]

CORPORATE OVER-STRETCH

These design flaws exist like errant genes within the corporation's DNA, and will be central themes of the rest of this book. For much of the time, these impulses may well be dormant, with the corporation simply too small to dominate others, for example. But when circumstances allow, they will seek expression until halted once more, not just risking social harm but the long-term interests of the corporation itself.

This prospect was not lost on the Company's contemporaries in Europe, Asia and the Americas. By the late 1760s, it had become a domineering threat to liberty – in the words of the *Gentleman's Magazine* – the 'imperious company of East India merchants'.[21] And yet we know that the apparent supremacy glorified in Spiridione Roma's huge tableau did not last. The Company quickly became over-extended financially and operationally, eventually resulting in its extinction as a commercial concern. For all its commercial sophistication and organisational complexity, the classical corporation lacks any intrinsic mechanism to hold it back from pursuing its own aggrandisement, nothing to say 'this is enough'.

Here lies the fundamental tragedy of the corporate form, the absence of an impulse for self-restraint that can temper its inherent drive for power. The very same year that it was being accused of imperious conduct, the Company Secretary, Robert James, was somewhat disingenuously telling Parliament that 'we don't want conquest and power; it is commercial interest only we look for'.[22] A more accurate statement would have been 'it is commercial interest only we seek, for which we are willing to consider conquest'. A hundred years later, as he reviewed Parliament's debates on the Company's final charter in the summer of 1853, Karl Marx put his finger on the essence of the Company's strategy, stating that it had 'conquered India to make money out of it'.[23] And, yet to invert Marx's famous quip, the Company's first attempt at conquest ended in farce, only to be followed much later by tragic success in 1757.

3
Out of the Shadows

THE ODOURS OF THE SPICY ORIENT

Looming above the down-at-heel shops and cafés that line Oude Hoogstraat in Amsterdam today stands the mighty Oostindisch Huis. This impressive three-storey brick-built edifice was the headquarters of the Verenigde Oostindische Compagnie (VOC) from 1606 to 1799, and still bears the company's monogram above its entrance. Perhaps it is the long-standing Dutch commitment to the environment that explains how the building has now been recycled to host a faculty of Amsterdam University. Sociologists lecture where the Heren XVII – the Company's board of directors – once met to determine business strategy.[1] What is striking about the humdrum atmosphere that now hangs over Oostindisch Huis is how this and other relics of the Company's past are still clearly visible parts of Amsterdam's landscape. A replica VOC ship – appropriately named *The Amsterdam* – is even moored beside the city's maritime museum, a far cry from the erasure of memory evidenced over the water in London.

For a hundred years, the VOC was the arbiter of European trade relations with Asia, overshadowing the efforts of its English namesake in both the scale and scope of its operations. The Dutch had been the first of the North European nations to break the Portuguese maritime monopoly of the Asian spice trade, with the Compagnie van Verre (Company of Distant Lands) sending its fleet to the East in 1595. Over the next six years, eight rival companies sent 15 fleets to tap the spice islands of Indonesia. Competition proved good both for the spice producers, who saw increased purchase prices, as well as Dutch consumers, who enjoyed falling sale prices. But it was a disaster for investors, and so, on 20 March 1602, the various companies put their differences aside and merged into a single body. The united company received a monopoly over all trade with Asia – just like the English Company – and worked diligently to channel trade for its own benefit.

Although England had launched its own East India Company two years earlier, the VOC had ten times the capital base, and quickly achieved a dominant position. It became the first joint stock to trade its shares on an open market, and in its lifetime the VOC would pay out 3,600 per cent in dividends based on the initial investment in 1602.[2] It took the lead in displaying its pre-eminence through the art it chose to commission for its headquarters, decorating its Great Hall with paintings depicting its Asian trading posts from Cochin on the Malabar coast of India, to Ayuthya in Thailand, Banda Neira in the Moluccas and on to Canton in China. Passers-by could also experience the Company's prestige in other ways as the aroma of the commodities stored within filtered into the street. For the poet Joost van der Vondel:

> The rich East Indies House grows addict, tired and drear
> And brings the odours of the spicy Orient near.[3]

Step by step, combining financial acumen with colonial brutality, the VOC achieved mastery of the Asia trade, managing fleets of more than a hundred ships and returning a fortune to its six founding cities. Jan Pieterszoon Coen, who had established Batavia (modern Jakarta) as the VOC's capital in Asia, symbolised the single-minded commercial aggression that brought it such success. Writing back to the Heren XVII in 1619, he was adamant that 'we cannot carry on trade without war, nor war without trade'.[4] Violence in the East was matched by corruption at home. Just 20 years after its foundation angry investors forced the directors to publish the accounts and introduce a modicum of responsiveness to shareholder concerns. For the next century, the VOC outstripped its English rival. But in the eighteenth century, it failed to diversify its product range and was weakened from within by administrative sclerosis and fraud. By the end of the century, its three initials were being used by critics to spell out its doom 'Vergann onder Corruptie'– 'perished by corruption'. Expelled from India by its English namesake, the rest of the VOC's Asian operations became untenable following the last Anglo-Dutch war in the 1780s, and, in 1799, the Compagnie ceased to exist.

COMMERCIAL SUPPLICANT

Understanding the VOC is essential if the English Company is to be seen in context. Indeed, the EIC was just one of many competing India companies launched by the nations of Europe in the seventeenth and eighteenth centuries. These ranged from important ventures from France and Denmark, as well as lesser operations launched from

Genoa, Ostend, Prussia, Russia, Sweden, Spain and Trieste. And for the first half of its existence, the English Company was the commercial supplicant, its trade with Asia at the mercy of both local rulers and rival Europeans.

When the London-based Company was established in 1600, Europe continued to live in the economic shadow of Asia, with England operating as one of its more marginal kingdoms. Spices and other luxury goods had been imported from Asia into Europe for thousands of years, carried overland across the Middle East. It was a trade dominated by local merchants, with Europeans in a dependent position at the end of the chain. The Ottoman capture of Constantinople in 1453 exposed this vulnerability, giving the Turks control of the Mediterranean and thus the ability to limit Europe's access to pepper and other spices, such as cloves, nutmeg, cinnamon and mace. So essential was pepper as a way of making preserved meat edible that the race was on to find alternative routes to the source of supply. The Spanish headed west across the Atlantic, and 'the Americas were discovered as a by-product in the search for pepper'.[5] The Portuguese sailed south along the coast of Africa and around the Cape of Good Hope. While Columbus presented a New World to the King and Queen of Spain, it was the Portuguese who successfully fulfilled their mission and found the source of the spice trade. Ironically, it would be silver from Spanish mines in the New World that would provide the bullion to pay for Europe's maritime imports of spice. In the two centuries after 1600, about one-third of the silver produced in America found its way to Asia to pay for Europe's imports.[6]

The arrival of Vasco da Gama's Portuguese fleet off Calicut (Kozikhode) in May 1498 marked a violent break with longstanding tradition of free trade in the Indian Ocean. When asked by an Arab trader why he had come, da Gama responded with precision, 'we seek Christians and spices'.[7] He found both, but focused his attention on filling his ships with pepper for the voyage home. Not content with being one trading nation among many, da Gama and his successors used their naval supremacy to impose a commercial monopoly in the Indian Ocean. Only merchants who bought Portuguese permits were allowed to do business on pain of confiscation and death, a measure justified on the grounds that the right to free trade was limited to Christians.[8] In a brutal extension of the wars of religion that raged between Christianity and Islam in the Mediterranean, the Portuguese enforced their monopoly with a savagery hitherto unknown in the region.

On his second voyage in 1502, da Gama dispensed with any attempt at negotiation. A large merchant ship bringing back 700 pilgrims from Mecca was taken, primed with gunpowder and sunk. He then moved on to Calicut, capturing 20 trading vessels and butchering their crews. More than 800 prisoners had their hands, ears and noses hacked off, the pieces piled into a boat and sent to the local ruler, the Zamorin, with a note telling him to make a 'curry' with what he found.[9] In light of these and other incidents, the economic historian Niels Steengaard has concluded that 'the principal export of pre-industrial Europe to the rest of the world was violence'.[10]

The Portuguese impact on the economies of the Indian Ocean should not be overstated. What is clear, however, is that for decades thereafter, Portugal's *Estado do India* would dominate European imports of pepper, accounting for as much as 75 per cent until the 1580s.[11] This was a state-managed affair, run from Portugal's Asian capital at Goa and a suite of bases across the Indian Ocean from Mozambique via Malacca to Macau. Portuguese dominance would, however, be ruined by religion – from within by the horrors of the Inquisition and from without by the insurgent Protestant Dutch. When he died in 1525, Vasco da Gama was buried in St Francis Church in Fort Cochin. Today, his grave is empty, but his memory lives on with a mural in the lobby of the Indian Government's Spice Board in Cochin, a peculiar choice for someone once described as 'a fiend in human form'.[12]

LOSING THE SPICE RACE

For a brief moment in the sixteenth century, the kingdoms of Spain and Portugal were united, bringing together their immense overseas territories in the New World, along with dominion over the Netherlands in north-west Europe. But Protestant revolt in the Netherlands led to the blockade of Antwerp, and the closure of Lisbon and Seville to Dutch traders, cutting off their spice supply. The Dutch response was rapid, and the successful return of Dutch ships laden with pepper in 1599 sent shockwaves through London's markets. The price of pepper almost tripled, rising from three to eight shillings a pound,[13] prompting a band of London merchants to petition Queen Elizabeth for exclusive trading rights. In many ways, the new company was seen a spin-off of the well-established

Levant Company, which saw its business threatened by the Dutch coup. 'This trading to the Indies', warned William Aldrich, 'have clean overthrown our dealings to Aleppo.'[14] Over £30,000 was raised to back the venture, which had a strikingly simple mission – 'let us be sole masters of the pepper trade',[15] declared the merchants. After much haggling the ailing queen eventually relented, awarding a charter on the last day of 1600, with the objective of bringing back valuable commodities from the East Indies, which should be 'bought, bartered, procured, exchanged, or otherwise obtained'. Alongside the pursuit of mercantile profit, Elizabeth's charter inserted the public policy goal of the 'advancement of trade'. In the end, the 218 investors who came together under this banner raised a total of £68,373 to finance a fleet of four small ships, which set sail in February 1601 to find an English niche in this lucrative business.

Their focus was the spice islands that now form modern Indonesia – pepper from Java, cloves from the Moluccas, as well as mace and nutmeg from the Banda Islands; India played no part of its early commercial strategy. The English Company's first trading base was established at Bantam in 1602, and the Company prospered in its first two decades as it struggled to gain a foothold. By taking the sea route to Asia, the Company was able to cut the prices of British imports of pepper, raw silk, cloves, indigo and mace by almost two-thirds compared with the overland route via Aleppo.[16] The Company's voyages between 1601 and 1612 generated returns of 155 per cent on invested capital of £517,784. Cloves sold from the Company's third voyage alone made profits of over 200 per cent. The first 'joint stock' then raised £420,436 to finance fleets for each of the four years between 1613 and 1616. But returns were much lower, though still substantial at 87 per cent. As time went on, a series of factors – including recession at home, mounting competition overseas and a growing glut of spices – meant that profits continued on a downward course. The second joint stock raised £1.6 million to finance annual voyages between 1617 and 1622, but could only offer 12 per cent back to investors, a rate of less than 1 per cent a year.[17]

What lives on from these times are tales of piracy and high adventure. Pirates have an ambiguous place in English folklore, part feared and part celebrated, and the first wave of East India traders simply continued an old English tradition: trade where necessary and plunder where possible. Though sometimes favoured by local people in the East Indies in their battles against the Dutch, the Company's motive was always the same: to secure exclusive control of local spice production. But the English Company progressively lost the 'spice race', outgunned and outclassed by the Dutch. Driven from the Moluccas following the massacre of English traders at Ambon (Amboina) in 1623, the Company gave up the prized nutmeg island of Run as part of wider negotiations following the second Anglo-Dutch war in 1667. In return, New Amsterdam in the Americas was transferred to British rule, and quickly renamed New York. The English Company would cling on to its residual bases in the spice islands, but was finally expelled from Bantam by the Dutch in 1682.

WINNING THE CALICO WAR

Forced from the spice islands, the Company refocused its gaze on India. The Company's ships had initially visited the Gujarat and Coromandel coasts of India in search of cotton textiles, which could then be bartered for spices in the Indies. A first embassy led by William Hawkins arrived at the Mughal port of Surat in 1608. His pleas for trade relations failed to interest Mughal Emperor Jahangir, who was still heavily influenced by the Portuguese. Persistence and military muscle paid off, however, and a naval victory over the Portuguese in 1612 resulted in the Company's first Mughal permit (*firman*) to trade from Surat, and thereafter at Ahmedabad and Agra. On the opposite coast, trading started at Masulipatam, the principal port of Golconda, in 1614. These early forays were capped in 1618, when England's ambassador Sir Thomas Roe finally won an extensive trade treaty from Jahangir. Hoping to distinguish the English from the Portuguese and Dutch strategy of conquest and fortification, Roe counselled the Company to avoid military entanglements. 'If you will profit,' he urged, 'seek it at sea and in quiett trade.' By 1625, 220,000 pieces of cloth were being exported by the Company from Surat.

One of the most memorable artefacts from this time is the 'Girdler's Carpet'. Eight metres long in deep blues and reds, the carpet was commissioned by Robert Bell from the Company's 'factory' in Surat, which then contracted the renowned Mughal workshop in Lahore to carry out the weaving. Bell was one of the first investors in the East India Company in 1600, and rose steadily through its ranks. But along the way he gained a reputation for murky accounting, and in 1630 was discovered smuggling wine to India. Four years later, things came to a head when he was accused of failing to pay for the 'very faire carpitt' that he had designed for his livery company, the Girdler's – the medieval guild of belt-makers. Bell claimed to have made the payment. But the Company's agent in Surat was by now dead. Many felt that Bell had cooked the books once more. By way of compensation, the Company confiscated 70 bags of Bell's pepper, and Bell withdrew from the Company under a cloud. His carpet remains on display in London's Girdler's Hall, and his mansion, Eagle House in Wimbledon, is now the home of the Al-Furqan Islamic Heritage Foundation. Bell was not the first – and would not be the last – Company executive to be fingered for ethical malpractice.

Maintaining a presence in Mughal India was a constant struggle. But, like the Dutch, the English Company succeeded largely by carving out a comfortable niche from the existing Portuguese empire, capturing its base at Hormuz on the Persian Gulf, for example, in 1622 and raiding Bombay in 1626. Permanent peace was signed with Portugal at Goa in 1635, giving the Company access to the Estado's ring of ports stretching all the way to Macao. It also paved the way for the establishment of the new base at Fort St George at Madras on the Coromandel coast in 1639. Bombay would follow in 1668, a wedding gift to Charles II from his Portuguese wife, Catherine of Braganza. The cash-strapped king promptly leased Bombay to the Company in return for a sizeable loan and an annual rent.

Before the benefits of this transfer could be realised, the Company almost ceased to exist, undermined by interlopers and civil war. For many in the seventeenth century, monopolies were regarded as the economic expression of royal despotism, powers to be opposed by the rising parliamentary forces. As early as 1604, a bill was introduced in Parliament to abolish all exclusive privileges over foreign trade. Supporting the bill, Sir Edwyn Sandys spoke out for the importance of commercial freedom: 'it is against the natural right and liberty of the subjects of England to restrain [merchandise] into the hands of some few'.[18] This was a spirit that would be echoed throughout the Company's career, with varying degrees of success. In 1604, the free trade bill failed. But the Stuart kings of England were always seeking additional sources of finance. As a result, the Crown was happy to back rival ventures, such as the short-lived Scottish East India Company of 1618 and the Courteen Association of 1636. Paradoxically, peace with Portugal became the excuse for William Courteen and a rival set of merchants to win a charter from the king to trade in the newly opened Portuguese zone. Courteen's venture would last for 15 years, disrupting the Company's monopoly presence. Yet, it would come together with the original Company in 1650 under the banner of the 'United Joint Stock' to found a permanent English factory in Bengal, at Hugli.

By then, however, the Company had been hard hit by the aftershocks of the British civil wars that raged from 1640 to 1647. The Anglo-Dutch struggles during Oliver Cromwell's protectorate in the 1650s also profoundly damaged Company interests. In addition, Cromwell refused to renew the Company's charter in 1653, allowing its monopoly to lapse. This produced a brief window of open commerce, boosting trade and reducing prices, yet crippling profits – a result almost exactly the same as the Dutch experience before 1602. On 14 January 1657, the situation had grown so bleak that the Company's directors voted to liquidate its affairs. This proved to be an effective ploy to force Cromwell's hand. By October, a new charter had been granted, and a permanent joint stock was established with capital to the tune of £740,000 – although only 50 per cent of this was actually subscribed at the time. It would take another half-century before the Company could match the invested capital of the second joint stock of 1617.

The Company could finally be called a modern corporation, and for the next three decades it experienced an economic boom. Between 1658 and 1688, the Company managed to complete 404 voyages between London and the East Indies, an average of 13 each season.[19] The return of King Charles II in 1660 secured its position, and from established bases at Surat and Madras, the new port of Bombay and the emerging trade with Bengal, Company imports surged. In 1664, it imported a quarter of a million pieces of cloth, almost half from the Coromandel coast, a third from Gujarat and less than a fifth from Bengal. By the end of the decade, cotton and silk textiles made up 56 per cent of Company imports, pushing pepper into second place, followed by raw silk, indigo, saltpetre, coffee and tea. Indian textiles hit an all-time peak of 1.76 million pieces in 1684, representing 83 per cent of the Company's total trade. This influx of cheap, easily washable clothing created a health and lifestyle revolution. By the end of the century, the value of the English Company's trade was fast catching up with the Dutch, with Bengal taking an ever-greater share. If the VOC was the commercial hare among the north European trading companies, the EIC was proving to be the tortoise.

The 1680s were the peak of the boom, when 200,000 pieces were exported from Bengal alone each year. This produced generous dividends and capital growth for the Company's investors. The Company's share price more than quadrupled in the two decades following the Restoration, growing from £60–£70 in 1664 to £245 in 1677 and £300 in 1680. Dividends were also substantial. For most of the 1670s, the Company paid out a 20 per cent dividend. But in 1680, fortunes improved and a 50 per cent payout was made, to be repeated in 1682, 1689 and 1691. And in 1682, so strong were the Company's finances that each proprietor received matching shares as a bonus, taking the Company's capital stock to £740,000. In all, from 1657 to 1691, proprietors received 840 per cent in dividends on their original investment. And for India, there was a steady influx of bullion, stimulating growth in income, output and employment. Between 1681 and 1685 alone, the Company exported 240 tonnes of silver and 7 tonnes of gold to India.[20] Financially, these were perhaps the best days of the Company's life.

A BID FOR DOMINION

It was at this point that the Company's directors in London made a fundamental shift in corporate strategy, a turnaround engineered by one of the most influential executives in its history, Sir Josiah Child. Born in 1630, Child made his first fortune as a victualler (supplier of food) to the navy under Cromwell's protectorate. His career took off in the early 1670s, when he became a member of the exclusive victualling syndicate for the Royal Navy, along with another rising star, Thomas Papillon. This lucrative venture gave Child the resources to become a founding shareholder of the Royal African Company, which had been awarded a royal monopoly to conduct the slave trade, and was headquartered, like the East India Company, on Leadenhall Street. In 1671, Child became a shareholder in the EIC for the first time, and only two years later he held 2 per cent of the entire stock, becoming the largest shareholder in 1679. Shares brought power in the Company, and for 17 years, from April 1674 until his death in 1699, Child was on the Company's board. Throughout the 1680s, he was either governor (chairman) or deputy-governor.

'As a practical man of business, he had few equals', wrote Thomas Macaulay in his *History of England*.[21] Child had a firm grasp of the essentials of business administration, making his intentions absolutely clear at home and abroad. Poor performance was not accepted, as the Company's executives in Madras soon realised when they received a severe rebuke in September 1687. 'The great trouble we labour under', wrote Child, 'is that you cannot get out of your old formes, and your cavilling way of writing or perverting, or misconstruing, procrastinating, or neglecting our plain and direct orders to you as if you were not subordinate but a coordinate power with us.'[22] Child was also a highly effective corporate advocate, producing a series of pamphlets under his own name and the pseudonym Philopatris, to persuade politicians of the Company's case. Early on in his career, he had also published *A New Discourse on Trade*, expounding the reasons for the Dutch success in trade, a model he wished to emulate.

Child's influence stretched to London's embryonic financial markets, where he had the reputation as 'the original of stock-jobbing'. Known today for his desert island story of Robinson Crusoe, Daniel Defoe was also a leading economic analyst of his age, and Defoe cast Josiah Child as a pivotal figure of his *Anatomy of Exchange Alley*. Published in 1719 as an investigation into the forces and figures that would soon drive the South Sea Bubble, Defoe examined the rising markets of the 1680s and 1690s, and made it clear that 'every Man's Eye, when he came to Market, was upon the Brokers, who acted for Sir Josiah', enquiring 'does Sir Josiah Sell or Buy?' But it was not just Child's wealth that moved markets, but his skill for manipulating the news from India. According to Defoe,

> there are those who tell us, letters had been order'd by private management to be written from the East Indies with an account of the loss of ships which have been arrived there, and the arrival of ships lost; of war with the Great Mogul, when they have been in perfect tranquillity, and of peace with the Great Mogul when he has come down against the factory of Bengal with 100,000 men, just as it was thought proper to call those rumours for raising and falling of the stock and when it was for this purpose to buy cheap or sell dear.[23]

Child's commercial vision was stark. Like many mercantilists, he saw wealth as being exclusively drawn from landed property. As a result, international trade was a zero-sum game with the goal of amassing as much of this wealth as possible for one's own nation.[24] Monopoly corporations such as the East India Company were therefore an essential part of England's commercial armoury. Child admired the tough-minded way in which the Dutch had achieved their supremacy and, echoing Coen, he fervently believed 'profit and power must go together'.[25] As he rose to prominence in the Company, Child put in place a radical plan to implement his vision. The first step was to make a new alliance with the Crown to guarantee the Company's privileges at home. Elected governor in 1681, Child quickly awarded Charles II 10,000 guineas to help smooth the renewal of the Company's charter, a payment that became an annual gift for the next seven years. Next he broke with his former partner Thomas Papillon, who was proposing to open up the East India trade to a much wider pool of investors and merchants. Papillon was also a leading 'exclusionist' who wanted to stop Charles's Catholic brother James from becoming king. Driven from his position on the Company's board and hounded by the court, Papillon was forced into exile in 1685. Child rapidly became a favourite at court, marrying his daughter to the eldest son of the Tory aristocrat, the Duke of Beaufort, and transferring £10,000 of Company stock into James's name. With his position at court secure, Child clamped down mercilessly on the growing band of interlopers who sought to break the Company's monopoly.

Having secured his position in England, Child then implemented the second part of his strategy: commercial conquest abroad. Child wanted the Company to become a sovereign power in India, forcing the Mughal Empire to trade with it on terms of equality. The prize was Bengal, where the Company had increasingly important trading operations but lacked a fortified stronghold like Goa or Batavia. This left it exposed to the fiscal exactions of the provincial governor, who, for example, in 1680 introduced a 5 per cent duty on imported bullion and a 3.5 per cent duty on exports – in spite of the Company's technical duty-free export status. In January 1686, Child gave his blessing to an expeditionary force of ten ships and six companies of infantry sent by the Company to force concessions from the Mughals in Bengal. Writing to the President of Fort St George in Madras on 9 June 1686, Child underlined the imperative for the Company to transform itself from 'a parcel of mere trading merchants' into a 'formidable martial government in India'.[26] The same tone filled his visionary call in 12 December 1687 for the new President and Council in Madras to 'establish such a politie of Civil and Military power, and create and secure such a large revenue to maintain both at that place as may be the foundation of a large, well-grounded sure English dominion in India for all time to come'.[27]

Child had begun what has become known as the Anglo-Mughal war – although it would perhaps be better described as first Company–Mughal conflict. His strategy was, of course, complete madness. The Mughal Emperor Aurangzeb was a military zealot, intent on asserting his power throughout the subcontinent. In 1686, for example, he took Bijapur, and the following year Hyderabad. In Bengal, the local forces of the Mughal's deputy, or Nawab, were equally overwhelming. Three years of skirmishing through the swamps of the delta followed, which 'only rendered our nation ridiculous', according to Job Charnock, the Company's chief in the region. Over in Gujarat, the Company raided Mughal shipping, provoking the capture of Surat and a full-blown siege of Bombay in 1689. Aurangzeb eventually restored the Company's trading rights, but at the cost of diplomatic humiliation and a fine of Rs150,000, plus damages. Only one piece of consolation could be drawn from the whole sorry affair. A new 'factory' was established among the villages of Kolikata, Govindapore and Sutanuti on the Hugli river in 1690, for which fortifications were begun in 1696 and *zamindari* rights purchased two years later. Calcutta had been born.

Yet, by then, Josiah Child's two-pronged strategy of corruption at home and aggression abroad had come crashing down. The Glorious Revolution of 1688–89 would not only replace Child's patron, James II, but would threaten the elimination of the Company itself.

A WHIRLWIND OF DISASTERS

On Guy Fawkes Day 1688, William of Orange, Stadtholder of the Netherlands, landed in England and ousted James II from the throne. Many forces were at work in this 'Glorious Revolution', most notably a convergence of a popular desire in England to be rid of a Catholic king with an urgent need in the Netherlands to remove James's pro-French threat. Yet commercial considerations were by no means secondary in the minds of the British elite as they constructed the unprecedented Bill of Rights that would bind the new joint monarchs, William and his English wife Mary, daughter of the deposed king. James's economic strategy, inspired by Child's aggressive mercantilism, had excluded whole swathes of the merchant class from the benefits of foreign trade. The result was a 'great grumbling in the City against a certain great East India merchant whose first name rhymes with Goliah'.[28]

Soon after the coronation in April 1689, the Convention Parliament began investigating the mounting complaints against the chartered corporations, most notably the African and Indian companies. Parliament quickly concluded in favour of establishing a new India company. This soon took shape at Dowgate in the City of London, with its base in the Skinners Hall. A fierce political battle began – 'the chief weapons of the New Company were libels; the chief weapons of the Old Company were bribes', wrote Macaulay.[29] Initially aiming for reform, the Dowgate Adventurers pressed for the Old Company to double its capital to £1.5 million to let other investors have a share of its riches and to limit individual holdings to £5,000 to prevent the concentration of power that Child had enjoyed. Papillon returned from Utrecht to join the triumphant Whigs who were pressing for change. But Child refused to budge, and the Commons voted to dissolve the Old Company. Yet, before this could be put into effect, while Parliament was in recess, in October 1693, the King suddenly granted a new charter to the Company for 21 years.

Parliament was furious, and in January 1694 passed an uncompromising resolution stating that 'all subjects of England should have equal right to trade to the East-Indies'.[30] This marked a profound break with the chartering process. Previously, a charter was the personal privilege of the Crown; now it would have to be confirmed through an Act of Parliament. Trade with India had been freed, and budding merchants chose to move north of the border to establish a new Scottish East India Company with £300,000 of capital. Child showed his contempt for the will of Parliament in a private letter to the Company's executives in India. 'Be guided by my instructions', he wrote, 'and not by the nonsense of a few ignorant country gentlemen who have hardly wit enough to manage their own private affairs, and who know nothing at all about questions of trade.'

But this breach of the Company's monopoly was not the end of the matter. Many had been suspicious at the circumstances that led to the charter grant in October 1693, and Parliament opened corruption investigations in March 1695. Even by the lax standards of the day, politicians were genuinely shocked by what they found. A team of MPs pored through the Company's accounts and uncovered a complex web of bribes, all emanating from the Governor Sir Thomas Cooke, Child's son-in-law. In the six years since the Revolution, £107,013 had been paid out for 'the special Service of the Company', including a massive £80,468 in 1693 to win a new charter. A further £90,000 had been lent to Cooke to buy Company shares to ease the chartering process. A crooked saltpetre import deal was also discovered that would transfer another £12,000. Initially, Cooke refused to explain these transactions. But a short spell in the Tower of London and an Act of Indemnity – effectively, a plea bargain – freed his tongue. The first slice of £10,000 had been delivered to Josiah Child, who passed it on to the King as a resumption of the traditional gift he had made in the 1680s. Other payments were made to a host of intermediaries to argue the Company's case at court. In front of a committee of both Houses of Parliament, Cooke was frank that 'the Inducements for giving this Money were, Fears of the Interlopers going out and Subscriptions for a new Company going on; by which they apprehended the Company would be ruined'.[31] With Josiah Child in the background, Cooke had orchestrated a whole series of intermediaries – a Mr Acton, Nathaniel Molineaux, Sir John Chardin, Paul Dockminique Esq and Captain John Jermaine – to press its case. The Attorney General received £545, and the Solicitor General just £218. Standing above all of these was Sir Basil Firebrace, who pocketed £40,000 in a series of contracts, which were designed to pay out only if the charter was won. Firebrace then commissioned others to sway the minds of key figures at court.

After interrogating Cooke, the MPs turned their attention on Firebrace. Like so many others broken by their own corruption, Firebrace sometimes stumbled in his answers, at one point pleading that he might postpone answering a particularly penetrating question to 'some other Time; being not well, not having slept Two or Three nights, and much indisposed as to his Health'.[32] Eventually, after persistent questioning, Parliament discovered that £5,500 had been received by Thomas Osborne, Duke of Leeds, and President of the King's Privy Council. The MPs expressed outrage at the 'dark practices in this affair', and feared that if someone so senior in government could take money for a commercial charter, he could also take money to betray the country to the French. But there was no law against taking money at court, and so a motion was prepared to impeach Leeds for abusing his office. A key witness fled the country, and before Parliament could start formal proceedings, the King commanded that the session be brought to a close, thereby ending the impeachment proceedings.

For John Pollexfen, a member of the parliamentary committee investigating the Company's affairs and a leading critic of its monopoly status, the conclusion was clear: 'companies have bodies, but it is said they have no souls; if no souls, no consciences'.[33] But Cooke, Child, Firebrace and Thomas Osborne all escaped punishment. As for the Company, its fate became ever more bleak. The post-Revolution stock market boom came to a shuddering halt, and the growing scandals cost the Company's shares 35 per cent during 1695 and a further 28 per cent in 1696. The situation was compounded by the onset of war with France, which disrupted the economy, hitting London's textile industry particularly hard. The Company had long been the target of protests from protectionist interests, critical of its growing imports of Indian calicoes. 'When the East India ships come in,' they argued, 'half our weavers play.' Others contended that competition from India kept wages in the wool and silk industries at starvation levels. The poor economic conditions of 1696 inflamed these passions, and in November several hundred weavers marched from Spitalfields in the East End of London to Westminster to push for legislation restricting Indian imports. The pressure was intensified the following January, when 5,000 weavers once again marched on Parliament. On their return journey, the weavers attacked East India House and broke open its doors, forcing the intervention of the local militia. In March, rioters ransacked the house of the Company's Deputy-Governor Thomas Bohun in Spitalfields, and two days later, the weavers marched to Hackney and threatened Josiah Child's mansion. The weavers had made their point, and three years later Parliament passed the first of a series of acts forbidding the use and wearing of all 'wrought silks, Bengalls and calicoes'.

The mood of financial crisis prompted the final denouement in the Company's long fall from grace. War had depleted the Crown's coffers, forcing it to turn to the City for cash. The Old Company offered the King a loan of £700,000 at 4 per cent interest. But the Dowgate Adventurers put forward a massive £2 million, though at a cost of 8 per cent interest. The King took the Dowgate offer, and in June 1698, the Commons passed an act awarding the monopoly of Asian trade to a new General Society. The Old Company's days appeared to be numbered.

The promise of commercial liberty that so many had entertained would be dashed, however. Two giant loopholes allowed the Old Company to regroup and recover its ascendancy. First of all, it was given a three-year period to wind up its affairs, and second, it also had the right to invest in the New Company, which it took advantage of by buying up £315,000 or 15 per cent of the new stock. The New Company was designed as an old-style regulated venture, enabling shareholders to trade under its umbrella up to the value of their holding. Shareholders were also able to form their own joint stock companies within the General Society, and so alongside the new 'English Company Trading to the East Indies', which accounted for the bulk of the shares, the Old Company continued to trade and its merchants in India stayed firmly in place. A valiant of bunch of independent traders also managed to subscribe to £23,000 of stock, creating something of a competitive market for the first time since the 1650s. Adam Smith would later observe that this window of relatively open trade brought rising prices for producers in India, cutting sale prices to consumers in England.[34]

Neither the Old nor the New Companies, however, had any intrinsic interest in competition, and to avoid commercial civil war, a scheme of amalgamation was agreed on 27 April 1702, brokered by none other than Sir Basil Firebrace. Seven years later, the new United Company of Merchants Trading to the East Indies was finally launched. In return for an exclusive charter, a further £1.2 million was raised and promptly loaned to the Crown at zero interest. This took the Company's invested capital to £3.2 million, all of which was lent to the government at 5 per cent. The United Company was 'on its way to becoming the prosperous and sound commercial and financial corporation which was not only far and away the biggest and most complicated trading organisation, but was the centre of the financial market rising in London'.[35]

Yet, not everyone was happy. One of the independent shareholders, writing anonymously to an MP in 1708, expressed his disgust at the merger, lamenting that there was 'not a man left that dare bring in a muslin neck cloth or a pound of pepper but themselves'.[36] The great hopes of the Glorious Revolution had come to nothing, he wrote, noting that it was 'strange after all our struggles for liberty that this monster, monopoly, should lift up its horns and shake his chains to the terror of the honest trading subject'. It was a 'wretched bargain' and a subject 'so melancholy, it makes my head ake'.

ON THE IMMENSE OCEAN OF INDIAN COMMERCE[37]

Once again, the East India Company had escaped extinction at the eleventh hour. By the time of the merger in 1709, external events had also begun to move in its favour. In India, Child's great adversary the Emperor Aurangzeb died in 1707, leaving behind a depleted treasury and a series of ineffective successors. Ten years later, on New Year's Eve 1716 the Emperor Farrukhsiyar made three imperial decrees (*firman*) granting the Company duty-free trading rights in the provinces of Bengal, Hyderabad – which contained the Coromandel coast – and Ahmedabad, which oversaw the ports of Gujarat. Imperial weakness, persistent negotiating and healthy bribes had succeeded where Child's frontal assault had failed. This *firman* provided the basis for a new era of corporate prosperity – as well as the seeds of perennial dispute with local rulers in India over its interpretation.

Perhaps more than any other of the Company's executives before or since, Josiah Child had demonstrated where an appetite for corporate power could lead. For contemporaries such as the diarist John Evelyn, he was the archetype of the 'suddenly monied', the new breed of merchant princes who had become both politically and economically dominant in the 1680s and 1690s. What makes his career so striking is the openness with which Child laid out his objective of commercial dominion and the consistency with which he sought to achieve it through a despotic alliance at home and aggression abroad. Like so many of his successors, he escaped unpunished, retiring to the calm of his walnut orchards at Wanstead, where he died in 1699 with £200,000 to his name, equivalent to just under £20 million in 2002 prices.[38] After Child, no-one either at headquarters or in the field would be as explicit in their intentions. But the desire would remain.

Turning its back on Child's adventurism, the Company's directors aimed to flourish by espousing high standards of corporate practice: 'righteousness is at the root of our prosperity', they urged their executives in India. Corruption still remained embedded in the Company's operations, but was kept to a manageable level. As for relations with India, the directors instructed its servants to 'take care that neither the broker, nor those under him, nor your own servants, use their authority to hurt and injure people'.[39] Its string of port cities flourished. In the case of Calcutta, Gulam Husain Salim, the Persian author of *Riyaz-us-Salatin*, argued that it was 'the liberty and protection afforded by the English', along with 'the lightness of duties levied', that explained its rise.[40]

'Trade, and trade only, was their business', and by the 1720s, the Company was outstripping its long-standing Dutch rival in terms of the Bengal textile trade.[41] Overall, it was now starting to match the VOC's share of the entire trade with Europe – a huge turnaround from the situation in the 1660s (see Table 3.1).

Table 3.1 Dutch and English East India Company exports from Asia 1668–1780 (in million florin)

	1668–70	1698–1700	1738–40	1778–80
English	4.3	13.8	23.0	69.3
Dutch	10.8	15.0	19.25	20.8

Source: Om Prakash, *European Commercial Enterprise in Pre-Colonial India*, New Delhi: Cambridge University Press, 2000, pp. 115, 121.

This commercial success was felt on the streets of London, where its main product line of Indian calicoes had become ubiquitous. Writing in January 1708, Daniel Defoe describes how calicoes 'crept into our houses, our closets and bedchambers' to such an extent that 'everything that used to be made of wool or silk, relating to either the dress of women or the furniture of our houses, was supplied by the India trade'.[42] For the Company, the initial ban on 'Bengalls' introduced in 1700 proved to be a temporary constraint. In response, the Company refocused its efforts towards supplying the British calico printing industry with raw materials, and located re-export markets for India's textiles. As part of the fast-growing African slave trade, Indian cottons became a vital item of barter for human cargoes. This was globalisation Georgian-style – a development enthusiastically endorsed by Joseph Addison in the pages of the *Spectator*. Addison gloried in the way that London had become an 'emporium for the whole Earth'. Writing in 1711, he described how 'the single dress of a woman of quality is often a product of a hundred climates ... the scarf is sent from the torrid zone ... the brocade petticoat rises out of the mines of Peru and the diamond necklace out of the bowels of Indostan'.[43] In India, this rapid growth in demand for textiles provided a valuable economic stimulus, bringing a flood of bullion into the region. Competition for the output of India's weavers between the English and other European companies, and, more importantly, with the dominant Asian merchant class, also ensured that this was a 'seller's market', boosting returns for local producers.

That eternal indicator of the Company's fortunes, its share price, reflected this recovery. A steady upward curve can be plotted from the low point of £39 in June 1698, just as the New Company was receiving its new charter, rising to over £100 as arrangements for the great merger began in 1702. Given the momentous nature of the deal, it was no surprise that the share price passed £200 in December 1717 as news of the *firmans* reached the London market. Inevitably, the Company's stock got caught up in the South Sea Company speculation of 1720, and in June of that year, it rose over 44 per cent from £290 to £420. Although John Company's shares plummeted by two-thirds as the South Sea Bubble imploded in 1721, it survived and became the undisputed 'blue chip' mercantile stock on the London exchange. In fact, the passing of the Bubble Act in 1720 made the Company's supremacy all the more noticeable, as the chartering of new joint stock companies came to a halt. After the dismal 1690s, when dividends had been suspended, payments to shareholders were resumed. During the 1730s and 1740s, the stock fluctuated between £150 and £200, and dividends were a modest, but predictable 7 to 8 per cent. This was a far cry from the huge returns of the 1680s, and still lagged those of the VOC, which awarded dividends averaging

20 per cent in the 1730s. But steadiness was now the key. In all, the Company earned a profit of £30,000,000 more from its sale of Asian goods in the three decades 1713–43 than it paid out in bullion and other goods.[44]

This apparently healthy equilibrium concealed major tensions, however. At home, the Company's monopoly remained a focus of dispute, and in 1730 petitions came in from London, Bristol and Liverpool to open up the Asia trade. In words that Adam Smith would echo half a century later, the petitioners argued that 'whatever is gained by the monopolising company, in the high prices at which it was enabled to sell, or the low prices at which it was enabled to buy, was all lost by its dilatory, negligent and wasteful management'.[45] An intriguing proposal was put forward to replace the Company's joint stock with a regulated company, which would manage the common infrastructure of the India trade, in return for a commission on all imports and exports; independent traders would then operate freely under this umbrella. But the Company had deep pockets and cut the rate of interest on its loan to the government from 5 to 4 per cent, and presented the state with a free gift of £200,000 in cash. In return, the charter was extended to 1766. In fact, the Company's monopoly would be secure until 1793.

In India, geopolitical turmoil had become a constant. The authority of the Mughals was visibly humbled following the sacking of Shahjahanabad (Delhi) in 1739 by the Persian Nadir Shah, who took the Peacock Throne back with him to Tehran. Political power fragmented, favouring the rise of autonomous regimes, notably in Bengal and Hyderabad. In the west, the Maratha confederacy asserted its military autonomy, raiding Bengal, for example, for the best part of the 1740s. And, although the Dutch no longer presented a threat, Britain's century-long conflict with France finally spilled over into India in the 1740s. In the mounting chaos of post-Aurangzeb India, the corporate needs of the Company and private interests of its executives would fuse together to produce the Bengal Revolution.

4
The Bengal Revolution

THE RISE AND FALL OF RAJAH NABAKRISHNA

Sovabazar in north Kolkata has a distinct and impressive atmosphere, the home to many of city's oldest commercial families. As the city expanded rapidly in the eighteenth century under the Company's protection, a powerful class of Indian merchants came to the fore. Called banians by the British – after the *bania* caste – they performed the crucial role of intermediary. These local traders would arrange the purchase of key commodities such as textiles, opium and saltpetre for the Company, and make loans to provide much-needed cash flow. In addition, the banians also went into business with the Company's executives on an individual basis, enabling the English to profit from the opportunities for private trade that the hazardous posting to Bengal provided. In the words of William Bolts, one of the Company's most successful and controversial traders, 'a Banyan is a person by whom the English gentlemen in general transact all their business. He is interpreter, head book-keeper, head secretary, head broker, the supplier of cash and cash-keeper, and in general also secret-keeper.'[1] The importance of this relationship is depicted in Thomas Hickey's late eighteenth-century portrait of John Mowbray with his banian. Deep in discussion, Mowbray is seated, listening intently as the banian, swathed in cloth, reads from his account log, a map of their commercial hunting grounds in north India strategically placed on the wall behind them.

One of the most powerful of these merchants was Rajah Nabakrishna Deb, whose palace stills stands on Nabakrishna Street in Sovabazar. Two lions guard the gateway, their paws resting on red-painted cannonballs. Beyond lies an inner courtyard around which rises a two-storey building that contained Nabakrishna's offices, library, living quarters and shrine to the goddess Durga. During the lavish parties (*nautchs*) that he threw for the British, the women of the household would retire to their *zenana* on the upper floor to observe the proceedings through wooden grills. For almost half a century, Nabakrishna was one of the pillars of the Company's success in Bengal, a key ally in the revolution that brought them control of India's richest province. When the new Nawab Siraj-ud-Daula confronted the Company in 1756, Nabakrishna took the Company's side, smuggling food into the besieged Calcutta before its fall. He then worked as Robert Clive's go-between in the negotiations that led up to Plassey, and, in its immediate aftermath, helped to loot the harem at Murshidabad of Rs80 million in gold, silver and jewels.

More than this, Clive and Nabakrishna apparently became close friends. Such was the depth of the friendship that when Clive was looking for a suitable location to celebrate Plassey in place of the destroyed church of St Anne's, Nabakrishna offered his own house as a substitute. Clive accepted and made an offering at the feet of Durga, Kolkata's local deity. To this day, 'the annual Durga Puja at 36 Nabakrishna Street is still known as Company Puja'.[2] In 1766, Clive awarded Nabakrishna the title of Maharajah, and a salary of Rs2,000 for his services to the Company. Returning home from the ceremony, Nabakrishna rode to his palace in Sovabazar on an elephant, scattering money in the streets. Ten years later, Warren Hastings went one step further and made him the perpetual *talukdar* of Sutanuti, one of the prime areas of Calcutta. So close was Nabakrishna to Clive that he would be accused by some of Clive's rivals of trumped-up charges of robbery and rape, charges of which he was quickly cleared.

But Nabakrishna's relationship with the British eventually soured. In 1780, Hastings needed to borrow Rs300,000 to cover a hole in his personal finances, and turned to Nabakrishna for help. Hastings wanted to transfer the money to the Company's account, and then use this to pay himself for the range of cultural activities he had funded out of his own pocket (including a mission to Tibet and the new madrasa in Calcutta). Nabakrishna insisted that the money should be treated as a gift rather than a loan, and Hastings accepted, recording it as a donation to the Company, from which he promptly started paying himself. Already murky, what made the deal extremely suspicious was that it coincided with Nabakrishna's request to be made one of the Company's key officials in the district of Burdwan in order to enable him to recover arrears from the local ruler. The appointment was made and the money changed hands. All this became entangled in the wider charges of malpractice and corruption that would later assail Hastings on his return to England. At his impeachment, the prosecution would argue that Nabakrishna's Rs300,000 was a bribe, and therefore contrary to Company rules.

Then, in 1792, in the middle of the trial, Nabakrishna changed tack and stated that it was a loan after all, for which he had never been repaid. Hastings was presented with a bill for £37,500 plus 12 per cent interest, which he refused to pay, prompting a second lawsuit that proceeded in parallel with the impeachment. Parliament's stamina for the marathon impeachment trial was fading fast, and in 1795, Hastings was acquitted of all charges, including of accepting a bribe from Nabakrishna. This should have put the Rajah in a good position in his parallel case; if the money was not a gift, then it must be a loan. But such are the vagaries of justice that it took a further nine years for the courts in London to conclude that Hastings had accepted a gift after all – and therefore had no obligation to repay the Rajah. By this time, Nabakrishna was no more, dying in 1797 and leaving Rs10 million (£1 million) – a fortune that would be worth over £70 million today.[3] The British mangled many Indian words in their time, but there is a special scorn in the anglicised version of Rajah Nabakrishna: Nobkissen.

Nabakrishna's career symbolises the ending of the mutual mercantilism that the Company initially pursued in India. The French historian Fernand Braudel concluded that the Company's rise to prominence only came about with the 'help, collaboration, collusion, coexistence, symbiosis' of the local merchant elite.[4] The Company simply could not trade without their contacts and their capital. And when the Company needed ready cash to resolve the liquidity crisis in England caused by the South Sea Bubble in 1720, it borrowed the money in India. Yet, beneath this mingling of Indian and British trading cultures, a fundamental battle was under way between the moral economy of Bengal's regulated marketplace and the Company's monopoly capitalism. The Company had lost the first round to crack the Mughal Empire in the 1680s. But in the Bengal of the 1750s, it was pushing every opportunity to advance its interests against the regulatory power of the local nawab, the commercial supremacy of the Asian merchants and the rising threat of the French. What Child had failed to achieve in the 1680s, Robert Clive would accomplish through a mixture of sheer audacity, military force and exquisite fraud.

The violence of the Company's takeover of Bengal – and the use of the Company's own private army to carry out the transaction – has meant that the battle of Plassey and all that followed have generally been seen as a simple example of colonial conquest. This view is given strength by the Company's subsequent evolution into an agent of the British state, administering its Indian territories in return for a secure profit for its shareholders. But the sheer strangeness of the Company's absorption of Bengal – and much of the rest of the subcontinent – should not blind us to the fact that this event is best understood as a business deal, as an extreme form of corporate takeover. Two words were used repeatedly by contemporaries to explain the peculiar transformation that took place. First, the Company had engineered a 'revolution' that not just replaced one nawab with another who was more amenable, but also changed the underlying dynamics of the Bengali state. Second, it had made a phenomenal 'acquisition' that placed the Company, its executives and shareholders on a totally new path to prosperity.[5] Adam Smith would later warn of the tendency of corporations to engage in a 'conspiracy against the public', using their economic muscle to erode the capacity of the state to regulate and tax for the common good. This was an age of revolutions, and alongside the better known American and French revolutions, the Company engineered its own revolution in Bengal. If evidence was needed of corporate conspiracy, this was it.

'THE RICHEST COUNTRY IN THE WORLD'[6]

For the first half of the eighteenth century, the Company's attention was focused on the prize that was Bengal. The Indian subcontinent was then the workshop of the world, accounting for almost a quarter of global manufacturing output in 1750, compared with just 1.9 per cent for Britain (Map 2).[7] Within the Mughal Empire, Bengal was the richest province (*suba*), described by Aurangzeb as 'the Paradise of Nations'. Proximity to good raw materials, a highly productive agricultural sector along with a sophisticated division of labour in cloth production gave Bengal an unbeatable combination of high quality and low prices. Such was the cost advantage that in the late eighteenth century Indian cottons could be sold at a profit in Britain, at prices 50 to 60 per cent lower than those fabricated domestically. Deeply embedded in the traditional village system, hand-woven cotton linked agriculture with industry, creating a diversity of income and providing goods that could be traded both locally and internationally. For millennia, Indian cotton cloths out-competed the rest of the world. Even in the first century A.D., the Roman historian Pliny was complaining that the extensive importing of cotton fabrics from India was draining Rome of gold. Similar complaints came from English weavers when Indian cottons once again began to enter Europe in bulk in the late seventeenth century.

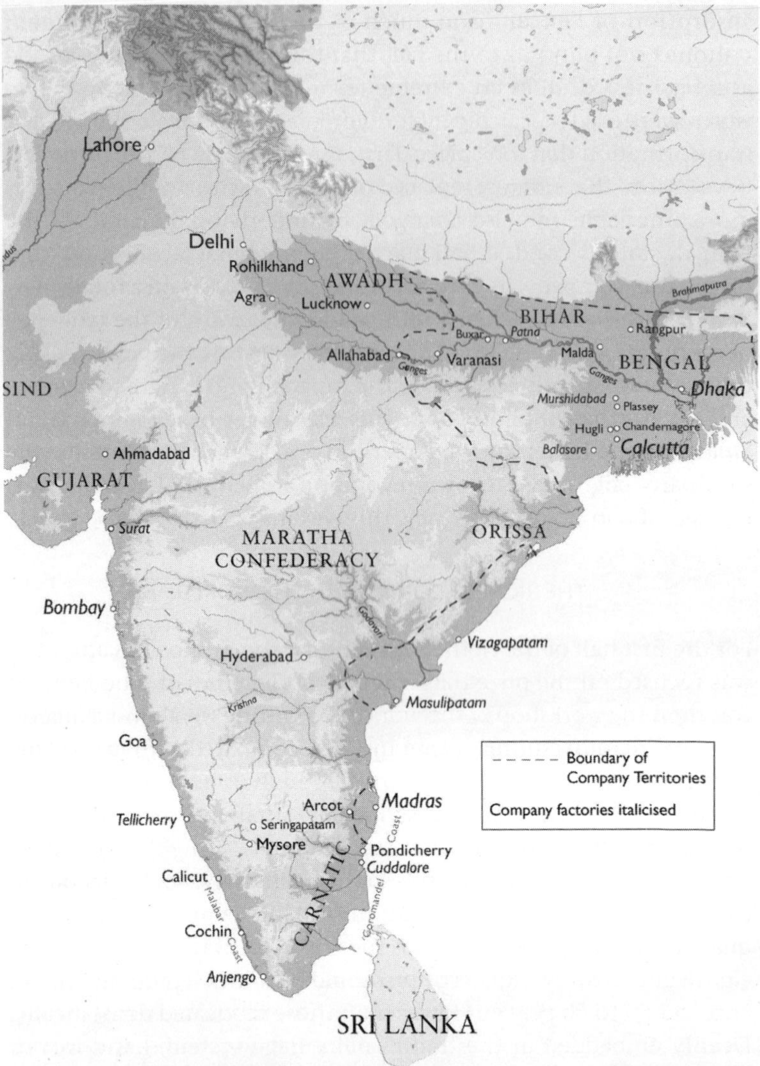

Map 2 India in the late 1760s

Bengal's production was also distinguished by immense diversity, with over 150 different names for the textiles bought by the Company, covering muslins, calicoes and silk, along with mixed cotton and silk goods. Different production centres would specialise in particular styles; for example, Dhaka was renowned for the transparency, beauty and delicacy of its muslins. So fine was the fabric that a pound of cotton could provide upwards of 250 miles of muslin thread. Quality and style varied from the finest *mull-mulls* and *allaballee* through to *shabnam* (morning dew) and *nayansukh* (pleasing to the eye). Essential for the feel of the muslin was the short-staple *phuti* cotton grown on the banks of the river Meghna, near Dhaka, described by the British Resident as 'the finest cotton in the world'.[8] One estimate from 1776 suggests that as many as 25,000 weavers were based in Dhaka producing some 180,000 pieces of cloth from thread spun by 80,000 women.[9] Along with its textiles, Indian names for cloth also entered the English language, not least bandana, calico and chintz, dungaree, gingham, seersucker and taffeta.

For the Company, the textile craze in Europe created immense wealth for its traders and shareholders. Although it had started trading textiles from the Gujurat and Coromandel coasts, Bengal steadily grew in importance. From just 12 per cent in 1668–70, Bengal's share of total Company imports climbed to 42 per cent in 1689–90, making it the largest single source of supply; by 1738–40, the proportion had climbed to 66 per cent.[10] But the Company was only one trader among many, and the trade of all the European companies put together probably represented only one-third of the Bengal's total exports, the bulk still being conducted by Asian merchants.[11] Not surprisingly, this immense source of demand created a powerful upward pressure on prices.

Access to this market was also tightly controlled, regulated by a Mughal trade policy that carefully delineated what could be traded and by whom on the basis of both economic functionality and social significance. The Mughals made clear distinctions between inland and international trade, with foreign companies being awarded the privilege of export in exchange for inflows of silver to enrich the treasury and lubricate the economy. Within Bengal's internal market, a range of prestige items, such as salt, betel and tobacco, were traded on the basis of social rather than market norms. 'European trading groups, people from the "hat-wearing nations" (*kulah poshan*) were admitted into these transactions of privilege and power as long as they did not disrupt the material hierarchy of exchange.'[12] This combination of strong demand and tight regulations meant that the terms of trade for the European traders drawn to Bengal were tough. Only bullion would do, and between 1708 and 1756 three-quarters of the Company's imports into Bengal were in the form of silver.

The foundations for the Company's operations in Mughal India were laid out in the succession of imperial decrees (*firman*), which defined the commercial privileges granted by the emperor. From the 1650s, the Company had won the ability to export goods from Hugli, the main port of Bengal, duty-free in return for an annual payment of Rs3,000. But it was only in 1717 that the Company managed to win imperial backing for this position through the famous *firman* of Emperor Farrukhsiyar. As part of this decree, the Company's President at Calcutta was given unprecedented authority to issue passes (*dastaks*), which would then exempt shipments from paying duty. Like many multinationals operating today, the Company had been awarded a tax status that favoured it over local traders. But the *firman* did not specify which goods were to be covered, although the general understanding was that it applied solely to export goods.

Almost as soon as the 1717 *firman* was agreed, the Company began to push the boundaries of acceptable business. The Company's president began issuing *dastaks* to its executives enabling them to engage in private trade at duty-free rates. Worse, it also sold the passes on to Asian merchants, thereby gaining an income stream that legally belonged to the Nawab. For the Bengali authorities, the Company's practices posed a two-fold threat, undermining its revenue base and threatening the local economy. In his dispute with the Company, Siraj-ud-Daula would claim in 1756 that the Company had defrauded the Mughal exchequer of Rs15 million since 1717 through the abuse of its *dastaks*. The Nawab was also highly conscious of the destructive effect that the Company's ability to undercut local traders was having on the wider Bengal economy. In 1727, for example, the Nawab's officials stopped the Company fleet from Patna and found that it was illegally carrying huge stores of salt downriver to Calcutta. Protesting to the Company's president, the Nawab Alivardi Khan stated that if it did not put a stop to its 'encroachments', it would 'undersell all others, engross the whole trade of the province, and thereby deprive vast numbers of the natives of the means of a livelihood'.[13] Alivardi Khan repeatedly clamped down on *dastak* abuse, forcing the Company to make additional duty payments in 1727, 1731, 1732, 1736, 1740, 1744 and 1749.

The dominant position of Asian merchants in the Bengal economy also rankled with the Company. Like the Company, local merchants were keen to win sole control over vital commodities. The Armenian Khwaja Wajid, for example, prospered through his monopoly over the salt and saltpetre trades, and had a powerful position in the Patna opium trade. More than this, the Company resented its dependence on local merchants for cash and connections. The Company simply did not have the skills or capacity to buy goods direct from the producers, and so had to commission local brokers to purchase textiles and other products on its behalf. In the case of textiles, the brokers would pay the weavers an advance (*dadni*), which was used to cover materials and living costs during the production of the cloth. This relationship generated considerable bitterness on the Company's part, its executives continually fearing that they were either being overcharged or supplied with sub-standard goods by the *dadni* merchants. The Company was also frustrated that these brokers were not wholly focused on its interests, but traded on their own account. Indeed, Asian trading houses, such as those headed by Jagat Seth and Amir Chand (Umichand), were often far richer and better connected than the Company. The relationship was further complicated by the huge extent of English indebtedness to local bankers. In the run-up to Plassey, almost all of Calcutta's English community had loans outstanding with Indian moneylenders.[14]

If this was not enough, competition from other European trading houses was threatening the Company's position. The English were just one of many foreign players in the Bengal market, and in the short stretch of the river Hugli north of Calcutta lay first Serampore (Denmark), Chandernagore (France), Chinsura (Netherlands) and the port of Hugli itself. Calcutta had become the leading port on the river in the 1720s, outstripping the long-established Dutch. In the 1730s, however, the French Compagnie Perpetuelle des Indes began to pose a serious threat. Under the leadership of Joseph François Dupleix as Governor of Chandernagore, the French took the commercial initiative from the English, most notably in the lucrative inland trade exploited by both companies' executives on their own account. Dupleix's commercial brilliance undermined both the corporate and private interests of his English rival, and it is with some accuracy that he was later able to claim, 'I made the English tremble for they saw their commerce dwindling and their merchants forced to declare themselves bankrupt.'[15] By the early 1750s, Company exports from Bengal were in decline, matched by a resurgence of Dutch trade from Chinsura. Back in London, the Company's shares also stumbled, commencing a slow slide from £197 in December 1752 to £133 in January 1757. Dividends also started to slip, falling from 8.6 per cent in 1752 to 5.8 per cent in 1756, a pathetic payout that was repeated in the two following years.

Revolutions often occur when a strong run of improving conditions comes suddenly to a halt. The shattering of expectations that this brings drives those affected to seek radical solutions. Bengal was no different in the early 1750s, where the Company was desperate to find a solution to its worsening commercial position. In 1751, the Company's *dadni* merchants refused to comply with new terms and conditions, and the Company suffered a severe procurement shortfall the following year. In June 1753, the situation had become a crisis, and the Company abolished the entire *dadni* system, introducing paid agents (*gomastas*) who would purchase goods directly from the production outlets (*aurungs*). By cutting out the middleman, the new approach also gave the Company's executives a chance of relaunching their own trading businesses; the road to Plassey was paved with the commercial adventurism of private trade. Relations with the Nawab continued to sour, and in August 1752 Robert Orme, one of the Company's leading merchants in Calcutta, wrote in frustration to a friend in Madras, ''twould be a good deed to swing the old Dog [Alivardi Khan]. I don't speak at random when I say that the Company must think seriously of it or it will not be worth their while to trade in Bengal.'[16] The friend was another Robert, Robert Clive.

THE SPIRIT OF WAR AND CONQUEST[17]

Frustration was one thing, the opportunity to realise these private thoughts quite another. What created the conditions for revolution to finally take place was the steady implosion of Mughal authority. Imperial over-stretch under Aurangzeb had left the Mughals vulnerable to repeated assaults from Afghan, Persian and Maratha invasions. Perpetual court intrigue and waning military might also began to undermine its highly effective system of imperial governance. At its heart had been strict control over provincial governors ensuring that appointments were made from the centre. In addition, the Mughals separated provincial powers between a *nazim*, who administered political and judicial matters, and a *diwan*, who managed tax and financial affairs. In Bengal, this elegant system began to break down in 1717 when both offices were merged under Murshid Quli, who promptly moved the capital from Dhaka to the self-styled Murshidabad. When he died in 1727, he was succeeded by his son-in-law, Shujauddin, who ruled until 1739. Then in a bloody coup that set the precedent for subsequent events, Shujauddin's son was deposed by his pipe-bearer (*hookahburdar*), Alivardi Khan. Bengal's economy had considerable strengths. But even these began to be shaken by the persistent Maratha raids throughout the 1740s, and the Nawab's growing use of arbitrary measures to raise revenues. And although Alivardi ruled for over 15 years, the regime he passed on to his grandson, Siraj-ud-Daula, was highly personalised and increasingly fragile. A weak ruler would leave Bengal exposed to the side-effects of the global war now being pursued by France and Britain.

Since the merger of Anglo-Dutch interests at the Glorious Revolution in 1688, France rather than the Netherlands had been viewed as Britain's primary imperial competitor. It would take a hundred years of on-and-off warfare to decide the outcome at the Battle of Waterloo in 1815. Initially, the countries' two East India companies were able to stand aloof from this geopolitical struggle, with both sides agreeing a neutrality pact during the War of the Spanish Succession (1701–14). But in the War of the Austrian Succession (1740–8), the British state propelled the two companies into open hostilities. After his term of office at Chandernagore, Dupleix had become Governor of Pondicherry. In 1744, when news of war reached India, Dupleix once again offered a neutrality pact to his counterpart in the English Company at Madras. The Company played for time, but offshore the Royal Navy raided the Compagnie's shipping. Hostilities had begun.

In the ensuing battles, not only did Madras fall to the French, but the French also defeated the Nawab of the Carnatic who had understandably forbidden the two Companies from fighting on his territory. Although Madras was returned to the Company at the Peace of Aix-la-Chapelle that ended the Austrian War, the conflict continued, with both firms now backing rival princes for control of the Carnatic. It is in these conflicts in South India that Robert Clive first showed his military prowess, and the Company saw a new source of income emerging from 'nabob-making' alongside commerce. Like other Company executives, Clive arrived in India as a young writer, landing in Madras aged 19 in June 1744. From a modest gentry background, Clive was keen to restore his family's social status, and used the proceeds of his first Indian fortune to pay off the mortgage for his birthplace, Styche Hall in Shropshire.

As a boy, he had been known for being 'out of measure addicted' to fighting, and it was only when war erupted in India that he showed any promise for the Company. Untrained as a soldier, Clive had an uncanny ability to pull off audacious guerrilla actions, capturing Arcot and holding it in the teeth of an overwhelming French force. The following year, he forced Trichinopoly to surrender, and in the eventual peace treaty, the Company acquired San Thome and Poonamallee, boosting the territorial revenues of Madras. Clive returned to England in October 1753 as a popular hero, receiving a gold-lined sword studded with diamonds from the Company's grateful directors.

Dislodged from Parliament in a disputed election contest, Clive returned to India in April 1755 as Governor of Fort St David at Cuddalore. His mission was to open a new front against the French on the west coast, attacking their interests in Hyderabad. By the time he reached Bombay, however, peace had been agreed, and Clive was en route to Madras when disturbing news arrived that the Company had been expelled from Bengal.

THE ROAD TO PLASSEY

Alivardi Khan's grandson, Siraj-ud-Daula, came to power in April 1756 aged 21. Generally portrayed by his opponents as a vicious and decadent individual, Siraj-ud-Daula's stance towards the British was perfectly consistent with the core principles of his grandfather's reign. Alivardi Khan had tried to clamp down on the Company's abuse of the *dastak*, and was highly suspicious of the growing military dimension of the Company's settlement in Calcutta. In particular, he objected to the defensive ditch that had been constructed to protect the city against the Maratha raids of the 1740s. 'You are merchants,' he told the Company, 'what need have you of a fortress?'[18] Both of these factors were also prime drivers of Siraj-ud-Daula's decision to teach the Company a lesson. He was particularly concerned by the Company's decision to strengthen Fort William in Calcutta, motivated in part by the threat of a coming global war against the French. The new Nawab had the added grievance of the Company's decision to give refuge to one of his leading opponents. Even one of the Company's own executives, Richard Becher, recognised that it had given the Nawab 'sufficient cause to be angry with the English'.[19]

For its part, under the wayward leadership of Calcutta's President Roger Drake, the Company wholly underestimated the determination of the new Nawab to curb its misdemeanours. As in previous disputes between nawab and Company, negotiation was the first option for resolving the conflict. Siraj-ud-Daula sent his ambassador

Narayan Singh to parley with the Company in Calcutta. But Singh was humiliated and unceremoniously expelled. Reporting back in Murshidabad, Singh was outraged, saying 'what honour is left for us men when a few traders, who have not yet learnt to wash their bottoms, reply to ruler's orders by throwing out his messenger?'[20] Yet still Siraj-ud-Daula pressed for a negotiated solution, declaring that 'if the English behave themselves like merchants they may rest assured of my favour, protection and assistance'.[21] The problem of course was that the Company no longer wanted to be just another merchant among many. It wanted dominion and refused to accept the Nawab's terms – the demolition of fortifications, the ban on the sale of *dastaks* to Asian traders and an end to harbouring the Nawab's enemies.

When all else failed, the Nawab sent his forces to capture Calcutta. The Company might have been commercially significant, but a combination of cowardice and lack of preparations meant that Fort William was quickly overwhelmed in June 1756. In an incident that became part of British imperial myth, that night anything up to a hundred Company prisoners died of asphyxiation in the 'black hole', a tiny cell in the grounds of Fort William. Just as in 1689, the Company was on the verge of total expulsion from Bengal, its most profitable subsidiary. Articles in the London press estimated that the Company lost £2,250,000 on the fall of Calcutta, more than half its nominal share capital. Siraj-ud-Daula underscored his position of supremacy by renaming Calcutta as Alinagar and demanding repayment from the Company of evaded customs duty for the past 15 years. In local markets, traders quickly drew their own conclusion from the Company's humiliation, and calico prices rose 50 per cent, with the price of European goods falling in proportion. 'This alarmed the Company's governors so much', commented one observer, 'that they took immediate measures for repossessing the settlements.'[22]

Unknown to Siraj-ud-Daula, the Company was rapidly constructing a counter-offensive deploying the forces sent with Clive for the Hyderabad expedition along with Royal Navy ships under the command of Admiral Watson. On 11 October 1756, Clive wrote back to the Company's Secret Committee in London that 'I flatter myself that this expedition will not end with the retaking of Calcutta only – and that the Company's estate in these parts will be settled in a better and more lasting condition than ever.'[23] In the instructions it gave to Clive two days later, the Madras Council highlighted the importance of winning back Calcutta (with reparations), but added that the mission should also 'effect a junction with any powers in Bengal that might be dissatisfied with the violence of the Nawab's government or that have pretensions to the nawabship'.[24] The Company was putting its experience in the Carnatic to good use.

Clive's expedition was small in number, but highly focused, ransacking Hugli in January 1757 and retaking Calcutta the following month. By the Treaty of Alinagar, the Company was empowered to mint its own coin and extend the use of the *dastak* to its private trade. Clive pushed on. Avoiding French overtures for a neutrality pact in Bengal and taking advantage of the incursion of Afghan marauders in the west of the province, Clive's forces bombarded and captured Chandernagore in March. The commercial significance of this victory cannot be underestimated. When news of the fall of Chandernagore reached London months later, the Company's share price rose by 12 per cent.[25] The first of the obstacles to the Company's domination of the Bengal economy had now fallen.

Intrigue would soon finish off both the Nawab and the Asian merchants. The story of the conspiracy that led to Plassey is obscured by claims and counter-claims about who was ultimately responsible. For one expert, it was the British who 'engineered and encouraged the coup'.[26] Clive in his letter to the Company's directors following the victory at Plassey reported that it was disaffected Bengalis who had 'made overtures to us'.[27] Whatever the precise allocation of responsibility, it is clear that there was a powerful convergence of interests between the English Company and sections of the Bengal court. If blame is to be attached, the Company was obviously guilty of fomenting illegal insurrection, while Mir Jafar, Jagat Seth, Amir Chand and the other conspirators were equally at fault for high treason.

All three of the major plotters on the Bengali side were significant figures in their own right. Mir Jafar was a leading soldier and Siraj-ud-Daula's paymaster-general (*bakshi*), but had been removed from office in the wake of Chandernagore. The Jagat Seths were unrivalled in northern India for their financial power. Known as 'banker of the world' (*jagat seth*), this *marwari* family had built up formidable economic resources on the back of its control of the imperial mint and extensive moneylending. They wielded this financial clout at the Bengali court and were judged to be 'the chief cause of revolutions in Bengal' by a French commentator at the time.[28]

Originally from Agra, Amir Chand was another of Bengal's leading merchant princes, controlling much of the trade in opium and saltpetre. He was also well known to the Company, working as one of its *dadni* merchants from the early 1730s. Relations had not always been harmonious between the two, and in 1735, the Company terminated its contract with him on account of fraud. Four years later, however, he was reinstated and later managed a full third of the Company's annual investment in Bengal.

The novelty of the Plassey coup did not lie in the raw fact of intrigue and treachery in the Bengal capital of Murshidabad. What was new was the willingness of the conspirators against Siraj-ud-Daula to ally themselves with what were in effect foreign mercenaries. Like the weak and greedy nobles operating in post-Roman Britain, leading aristocrats and merchants at the Bengal court believed that they could control the foreign barbarians to their own ends. They proved to be catastrophically mistaken. Bengal was certainly rich, but its governing and merchant elite had little depth, basing their primacy on personal contacts and loyalties. Set against this was a robust impersonal institution with a highly focused set of priorities. The Company's corporate structure gave it 'a collective strength and unity of purpose [that was] not available' either to Asian merchants or post-Mughal nawabs.[29] This single-mindedness would soon be on display in Bengal.

During the intense negotiations of the deal that would overthrow Siraj-ud-Daula, Amir Chand once again overstepped the mark, in the process becoming the original 'Mr Five Percent'. Threatening to expose the plotters, Amir Chand demanded a full one-twentieth of the Bengal treasury for his continued support. One hundred and fifty years later, in 1914, another more successful corporate intermediary, Calouste Gulbenkian, earned the title 'Mr Five Percent' for the share he received of the Turkish Petroleum Company for arranging the deal between an Anglo-Persian syndicate, Shell and Deutsche Bank. Back in 1757, both the other Bengali conspirators and the Company were outraged by Amir Chand's audacity. In a sleight of hand that would become legendary, Clive drew up two treaties with Mir Jafar. In a fake treaty inscribed on red paper, Clive agreed to Amir Chand's demand, forging the signature of Admiral Watson, the leader of the expedition. In the real treaty written on white paper, however, no mention was made of this transfer. When Amir Chand learned of the trick in the aftermath of Plassey, he fainted and died in despair shortly afterwards.

The conspiracy that culminated at Plassey was a close-run thing and almost ended in disaster. Siraj-ud-Daula actually discovered the plot. But in a bout of indecision that proved his undoing, the Nawab decided not to crush the conspiracy and sought reconciliation instead. In addition, his attention was divided, fearing both incursions of Afghan troops in western Bihar and the aggressive Company to the south. On 23 June 1757, the Nawab's larger but poorly organised and internally divided forces met the Company's much smaller yet better-disciplined troops near a grove of mango trees at Plassey. Perhaps as many as 50,000 Bengalis faced the Company's forces of 3,000 infantry, of which only a third were British. Luck, pluck and treachery all came together to bring about the Nawab's defeat, which was swiftly followed by his assassination. The Company installed Mir Jafar as its puppet and proceeded to implement the terms of its treaty.

The payback began immediately. French factories were eliminated from Bengal, substantial damages were paid as compensation to the Company, as well as to the English, Indian and Armenian inhabitants of Calcutta, and the Company received grants of lands surrounding the city, known as the 24 *parganas*. In an extraordinary deal, Clive had won an immediate £2.5 million for the Company to be followed by enhanced revenues into the future. Writing in triumph to the Company's directors on 26 July 1757, Clive concluded that 'this great revolution, so happily brought about, seems complete in every respect'.[30]

REAPING THE REWARDS OF REVOLUTION

Almost immediately after the Plassey coup, the techniques that Clive had deployed were subject to substantial scrutiny, and have been the focus of controversy ever since. Many criticised Clive for stooping to so-called 'Oriental' practices of corruption and deceit. Surveying Clive's career many years later, Thomas Babington Macaulay concluded that he had become an 'Indian intriguer', and his trickery of Amir Chand was 'not merely a crime, but a blunder'. Clive's most recent English biographer, Robert Harvey, takes a more Machiavellian approach and argues that Clive 'deserves enormous credit for his skill in deceit'.[31] There can be little real sympathy for Amir Chand, outwitted by someone more underhand than himself. But Clive's great deception forms part of the original lie that underpinned British rule in India. The 'black hole' incident would later be blown up as a crime that justified the Company's fullest retribution. But the Company would remain wide open to the charge of hypocrisy when it later extolled its 'plain dealing' (in Clive's own words) as providing the foundations for its rule.[32]

More serious are the charges of corruption levelled at Clive. Along with other leaders of the expeditionary force, Clive profited enormously from the Plassey Revolution, gaining Rs200,000 as a member of the Bengal Select Committee, a further Rs200,000 as commander-in-chief, and another Rs1,600,000 in the form of private donations from the Bengal nobility, in all amounting to £234,000 – some £22 million in 2002 values. Aged 33, Clive had suddenly become one of the richest men in England. Defending himself in Parliament many years later, Clive declared himself innocent of all charges: 'Mr Chairman, at this moment, I stand astounded at my own moderation.' Unseemly as these payments may well have been, Clive was breaking no law in accepting them. He was merely setting 'an evil example' to others, according to Macaulay. Furthermore, his rewards are in many ways not that different from the success bonuses awarded to the chief executives of 1990s corporations for pulling off high-stakes acquisitions. Vodafone's Christopher Gent, for example, won an extra £10 million in 2000 for securing the capture of Germany's Mannesmann, a reward that one shareholder described at the time as behaviour akin to 'the robber barons of old'.[33]

What Clive had started, others would copy. In the eight years that followed Plassey, the Company placed four nawabs on the throne of Bengal. Each 'revolution' was accompanied by the transfer of more land to the Company to reschedule the Nawab's now-hefty debts, along with lavish presents for leading Company executives, totalling £2.2 million, along with another £3.8 million in reparations. In 1760, Mir Jafar was toppled by the Company in favour of his son-in-law Mir Kasim, who in turn was overthrown in 1763 when he tried to stop the cancer of the Company's private trade. Mir Kasim's solution was bold – abolishing all internal customs duties, thereby negating the value of the Company's duty-free *dastaks*. This reform could not be allowed to stand, and so the Company went to war once more.

Such was the hatred of the Company that a group of English prisoners held in Patna were murdered by Mir Kasim's troops in 1763, a deliberate act of vengeance far more brutal than the 'black hole' incident six years earlier. The once pre-eminent Jagath Seths were also beheaded for their complicity with the British. In addition, armed bands of holy men (*sannyasi*) contributed to the turmoil, with one group raiding Dhaka and looting the Company's factory at Baiganbari. Mir Kasim joined forces with the Nawab of Awadh and the Mughal Emperor Shah Alam II to challenge the Company for control of Bengal. In this second 'Company–Mughal War', the original outcome was reversed. At the battle of Buxar in October 1764, the Company's forces triumphed in a victory that was perhaps more decisive even than Plassey. Mir Jafar was returned to the throne for a pitiful last few months before his son Najim-ud-Daula took over in early 1765. Not for nothing has this period been described as 'one of the worst chapters in English history'.[34]

Beyond the sordid details of the repeated coups that the Company inflicted on Bengal lies the fundamental motivation for the deed – the establishment of market dominion for the benefit of the Company and its executives. As Macaulay acknowledges, Clive 'considered himself as the general, not of the Crown, but of the Company'.[35] And what had the Company gained by this revolution? The regulatory authority of the Nawab was broken, enabling the Company to achieve its long-desired monopoly over the export trade, expand into the internal market and appropriate the public revenues of Bengal for its own benefit. One estimate suggests that in the decade after Plassey, Bengal lost two-thirds of its revenues to this commercial plunder.[36] As Luke Scrafton – Clive's right-hand man – would later comment, Plassey allowed the Company 'to carry on the whole trade of India (China excepted) for three years, without sending out one ounce of bullion'.[37] The reversal of global economic eminence had begun.

Within Bengal, the Nawab's ability to enforce rules against the abuse of *dastaks* was severely weakened. Exerting his new-found power, Clive insisted that the Company's executives (himself included) should have free rein to exploit the internal market. Bengali fears that this would mean that the English would 'engross' the market were soon proved right. By 1762, the Nawab Mir Kasim was protesting to the Company in Calcutta that its *gomastas* 'forcibly take away the goods and commodities of the *ryots*, merchants etc for a fourth part of their value; and by ways of violence and oppression they oblige the *ryots* to give five rupees for goods which are worth but one'.[38]

With the regulatory capacity of the Bengal state eliminated, the Company was able to remove the competitive threats posed by both the other European trading companies as well as local Asian merchants. The French challenge had already been eliminated with the capture of Chandernagore in the run-up to Plassey. Although the French returned to the port (and stayed until 1947), the Compagnie Perpetuelle was a shadow of its former self, and would be liquidated in 1769. As for the VOC, only a few months after Plassey, Company traders were using their new position to undermine their Dutch rivals. Company agents became infamous for invading the textile districts, and ripping away pieces of cloth being woven for the VOC. Faced with commercial annihilation, the Dutch staged a desperate rearguard action. In June 1759, the VOC sent a fleet from Batavia to Bengal. But the expedition was bungled, and the Dutch were forced to pledge never to bring troops to Bengal again. The Dutch monopoly of the Bengal opium trade – exercised through a private company, the Opium Society – was also overturned and replaced by the Patna Group of English traders, who quickly became infamous for their underhand practices and the wealth they generated. For example, Company executives were known to 'order a peasant to plough up a rich field of poppies, and sow it with rice' to reduce supply and thus boost the opium price.[39]

As for the Asian merchants, Amir Chand's fate was merely an extreme example of what was to strike the Asian merchant class. Key areas of the inland economy that had once been controlled by Asians were now formally transformed into a Company monopoly. In 1758, for example, Mir Jafar gave the Company the rights to the valuable saltpetre sector, a business that Amir Chand had himself once dominated. In addition, the Company pushed forward with the system of salaried *gomastas*, eliminating the need for Asian business partners.

AN UNREQUITED TRADE

After Buxar, all of Bengal was at the Company's mercy. Its competitors had been dealt with, and the Nawab was no longer any threat. But there was still one final acquisition that would complete the revolution: the absorption of Bengal's treasury into the Company's accounts. The transfer of 24 *parganas* following Plassey had added £58,000 in taxes to the Company's revenues. Soon Clive was being approached by the Mughal Emperor, requesting that the Company assume the office of tax management (*diwani*) in order that Bengal's regular tribute to Delhi could be resumed. Writing to the Prime Minister, William Pitt, in January 1759, Clive explained that he had declined 'for the present'. Clive then sailed home with a £300,000 fortune – worth over £34 million today – and a lifetime award (*jagir*) from Mir Jafar worth some £30,000.[40]

The installation of Mir Kasim in 1760 brought the districts of Midnapore, Burdwan and Chittagong under Company control, yielding another £650,000. When Clive returned to India for the third and final time in May 1765, he threw off his initial caution and forced the enfeebled Shah Alam II to formalise the Company's control. On 12 August 1765, the Emperor granted the Company the *diwani* rights for Bengal, Bihar and Orissa, in return for an annual tribute of Rs2.6 million, equivalent to £325,000. When all the costs of the Nawab's administration had been deducted, Clive calculated that from Bengal's annual tax revenues of Rs25 million, there would still be 'a clear gain to the Company' of Rs12 million or £1,650,900.[41] In twenty-first-century terms, this amounted to an annual surplus of over £150 million, a profit margin of some 49 per cent.

For the cost-conscious directors back in Leadenhall Street, who had obsessively managed the export of scarce bullion to the Asia for over 150 years, Clive painted a wondrous picture of bounty. The acquisition of *diwani* rights would now 'defray all the expenses of the investment, furnish the whole of the China treasure, answer the demands of all your other settlements in India, and leave a comfortable balance in your treasury besides'.[42] Clive cleverly maintained the fiction of Mughal authority by ensuring that taxes continued to be collected by local officials, 'a perfect example of income without investment', according to Professor Sirajul Islam of Bangladesh's Asiatic Society.[43] In the next six years, the Company would collect over £20 million, generating a surplus of £4 million, less than initially expected. But this was still a substantial haul at a time when the Company's total exports from Asia before the *diwani* amounted to just £1 million each year.

The corporate state had arrived. Contrary to later rationalisations by imperial historians, Clive had not acquired the *diwani* to promote the interests of the British Empire. His motivation was far more straightforward. 'Though never inattentive to his own interests', wrote James Mill in his *History of British India* in 1817, Clive was 'actuated by a sincere desire to promote the prosperity of the Company'.[44] The directors could not believe their good fortune and instructed its officials in Bengal to split the surplus between the purchase of Bengal textiles for shipment back to England, sending the remainder to Canton to buy tea. This arrangement would progressively beggar Bengal in what was known somewhat poetically as the 'unrequited trade'. More prosaically, by the end of the century, 85–90 per cent of Bengal's external trade was in the Company's hands.[45]

THE WEAVERS' THUMBS

It was the wealth of Bengal's textile industry that had first lured the Company to Bengal, and it would be Bengal's weavers who felt the full force of the Company's new-found market power. Never rich, Bengal's weavers still had a better standard of living than their counterparts in contemporary England, largely owing to their ability to determine their terms and conditions. According to Prasannan Parthasarathi, there is compelling evidence that India's weavers had 'higher earnings than their British counterparts and lived lives of greater financial security'.[46] Economic tradition in India supported the position of the weaver against the merchant. At a time when the British state was intervening on the side of the employer – for example, to set maximum levels for wages – Indian weavers were able to act as a collective body, improving their ability to negotiate favourable prices. This bargaining power combined with strong European demand for cloth in the first half of the eighteenth century created a seller's market, enabling Indian weavers to enjoy a 'golden age' of low costs and high prices.

All this ended following Plassey. From a situation of relative economic independence, Bengal's weavers were forced into a position of near slavery, unable to sell to others and obliged to accept whatever the Company's agents (*gomastas*) would offer for their cloth. 'The Company went to market as Sovereigns and Tyrants', argued a revealing briefing written for Philip Francis in the 1770s. 'Instead of seeking a preference by paying better,' it added, 'they forced the manufacturers to Work for them and to work at an under price, at the same time that they prohibited all private merchants from dealing in the Assortments required for their Investment.' The outcome was inevitable: 'thus a general Monopoly was at once rigorously established'.[47]

The Company employed all kinds of subterfuge to squeeze prices ever lower. One practice that was particularly resented was the classification of perfectly good quality cloth as sub-standard (ferreted). These pieces would then be sold on to the open market at price substantially higher than that given to the weaver, in the process making a tidy profit for the Company's *gomasta* and Resident. As prices fell, weavers became unable to cover the costs of production, leaving themselves increasingly unable to earn enough to pay back the advances they had received from the Company. Further poverty and indebtedness followed. For Bangladeshi scholar Hameeda Hossain, it was 'the corporate buyer, who had provided the weaver with his working capital and access to the market [that] became the root cause of his pauperisation and alienation from his occupation'.[48]

Some weavers resisted this abuse of power. For example, in 1767, a group from Khirpal sent a delegation to Calcutta with a petition requesting an increase in the purchase price of cloth. Remarkably, the Company authorities agreed. But the local Company Resident not only ignored the order, but threatened to have the troublesome weavers arrested if they pursued their case. Yet, this was a rare example of resistance, and by the early 1770s, the Company was earning impressive returns from its policy of oppressive exchange. One estimate suggests that the Company's *gomastas* were able to pay 'in all places at least 15 per cent and in some even 40 per cent less' than the weaver would receive in the public bazaar.[49]

These price cuts were achieved at the cost of a brutality that became infamous at the time. According to William Bolts's celebrated account, 'various and innumerable' were 'the methods of oppressing the poor weavers, such as by fines, imprisonments, floggings, forcing bonds on them etc'.[50] For some of the weavers, the reaction to this abuse was simply one of despair. Among the winders of raw silk, called *nagaads*, Bolts reported that the Company's practices led to a shocking form of self-mutilation, stating that 'instances have been known of their cutting off their thumbs to prevent their being forced to wind silk'.[51]

It is difficult to imagine the scale of economic violence required to force skilled workers to harm themselves in this way. Apart from Bolts, however, no other evidence exists for this or similar incidents. This has not stopped it achieving apocryphal status as a symbol of the physical and psychological pain inflicted by the Company's takeover of Bengal. Indeed, the image remains alive in popular memory across the subcontinent, as poet Shahid Ali expressed in his 1980s poem, 'Dacca Gauzes':

> In history, we learned: the hands
> of weavers were amputated,
> the looms of Bengal silenced,
> and the cotton shipped raw
> by the British to England.
>
> History of little use to her,
> my grandmother just says
> how the muslins of today
> seem so coarse and that only
> in autumn, should one wake up
> at dawn to pray, can one feel that same texture again.[52]

AN OPULENT REVOLUTION

When Clive headed for England for the final time in February 1767, the long-term consequences of Plassey were obscure. Bengal was now the Company's star possession. But Madras remained hard-pressed, threatened by French intervention, Maratha incursion and the rising force of Mysore; it would take another three decades to secure southern India. Clive was confident, however, that his actions over the preceding ten years had endowed the Company with an unrivalled 'estate'. In spite all the 'envy, malice, faction and resentment' that was now building up against the Company, Clive was proud of his accomplishments and believed that the Company could justly claim to be 'the most opulent company in the world'.[53] In practical terms, this opulence was worth an estimated £38,400,000 for the Company between 1757 and 1780 in terms of goods transferred back to Britain on an unrequited basis.[54] Clive took with him a fortune worth approximately £400,000 and left behind a beloved mansion four miles north of Calcutta at Dum Dum. Currently being restored by the Archaeological Survey of India, there is talk of establishing a museum on the site. Two hundred and fifty years on, however, disputes still rage over how this 'little Mogul' should be remembered in his former home.

For some, Clive was a single-minded genius, for others an unethical rogue. Of course, he was both and more. It was his guile that enabled the Company first to regain Calcutta and then execute the Plassey master-stroke that humbled the authority of the Bengal state, smashed the Asian merchant class and eliminated the competitive threat from France. All of this can be traced back to Clive's calculated opportunism, a willingness to break any rule to achieve his goal. Rather than being somehow 'sucked in' by an internal crisis within the Bengal elite, Clive and the Company executives who worked with him were quite deliberate in their efforts to exploit every opportunity for promoting their own and their employers' interests. He was the great 'revolutionist', the 'nabob-maker' extraordinaire.

But Clive was more than just a powerful individual; he was the chief representative of a corporate machine that worked with remorseless logic to achieve its ends. It may have seemed luxurious, but the nawabi state was distracted by multiple enemies, divided internally by intrigue at court and lacking the institutional resilience to protect it against external assault from a single-minded opponent. Imperial historians have made much of the fact that the Company's directors had not drawn up a prearranged plan for conquest, making the Bengal Revolution somehow 'accidental'. But Clive's actions were entirely consistent with long-standing instructions from London to secure its possessions overseas. With the acquisition of the *diwani* rights, he had gained a windfall of immense proportions, attracting praise from everyone.

The Company's 'great revolution' in Bengal deserves to be placed alongside other better-known revolutions – the American, French and Russian – for the way that it shaped the modern world. In the space of less than a decade, the Company had rerouted the flow of wealth westwards. Yet, this was a corporate revolution, designed to acquire the riches of an entire people for the benefit of a single company. It was not patriots, republicans or Bolsheviks who had taken power, but a company of merchants answerable to persistent shareholders in London. Even its own deputy-chairman, Laurence Sulivan, confessed that this was a situation 'monstrous in reason'. No wonder that the house these merchants had built soon came crashing down.

5
The Great East Indian Crash

TO THE WAREHOUSE

The question, of course, was where to store all this Indian loot. Back in England, the Company jealously guarded its imports from the East in warehouses across the City of London. As well as being a financial centre, eighteenth-century London was also a site of physical exchange, and the warehouse was its archetypal building. The Company's warehouses were situated throughout the City on Lime Street, Fenchurch Street – next to where the East India Arms still stands – Seething Lane, Still Yard and Crutched Friars. But with the boom in imports that followed Plassey, the Company simply ran out of space. Shipping the treasure out of Bengal in the form of silver bullion was impractical, and so the Company decided to return wealth to its shareholders by expanding the scale of its purchase of Bengal goods, notably textiles.

The acquisition of the *diwani* in 1765 further accentuated the pressure to use physical trade as the mechanism to transfer Bengal's taxes back to England. As the Bengal Council wrote to the Company's directors in 1769, 'Your trade from hence may be considered more as a channel for conveying your revenues to Britain, than as only a mercantile system.'[1] To cope with this surge in goods, the Company constructed new warehouses at Brown's Yard near the Tower of London, and in 1771, it opened the Bengal Warehouse in Bishopsgate to hold muslins, calicoes and raw silk. Word of what lay within soon spread, and the Bengal Warehouse became the target for London's criminal fraternity, eager to get their hands on the valuable materials that were stored inside. In January 1773, for example, three thieves were brought to trial at the Old Bailey for the theft of 628 silk handkerchiefs from the warehouse, for which they were transported overseas, probably never to return.

Twenty years later, the Bengal Warehouse became part of the massive Cutler Street complex, much of which still stands today. Six stories high, the buildings are well-designed and surprisingly elegant – with Doric windows and Piranesian staircases – and yet tough enough to survive more than two centuries of wear and tear.

After the East India Company lost its commercial monopoly in 1833, the warehouses were sold off, but were kept in use right up until the 1970s. Redeveloped as office blocks – the warehouses of the financial age – the buildings continue to communicate something of the power they would have exuded in the wake of Plassey. The stairway that winds its way up through the Old Bengal Warehouse is still the original, constructed of granite and ironware, eight feet wide to allow the easy passage of bales of cloth and chests of tea. No goods are on display today. But in the early part of the twentieth century, the poet John Masefield toured the complex, and left these lines describing the impression it made:

> You showed me nutmegs and nutmeg husks
> Ostrich feathers and elephant tusks
> Hundreds of tons of costly tea
> Packed in wood by the Cingalee
> And a myriad drugs which disagree
> Cinnamon, myrrh, and mace you showed
> Golden paradise birds that glowed
> And a billion cloves in an odorous mount
> And choice port wine from a bright glass fount
> You showed, for a most delightful hour
> The wealth of the world, and London's power.[2]

These solid buildings could also tell another story. When the Company commissioned the Bengal Warehouse, it was at the height of its powers. For almost ten years following Plassey, East India Company shares had become the focus of intense international speculative activity, pumped up by successive announcements of ever-grander acquisitions in the East. Between February 1758 when news of the victory at Plassey reached London and December 1768, when the Company bought the land for the Bengal Warehouse, the Company's shares had doubled to stand at £276. But this was to be the peak of the boom. Five months later, in May 1769, news reached London that not only had a French fleet entered the Indian Ocean, but that Hyder Ali, Sultan of Mysore, had invaded the Company's possessions in south India. The share price fell 16 per cent in a single month, and would continue a downward course for the next 15 years, reaching the depths of £122 in July 1784, a fall of 55 per cent. Although the Company went ahead with the construction of the Bengal Warehouse, all other plans were put on hold until its fortunes had turned in the 1790s. It would only be in 1824, a full 40 years after prices had reached the bottom, that the Company's shares would regain the heady heights of 1768. The scale of the Company's financial slump can be measured by the fact that it took only 30 years for the New York exchange to regain the value it had reached on the eve of the Great Crash of 1929.

ROTTING FROM THE HEAD

What brought about this collapse in the Company's fortunes was the convergence of a whole series of forces. Unexpected events and the actions of individuals certainly played their part. But much of what took place was encoded into the Company's institutional structure. Perhaps the most fundamental challenge that all institutions face is to ensure that employees promote the collective rather than their individual self-interest. With joint stock companies, this primordial tension is accentuated by two additional forces: the separation of ownership from executive control, and the speculative potential of publicly traded shares. For the East India Company, the challenge of control went further still, as its directors needed to maintain an uneasy balance between the Company's own concerns and the private trading of its executives.

Private trade became one of a series of cancers that gnawed at the Company's ethical fibre. The taking of bribes from local merchants to secure business was commonplace, and these 'presents' would influence the quality and costs of the commodities the Company purchased. The Company laid down clear rules of behaviour to its staff, and made each pledge covenants, backed by sizeable bonds. But through both a lack of will and a lack of means the Company 'was very unsuccessful in checking corruption even when it was discovered' and 'found it hard to punish the guilty'.[3] Nevertheless, these perennial problems could be kept in check when the Company was just one of many companies battling to secure their slice of the Asia trade, and when local rulers retained a degree of regulatory capacity.

Plassey changed all this, removing all constraints on good practice. More than this, the intensification of corrupt practices was driven by the Company's own leaders in both the Calcutta Council and the London Directorate. A new catchphrase entered the language – 'a lass and a lakh [a *lakh* being Rs100,000] a day' – to describe the lifestyle of the Company's executives in Bengal enjoying voluptuous mistresses (*bibis*) and their generous presents from state officials and Asian merchants. In London, the hot breath of Plassey was felt immediately at East India House. For the first time since the battle between Child and Papillon, the board was split into competing factions. Hitherto, elections to the Company's board had generally been uncontested, with shareholders happy to support the slate of house candidates on the back of steady capital gains and healthy dividend payments. But the prospects of opulence that Plassey presented meant that control of the Company had become a valuable source of plunder and patronage. Civil war broke out among the shareholders, as rival groups sought to seize the helm. Meetings of the Court of Proprietors soon became 'large, stormy, even riotous', with 'indecently virulent' debates.[4]

On one side stood Laurence Sulivan, and on the other, the rising power of the Bengal Squad, led by Robert Clive. Sulivan had made his fortune in Bombay and first became a director in 1755 at the age of 52. Sulivan was no saint. Yet, by the standards of the day, he was generally regarded as competent and relatively clean-handed. In April 1758, he was elected chairman for the first time and would dominate affairs for the next five years. Almost immediately he took steps to rein in Clive and his band of adventurers. In words that echo the earlier critique of Alivardi Khan, the directors wrote to Clive, 'you seem so thoroughly possessed with military ideas as to forget your employers are merchants and trade their principal object'.[5] What really enraged Sulivan, however, was Clive's *jagir*. This had been awarded by Mir Jafar in return for Clive's assistance against yet another invasion of Bengal. Along with a grand-sounding Mughal title, the *jagir* came with an endowment of land that yielded annual revenues worth around £30,000. Mischievously, Mir Jafar had indicated that the land which would provide these revenues was none other than the Company's own 24 *parganas*. Not only was Clive already far richer than any of the directors back in Leadenhall Street, but he was now also the Company's landlord in its Bengal heartland.

Open conflict broke out in 1761 when Sulivan warned Clive that his *jagir* was unjustified. Two years later, Sulivan suspended payment. Clive reacted with fury and mobilised his personal fortune to overturn the decision. To do this, Clive had to break the rules that limited each shareholder to a single vote regardless of the size of their holding. By splitting his holding into £500 chunks, Clive was able to create an army of over 220 artificial shareholders voting for his case. Sulivan followed suit, creating another 160 votes and called on Lord Shelburne's ministry to use its resources to stem Clive's bid for power. In March 1763, this stock-splitting ensured that the numbers of votes cast in the Court of Proprietors was more than triple those in 1758, representing an unprecedented 1,400 shareholders.

Sulivan scraped through, and quickly ordered a halt to all payments of Clive's *jagir* from Company lands. But Sulivan's reign was coming to an end. At the beginning of February, news of Mir Kasim's attempts to quell the anarchy of private trade reached London. Sulivan backed the cause of regulation and demanded that 'a final and effectual end be forthwith put to the inland trade in salt, betel-nut and tobaccos'. The Bengal Squad had other ideas. At the shareholder meeting in April 1764, Sulivan was overthrown, Clive's *jagir* reinstated and the hero of Plassey made President of the Calcutta Council with a mission to restore order in Bengal. The proprietors also passed a resolution forbidding Company executives from receiving presents – a ban that was ostentatiously ignored by the Calcutta Council who engineered a final flurry of £114,000 in gifts when Mir Jafar's son, Najim-ud-Daula, became Nawab in February 1765.

AN EXCLUSIVE TRADE

Clive stage-managed his mission to Bengal, piously presenting himself as an avenging-angel sent to clean out the 'Augean stables' of corruption. Writing back to the Company's directors in September 1765, he proclaimed that the tyranny and oppression he found 'will, I fear, be a lasting reproach to the English name in this country'.[6] Contrasting his own conduct with the rapacity of his fellow executives, Clive would later confess to Parliament in May 1772 that he did not gain 'a single shilling' from his spell in Bengal. But his actions told otherwise.

Insider trading was the first arena that Clive chose to exploit his position. Even before he had fixed the *diwani* settlement, Clive was writing back to one of his attorneys, John Walsh, to buy as much Company stock as possible. After the acquisition had been made, his instructions became more urgent, pressing his agents and friends 'to lose no time in purchasing all the stock you can, for I am persuaded the stock of the Company must be doubled in three years by the surplus of the country only'.[7] Historian Huw Bowen has charted how Clive's agents back in England acted on his persistent urgings, buying stock before the news of the *diwani* hit London's stock markets. In all, £30,000 of nominal stock worth over £51,000 was bought for Clive in the months that followed, taking his total stake to £75,000.

This put him in a fantastic position to benefit from the uplift that the shares received when the markets digested the implications of the *diwani*. He would later make a well-timed disposal of some of his shares in May 1767, doubling his money in the process.

Clive also turned his hand to private trade, despite the directors' insistent ban on all involvement in Bengal's internal market. A month after his arrival in Calcutta, he formed a syndicate that turned a profit of 45 per cent from the trade in salt over the next six months. Then in August 1765 came his cunning plan to eliminate the anarchy of private trade by installing an exclusive business in its place. A peculiar 'special purpose vehicle' known as the Society of Trade was established with monopoly rights over the trade in betel nut, salt and tobacco, with shares allocated free to the Company's leading executives in Calcutta. Out of 56 shares, Clive allocated himself five, or just under 10 per cent of this elite enterprise. The ten other members of the Council received two shares each, but lower down the chaplain only got two-thirds of a share, and the poor sub-export warehouse keeper a measly one-third of a share. By this measure, a tiny gang of 60 executives simply engrossed the whole of the inland trade, excluding not only Asian merchants, but also junior executives and independent European traders. In theory, the scheme would provide the Company's elite with sufficiently high returns that they would not be tempted by private trade; the Company would also receive a guaranteed flow of revenues from duty payments. The reality was scandalous, doubling prices for salt, defaulting on duty payments and siphoning off profits for a select few. Clive alone received £21,000 in profits from the first year of trading.

When the Company's directors learned of this novel money-making machine in 1766, they protested that it was 'a determined resolution to sacrifice the interests of the Company and the peace of the country to lucrative and selfish views',[8] forbidding any executive from taking part. Just as with the ban on presents, however, Clive and the Calcutta Council studiously ignored the directors' orders for as long as they could, only winding up its affairs in September 1768. Public opinion back in London was incensed by Clive's Society of Trade scam. For the *Gentleman's Magazine*, Clive's establishment of a monopoly over the necessaries of life had 'signed the death warrant for two millions of his fellow creatures'.[9]

As Machiavelli would have warned, Clive may have been brilliant as a 'merchant prince' winning Bengal for the Company, but he was precisely the wrong person to establish durable systems of governance.

Boosting his own interests on one hand, he cracked down hard on the perks enjoyed by others, generating a vast store of bitterness that would soon transfer back to the Court of Proprietors. More serious perhaps was his persistent overestimation of the financial value of his acquisitions, creating the expectation back in London that 'a torrent of treasure' was about to flow into the Company's coffers'.[10] If Spiridione took inspiration from anyone in his grandiose depiction of Asian wealth it was from Clive.

THE BENGAL BUBBLE

It was not just Clive who became entangled in this speculative whirl. For London's investors, the temptation also proved irresistible. During the 1750s, the Company's declining fortunes had propelled its share price downwards to just £133 in January 1757. Shares rallied 7 per cent when ships reached England with word of Plassey. But the dislocation caused by the Seven Years' War meant that the Company's shares fell back to just £112 in January 1762. The onset of peace in 1763 brought renewed confidence to the markets, and a slow upward trend (see Figure 5.1).

When news of the *diwani* reached London on 19 April 1766, the Company's shares stood at £165. Following Clive's lead, British and foreign investors piled into East India stock. Looking back from his vantage point 70 years later, Macaulay describes the time as one of 'feverish excitement', driven by 'an ungovernable impatience to be rich', and 'a contempt for slow, sure, and moderate gains'. By the middle of June, the price had surged to £187, buoyed up by expectations of an enhanced dividend. Initially, the speculators were disappointed when the directors managed to defeat a motion increasing the dividend from 6 to 8 per cent at the June quarterly meeting. But this hungry force could not be stopped. Speculators continued to buy into Company stock over the summer, this time determined to form a majority to win returns on their investment. At the next meeting in September, these efforts were rewarded when the Court of Proprietors voted to increase the dividend from 6 to 10 per cent against the directors' wishes. By Christmas, shares were trading at £223, a gain of 33 per cent.

Soon all London was obsessed with the wealth that the Company's acquisitions in Bengal would generate. Foreign interest was also strong with over a fifth of the Company's shareholders residing in the Netherlands. In May 1767, shareholders met once more to take

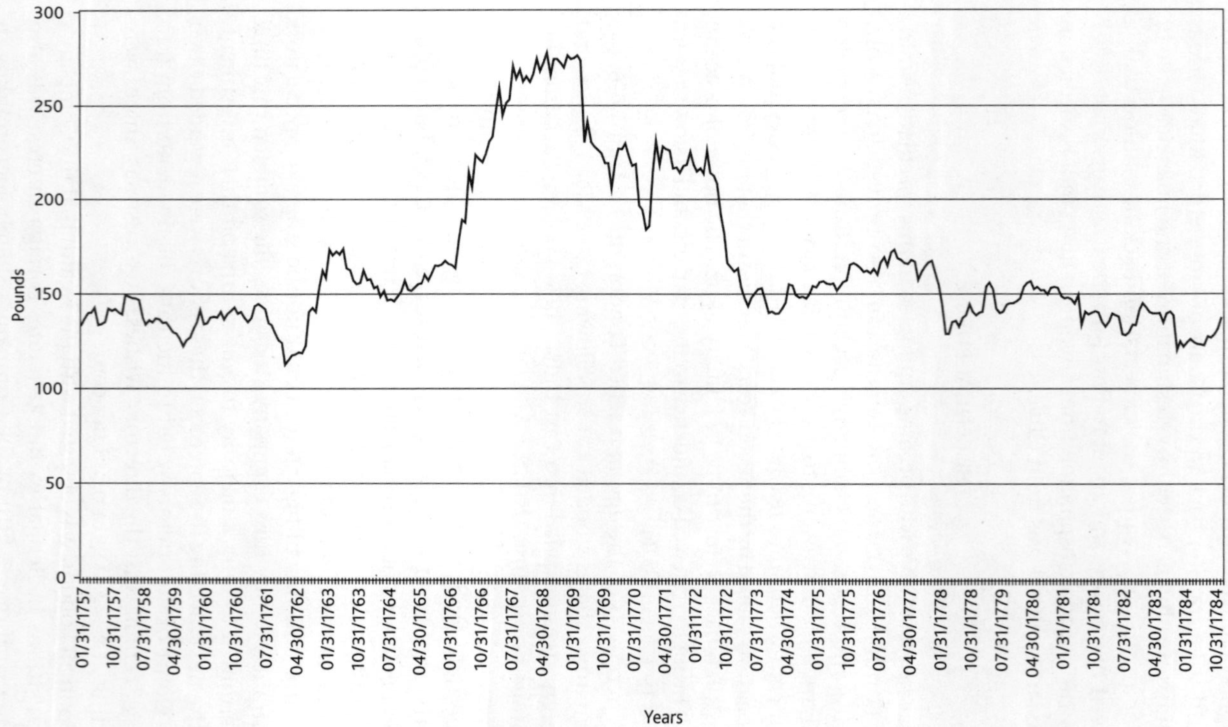

Figure 5.1 The Company's share price 1757–1784

a larger slice of Bengal's wealth. In one of the longest meetings in the Company's history, shareholders debated from noon on 18 May to 4 a.m. the following day on the dividend rate, eventually voting themselves an increase from 10 to 12.5 per cent. But before this could be paid, the government intervened, itself eager to profit from the *diwani*, not least to pay off its massive war debts. The Company was forced to make an annual payment of £400,000, and Parliament passed an unprecedented Dividend Act in June fixing the dividend to 10 per cent. But the Company's share price barely flickered, continuing its upward trajectory.

Prices were also being driven by the actions of market intermediaries, the 'bulls' and 'bears', who had had such a hand in the South Sea Bubble. The goal of the bulls was to pump up the price: 'today a man appears as a bull and endeavours to magnify every circumstance to obtain a momentary rise'. But shifts in market sentiment could change the same person into a 'bear', aiming to push down the shares so that he could later buy cheap, all for 'clogging and multiplying every expense of the company and for depreciating every advantage she possesses'.[11] For market observers, it was the innocent who were gulled by these shifting moods. 'To see sheep driven to the butchery', wrote one, 'is not more affecting than to see those innocent dupes, male and female, hurried into India House to vote away the value of the little property they possess.'

April 1769 was the peak of the frenzy. At a cost of continuing the £400,000 transfer to the government, Sulivan had managed to win back the right to increase the dividend up to a maximum of 12.5 per cent. The stage was set for the April elections of the directors, which surpassed all others in stock-splitting, 'the most extraordinary piece of jockeyship', when large holdings were split by contending factions with 'Machiavellian finesse'.[12] Then on Tuesday 23 May 1769, the East India ship, the *Valentine*, was reported safely home. But the news it brought of renewed conflict in south India was devastating, and share prices plummeted from £273 to £230 in a month. Writing to the leading politician Lord Shelburne in July of 1769, the financier Israel Barre concluded that 'there never was since the South Sea year so great a crush in stock matters'.[13]

Many of London's elite were nearly ruined in the crash, not least Laurence Sulivan who had increased his holdings to win the April elections. He would send his son, Stephen, to Bengal to redeem the family fortunes under the watchful eye of his protégé, Warren Hastings. The Burkes – brothers Edmund and Richard, and namesake

William – were also left severely embarrassed by the slump. William Burke had been among the first to bull the Company's stock in 1766 in a consortium with the Burkes' patron, Lord Verney. Following the crash, William would seek to regain his fortune in India, eventually becoming the agent of the Rajah of Tanjore, while Richard would head for the West Indies. Neither was able to shake off a reputation for unprincipled share-dealing. Edmund, author of *The Sublime and the Beautiful*, and rising star of the Whigs, protested his innocence of all malpractice. But his new-bought country estate in Beaconsfield was placed at risk by the Company's reversal of fortunes, and for the next few years, Edmund would be a strong advocate of both Robert Clive and the Company's chartered privileges against the increasing assaults from Parliament.

THE PERISHING

While the London establishment were contemplating the costs of its financial excesses in the summer of 1769, across the world in Bengal a drought of unprecedented ferocity was just commencing. For six whole months from August 1769 to January 1770, the monsoon rains failed to arrive, delivering a chronic water shortage that destroyed up to half the crops, particularly in the west and north-west of Bengal. With the New Year, drought started to turn into famine. Plentiful rain fell in June 1770, but 'hopes of relief were disappointed by the overflowing of the rivers in the eastern provinces', adding flood to famine.[14]

Famine had been an established part of India's social reality for thousands of years, and was only truly defeated following Independence in 1947. Early English travellers had commented with horror on the scale of the terrible famine of 1631, which had severely disrupted normal trade. Yet, the incidence of famine expanded dramatically, first under Company and then under the British Crown. In fact, British control of India started with a famine in Bengal in 1770 and ended in a famine – again in Bengal – in 1943. Working in the midst of the terrible 1877 famine that he estimated had cost another 10 million lives, Cornelius Walford calculated that in the 120 years of British rule there had been 34 famines in India, compared with only 17 recorded famines in the entire previous two millennia.[15] One of factors that explained this divergence was the Company's abandonment of the Mughal system of public regulation and investment. Not only did the Mughals use tax revenues to finance water conservation, thus boosting food production, but when famine struck they imposed 'embargos on food exports, anti-speculative price regulation, tax relief and distribution of free food'.[16] More brutally, if merchants were found to have short-changed peasants during famines, an equivalent weight in human flesh would be taken from them in exchange.

Like previous failures of the natural cycle, the inadequate monsoon of 1769 in Bengal could have been managed without great loss of life. But the Company had significantly increased Bengal's vulnerability to natural disaster. Bengal had been picked clean by the Company and its executives in the preceding decade. Revenue collection had increased dramatically from just £606,000 the year before the Company took over the *diwani* to a peak of £2,500,000 two years later. Flows of bullion into Bengal fell from £345,000 in 1764 to £54,000 in 1765, and ceased entirely in 1766. Instead, silver started leaving Bengal to pay for the Company's tea trade. By 1769, Richard Becher, the Company's Resident at Murshidabad, admitted with some shame that 'the condition of the people of this country has been worse than it was before', arguing that 'this fine country, which flourished under the most despotic and arbitrary government, is verging towards its ruin while the English have so great a share in the Administration'.[17]

Throughout 1769, the Company monitored the situation, and in November, the Calcutta Council wrote back to London that revenues would be reduced in the year ahead. A harrowing letter published under the name of J.C. in the *Gentleman's Magazine* in September 1771 reveals the unrelenting pursuit of self-interest that governed the Company's approach to the crisis. Rather than take action to curb price speculation in grain, 'as soon as the dryness of the season foretold the approaching dearness of rice', wrote J.C., 'our Gentlemen in the Company's service were as early as possible in buying up all they could lay hold of'.[18] The peasants quickly complained to the Nawab that the English had 'engrossed all the rice'. But when these accusations were put before the Company's Calcutta Council, the complaint was met with howls of laughter and thrown out. Huge fortunes were made as Company staff cornered the market. One junior executive accumulated over £60,000, as rice prices soared from 120 *seers* of rice per rupee at the beginning of the famine to just three *seers* a rupee in June 1770. At the time, a *seer* was equivalent to about 2 lb in weight. The Nawab and other Bengali nobles tried to respond in the traditional way and distributed rice free of charge. But because of the hoarding by the Company's executives, their stocks were soon depleted.

As the famine intensified, thousands flocked to Calcutta, many dying in the streets. Whoever he was, J.C. clearly had humanitarian feelings and would hand out food to the starving who gathered near his Calcutta residence. But he was also squeamish. On one occasion, he sent his servants to get the starving to move away from his house. But one of the near-dead rebelled, and cried out: 'Baba! Baba!, my Father, My Father! This affliction comes from the hands of your countrymen, and I am come here to die, if it pleases God, in your presence.'[19] J.C. concludes his letter by describing Calcutta's good fortune of having both vultures and dogs to deal with the dead – the first to take out the eyes and intestines, and the latter to gnaw the feet and the hands.

With no pictures or photographs to drive home the horror of the event, we are left with eye-witness accounts of the living feeding off the dead, of the Hugli full of swollen bodies and, in the words of Karim Ali, author of *Muzaffarnamah*, of whole families being yielded up to the 'talons of the wrath of the godless'.[20] However, the Company's first concern was to feed its army and then to ensure that its taxes were secure. Not only did the Company continue to collect its land revenues throughout the famine – instead of introducing some form of relief in the Mughal fashion – it actually increased the rate. In February 1771, Calcutta reported back to the directors that 'notwithstanding the great severity of the late famine and the great reduction of people thereby, some increase has been made' in revenue collection.[21] Many of the Company's leading executives used their position to purchase grain by force – even seed for the next year's planting – and then sold this at famine prices in the big cities of Calcutta and Murshidabad. Eventually, the Company did act, providing Rs90,000 in relief, a pittance in a land of some 30 million people with annual revenues of over Rs17 million. Even later imperial historians admitted that the Company did not even 'attempt to cope with the disaster'.[22] This was a man-made catastrophe.

The absence of comprehensive records means that it is impossible to calculate accurately the numbers of those who died in the famine. In 1772, Warren Hastings estimated that 10 million Bengalis had starved to death, equating to perhaps a third of the population. Hastings also concluded that the famine was caused by an artificial shortage of food supplies caused by market manipulation. For this, Hastings blamed the local merchants, ignoring the role of the Company executives themselves. Mortality was highest among low-income groups, the rural artisans and urban poor, neither of whom had direct access to food stocks. In Purnea, one of the worst-affected districts, the Company's agent reported that 'on the high and sandy soils, more than half the *ryots* are dead'.[23] Mortality in Malda also approached 50 per cent, while in Rajshahi between a third and a half of the people died, and in Birbhum up to a quarter perished. Re-examining the data, Rajat Datta has recently argued that the accepted estimate of 10 million deaths is inflated, suggesting a death toll of 1.2 million instead.[24] Yet, even if this more conservative figure is taken, the terrible outcome of the famine can still be barely understood. This was a time when the population of London was well under a million. All of these and more would have been wiped out if the famine had hit the Company's home town, instead of far-off Bengal. In effect, London would have been left a ghost town. Instead, it was Bengal that was depopulated, with one-third of the Company's territory lying 'as jungle inhabited only by wild beasts'.[25]

The sheer barbarity of the Company's conduct during the 1770 famine lies in its refusal to temper its demands for taxes with a sense of responsibility for the people of Bengal. As Warren Hastings acknowledged in a letter to the Company's directors in November 1772, 'it was naturally to be expected that the diminution of the revenue should have kept an equal pace with other consequences of so great a calamity'. The reason that revenues were maintained was 'owing to its being violently kept up to its former standard'.[26] Tucked away in the engaging autobiography of Dean Mahomet is a description of what this violence meant in practice. Better known for pioneering Indian cuisine in England and becoming the 'Shampooing Surgeon to His Majesty King George IV', Mahomet had initially followed his father in a career with the Company's army. In the opening section of his book, Mahomet describes how his father had helped to suppress a rebellion by Rajah Budhmal in 1769. Complaining of the 'great dearth', the Rajah had argued that it was impossible for him to pay his allotted share of taxation. The Company rejected this plea, and sent in troops to imprison the Rajah. But the violence spiralled out of control, eventually resulting in the death of Mahomet's father.[27] The following year Mahomet himself joined the Company's forces, and he describes a series of engagements between Bhagalpur and Rajmahal to eliminate the Pahareas, who opposed Company rule and robbed travellers. To 'strike terror', the Company suspended some of its captives 'on a kind of gibbet, ignominiously exposed along the mountain's conspicuous brow'. Mahomet's band of sepoys moved on, and 'as we proceeded on our march, we beheld the lifeless bodies of these nefarious wretches elevated along the way for a considerable distance'.[28] For the Pahareas, their fate was equivalent to Spartacus' defeated slaves, crucified and staked along the roads of Rome. But the Pahareas were not the only rebels against famine taxation. There is some evidence that peasants joined the *sufi* rebels of Shah Manju in his *sannyasi* revolt against the Company.[29]

A CATASTROPHIC FAILURE OF MANAGEMENT

The Bengal Famine stands out as perhaps one of the worst examples of corporate mismanagement in history. Yet, the preconditions for such a disaster had been in place for decades. The onrush of easy money from coups and corruption extinguished the scrupulous concern for trade that had previously characterised the Company's management. While those in England squabbled over how to divide the spoils, in India all systems of administrative control broke down, allowing abuse to flourish at the expense of both the people of Bengal and the Company itself. William Bolts captured this dual collapse perfectly when he wrote in 1772, 'while this nation is gazing after the fruit, the Company and their substitutes are suffered to be rooting up the tree'.[30] Remittances home from the Company's executives stood at just £79,000 in 1756. But following the victory at Plassey, they would average an annual £500,000 in the years to 1784.[31] In 1770–71, in the midst of the Bengal Famine, a staggering £1,086,255 was transferred home by the Company's executives – equivalent to nearly £100 million in twenty-first-century terms.[32]

Executives in India lost sight of their commercial purpose, and observers in London lamented the declining quality of the textiles that were now sent back from Bengal, which exhibited 'no assortment, no taste, nothing new either to furnish variety to the old or to engage new markets'.[33] Added to this, embezzlement became widespread. Writing much later, Warren Hastings would complain in 1782 that 'every article of the investment is provided for the Company at 30 or 40 or even 50 per cent beyond its real cost'.[34] All notions of cost control evaporated as military force became a vital part of the Company's operations, and membership of the officer corps purchased a share of the plunder following a successful military adventure. While the numbers of soldiers under Company command grew four times during the 1760s, the numbers of officers expanded ten-fold to take advantage of the plunder of war. By 1770–71, the Company's military and commercial spending in Bengal had reached £3,210,000, 50 per cent more than its revenues.

Far-sighted observers quickly concluded that the scale of the Company's acquisitions overwhelmed its management capabilities. Even before the acquisition of the *diwani*, Charles Jenkinson was writing that 'the affairs of this Company seem to become much too big for the management of a body of merchants'.[35] Crucially, the boardroom battles in London had made the Company a plaything of competing shareholder forces, sending a clear signal to the management of its subsidiaries in the East that the Company was now ripe for liquidation from within. In a revealing minute written by Clive in September 1766, the hero of Plassey traced the problem to 'the conduct of governors, who, too eager in the pursuit of private interest, have involved themselves in affairs which could not be reconciled to the strict principles of integrity' – as ever, excusing his own conduct from criticism.[36]

What had allowed the 'get rich-quick' appetites of the Company's executives to take hold so disastrously was the removal of the Nawab's regulatory authority. Just as a great oak or deodar provides valuable shade in a forest, so strong regulation provides the framework within which the economic ecosystem can flourish; weaken or remove it and anarchy and oppression will follow. In so many ways, the long-term interests of the Company as a trading concern would have been better served through partnership with a strong local ruler rather than market domination. By the end of the 1760s, the Company's directors were recognising that Bengal had been a hollow acquisition. Instead of the untold riches they had expected, the Company had 'only exchanged a certain profit in commerce for a precarious one in revenue'.[37]

In London, news of the famine generated a genuine sense of horror and humanitarian concern. The first inklings of what was taking place reached London in December 1770, when the *Gentleman's Magazine* reported that 'provisions were so scarce in the Company's new acquisitions that parents brought their children to sell them for a morsel of bread'.[38] When the full story became known, horror turned to outrage at the Company's negligence. As Horace Walpole said at the time, 'we have murdered, deposed, plundered, usurped – nay, what think you of the famine in Bengal, in which three millions perished, being caused by a monopoly of provisions by the servants of the East Indies'.[39]

DUPES FOR A DIVIDEND

But business was business. As the famine intensified, Company shareholders were focused on making up for their losses, and in December 1769, the Company's proprietors had taken advantaged of Sulivan's deal with the government and raised the dividend to 11 per cent. In September 1770, this was boosted to 12 per cent. And then in March 1771, the same month as the *Gentleman's Magazine* reported the 'great miseries to which the inhabitants are reduced by famine and pestilence', the Company's shareholders voted to raise the dividend to 12.5 per cent.[40] The share price started to recover, hitting £226 once more in May 1771. But this was a fool's bounce. The Company's finances were being consumed from within. Although the Company's imports from Bengal certainly appeared healthy, they were now being financed in part by loans from its own executives in India, who were flush with the gains from private trade and plunder. Made out in the form of bills of exchange, these loans were then redeemed back in London. Theoretically, the Company should have easily been able to afford to honour these bills of exchange. But the means at its disposal was being eroded by the boycott of its once prosperous tea trade with the American colonies. Furthermore, the share price fall of 1769 was still working its way like acid through Europe's financial system. Many speculators had bought the Company's shares on credit, and when the stock price fell were left ruined.

The Company's political status was also under fire as revelations of corporate conduct started to roll off London's printing presses. In January 1772, William Bolts's explosive *Considerations on Indian Affairs* was published in London. Bolts had been a rising star of the Company's Bengal operations, but had been expelled after clashing with the governing elite. Bolts's revenge was sweet and came in the form of a penetrating assault on the Company's systems of governance. 'The Company may be compared to a stupendous edifice', he wrote, 'suddenly built upon a foundation not previously well examined or secured, inhabited by momentary proprietors and governors, divided by different interests opposed to each other; and who, while one set of them is overloading the superstructure, another is undermining the foundations.'[41] The 'momentary proprietors' that Bolts scorned so intensely voted themselves another 12.5 per cent dividend in March, and then, three months later, the foundations started to give way.

On 8 June, a Scottish banker called Alexander Fordyce working in London disappeared. Fordyce had been intimately involved in the

London markets, and had sold the Company's shares short, expecting them to fall further. The fool's bounce had ruined his plans, and he left debts of £550,000. Many of these were owed to Scotland's banking firm, Douglas, Heron & Co., popularly known as the Ayr Bank. The Ayr Bank promptly imploded, the start of a financial crisis across Europe. Another 30 banks collapsed in less than three weeks, creating a huge shortage of ready money, depressing business confidence and bringing trade to a standstill. In an unprecedented move, the Company postponed its September sale until November in the hope that purchasing power would recover. But it now faced a three-fold crisis, with more than £1.5 million in outstanding bills of exchange, a long-overdue repayment of a £300,000 short-term loan from the Bank of England, along with nearly £1,000,000 in unpaid taxes to the government. On 15 July, the directors applied to the Bank of England for a loan of £400,000. Two weeks later, they were back, asking for another £300,000. This time the Bank could only produce £200,000. By August, the directors were secretly telling the government that it needed at least £1 million to bail it out. A story as big as this couldn't remain hidden for long, and on 18 September news of the Company's financial distress leaked out to the market, sending the shares down 10 per cent.

As accusations flew, the directors, who had kept the true state of affairs from their shareholders, announced that the precious dividend would have to be delayed. They also begged the government to waive the taxes the Company owed, and provide a loan to plug the gaping hole in its accounts. The traditional relationship of state and corporation was being reversed, with the government for once becoming the source of much-needed cash. Parliament was recalled early to consider what legislation was needed to prevent the situation spiralling out of control like the South Sea disaster had half a century before. A mood of vengeance was in the air, with parliamentarians in a mood to have 'hanged both Directors and servants'.[42] When the directors finally came face to face with the Court of Proprietors in December, two days before Christmas, all they could offer was a paltry 6 per cent annualised dividend. Furious shareholders 'arraigned the conduct of the Directors'. Six days later, facing the reality of empty coffers, the shareholders were forced to accept their measly offer.

How things had changed from the heady days of high prices and rich dividends. As one bitter observer concluded, 'the real dupes have been the steady, permanent old proprietors who look to the dividend as the means of their subsistence'.[43] In less than a decade, the Company had charted the classic boom-and-bust cycle, described so elegantly by the nineteenth-century economist, Walter Bagehot, as 'quiescence, improvement, confidence, prosperity, excitement, overtrading, CONVULSION, pressure, stagnation, ending again in quiescence'.[44] The tragedy then and now is how quickly memories of this cycle are smothered by the next surge, and how the real human consequences are sidelined. For the people of Bengal, the 'quiescence' following the East India Crash invariably meant the peace of the grave. Thousands lost jobs and savings at the end of the stock market bubble in the late 1990s; in the Great East India Crash of the 1770s, millions lost their lives.

On the walls of the redeveloped Cutlers Gardens, circular plaques have been placed to mark its former use. An unnamed ship stands in the centre, and around the rim are marked the names of the commodities Masefield had wondered at: silks, skins, tea, ivory, carpets, spices, feathers, cotton. The plaques are discreet and neatly designed. But they say nothing of the human costs of these exotic commodities, nothing of the crash that once shook the world. Two hundred and thirty years ago, millions of pounds of unsold tea were piled high in the Company's warehouses across the City of London, a consequence of a successful boycott across Britain's American colonies. In the global economy of the late eighteenth century, one thing united American patriots, English parliamentarians and Indian peasants: it was now time to tame the beast.

6
Regulating the Company

THE SEISMOGRAPHER

One of those caught up in the backdraught of the East India crash was Adam Smith. Hard at work in the Fife seaport of Kirkcaldy, researching the mysteries of the global economy, Smith, along with much of the Scottish establishment, was knocked off balance by the precipitate collapse of the Ayr Bank. Writing from London, Smith's friend, the philosopher David Hume, enquired in June 1772 after the crash, 'do these events affect your Theory? What say you? Here is Food for your speculation.'[1] Smith had been close to completing what would become his masterpiece, *An Inquiry into the Nature and Causes of the Wealth of Nations*. But the mood of financial chaos was so great that he confessed to William Pultenay in September that the book had been delayed owing to his efforts to extricate some of his friends from this 'public calamity'.

Eventually released to the world in March 1776, Smith's *Wealth of Nations* is one of the few books from the eighteenth century that still hold sway over the modern mind. In it, Smith puts forward an 'obvious and simple system of natural liberty', arguing that the open market was the most effective way of raising standards of living. Smith regarded the pursuit of individual improvement as an eternal (and entirely positive) feature of economic life, stating that 'it is not from the benevolence of the butcher, the brewer, or the baker that we expect our dinner, but from their regard to their self-interest'.[2] But Smith's outlook was far broader than the simply economic, and it was critical for him that transactions respected the 'laws of justice'.[3] This icon of the Scottish Enlightenment was Professor of Moral Philosophy at Glasgow University and viewed his discovery of the natural laws of wealth creation not as ends in themselves, but as stepping stones to the good society. In Smith's utopia, the relentless pursuit of self-interest is guided by 'an invisible hand' to produce outcomes that are beneficial for society as a whole.[4] By setting out an internally consistent model, Smith hoped to overturn the theoretical pillars of the prevailing mercantilist order that still tightly circumscribed economic life. But two institutions stood in the way: the state and the corporation. The over-mighty state was a natural target for Smith, but so was the over-mighty corporation.

In striking contrast to those who have appropriated *The Wealth of Nations* for their pro-corporate policies, Smith had little place for the corporation in his vision of economic liberty. He was deeply suspicious of the commercial class as a whole, arguing that they 'come from an order of men, whose interest is never exactly the same with that of the publick, who have generally an interest to deceive and even to oppress the public, and who accordingly have, upon many occasions, both deceived and oppressed it'.[5] And while he viewed profit as a necessary output from economic activity, he argued that it would be 'naturally low in rich and high in poor countries, and it is always highest in the countries which are going fastest to ruin' – something of a slap in the face for those today who view high profits as the measure of everything.[6] But it was to the corporation that Smith was particularly opposed, a stance that was founded on a combination of theoretical antipathy, strengthened by the evidence of contemporary malpractice.

Here, the East India Company's fall from grace provided a mass of material for Smith's overall case. *The Wealth of Nations* had been written during the period when the Company's aggression overseas and speculation at home had dominated British public life, and it is no surprise that it features extensively in his pages. Smith was also well-connected in London's political circles, and his name was even put forward as a potential member of a committee of inquiry into the Company's collapse in 1772. For Smith, the Company's rise and fall held the secret to one of the greatest puzzles of his time: explaining the distribution of benefits from the rapidly increasing integration of the world economy. 'The discovery of America, and that of a passage to the East Indies by the Cape of Good Hope', argued Smith, 'are the two greatest and most important events recorded in the history of mankind.'[7] Smith's belief was that the full potential of this dramatic opening had not been realised, owing to a combination of colonies and corporations. For the natives of both the East and West Indies, 'all the commercial benefits have been sunk and lost' in a series of 'dreadful misfortunes'. In Asia, the agents of this pain were the Dutch and British East India Companies, monopoly corporations that he condemned as 'nuisances in every respect'.[8]

Earlier than most, Smith recognised that commercial success often comes not just from meeting consumer demand, but also from building up market power to generate excess profits. 'To widen the market and to narrow the competition is always in the interest of the dealers,' Smith argued. The result of this anti-competitive behaviour was to raise profits above the natural level, amounting to 'an absurd tax upon the rest of their fellow citizens'.[9] Cartels are thus an ever-present danger in a market economy, and in Smith's immortal words, 'people of the same trade seldom meet together, but the conversation ends in a conspiracy against the public or in some contrivance to raise prices'.[10] Here, Smith gave an accurate description of the East India Company's shipping interest, the collection of ships' masters that leased the Company its vessels. The power of this 'confederacy' was such that the Company ended up leasing more ships than it needed at higher prices than were justified. This was an outcome explained in part by the fact that many of the ships' masters were also Company directors, a conflict of interest prohibited by Company by-laws but wholly ignored.[11]

More dangerous still was the establishment of exclusive corporations, such as the East India Company, which destroyed any pretence at competition. Monopoly corporations defied the logic of the market and resisted the 'reduction of price and consequently of wages and profit that free competition would most certainly occasion', according to Smith.[12] In this conclusion, Smith was drawing on the repeated experience of Asian commerce, when those scarce periods of open trading – such as in the Netherlands between 1595 and 1601, and in England between 1694 and 1702 – had resulted in higher prices for producers and lower prices for consumers, enhancing general welfare. Smith once again laid out the obvious defects of the Company's market dominance – not least the unjust exclusion of other English traders from the East, as well as the added expense for European consumers. But not only did the inhabitants of England pay 'for all the extraordinary profits which the company may have made upon those goods in consequence for their monopoly', but they also suffered from 'all the extraordinary waste which the fraud and abuse, inseparable from the management of the affairs of so great a company, must necessarily have occasioned'.[13] The Company's descent into malpractice was therefore no accident, but the inevitable and *necessary* product of a faulty institution. Monopoly didn't just create economic injustice, it was also 'a great enemy to good management'.[14] In Smith's vision of an open economy, entrepreneurs could not afford to displease their customers as these could easily choose alternate sources of supply. A monopoly corporation, like the East India Company, faced none of these pressures for good conduct, and would therefore continue to condone practices that would have otherwise have been stamped out.

For Smith, the Company was not just flawed as a commercial operation. After Plassey, political tyranny was added to the mix through the 'strange absurdity' of a joint stock corporation holding sovereign powers. For Smith, government by merchants was 'incurably faulty', stunting the natural growth of Bengal 'to what is barely sufficient for answering the demands of the company'. Sick of the callousness this engendered, Smith described the way in which the Company's executives sought to make a fortune and then leave Bengal as quickly as possible, 'perfectly indifferent though the whole country was swallowed up by an earthquake'.[15] In the form of the Bengal Famine, this earthquake had already struck.

FREEDOM OR SLAVERY

Smith was not alone in his criticism of the Company. Almost immediately after Clive's acquisition of the *diwani*, concerns arose about the social, political and ethical implications of this dramatic change in the Company's circumstances, concerns that would become more acute as evidence of gross mismanagement accumulated. After an initial rush of euphoria, real fears emerged about the raw political implications of the Company's rapid growth in wealth and power. This was a time of mounting discontent at the rottenness of the Georgian state, a struggle epitomised first by John Wilkes, the fiery MP for Middlesex, and then the series of letters penned by Junius. With its tight financial and political links with the ruling establishment, the Company was easily seen as yet another manifestation of 'old corruption'. Well-versed in the history of the Roman Republic, politicians and pamphleteers feared that just as the proceeds of Rome's conquest of Asia (western Anatolia) had been used to subvert its ancient freedoms, so the Company's takeover of Bengal would bring tyranny in England. 'The riches of Asia have been poured in upon us,' declared Pitt the Elder, 'and have brought with them not only Asiatic luxury, but, I fear, Asiatic principles of government.'

For many, the Company had become a monstrous hybrid, part Leadenhall Street merchant, part Oriental despot. As the *Gentleman's Magazine* concluded in April 1767, the issues at stake were not just about the wealth that the Company had acquired, but 'whether the freedom or the slavery of this island shall result'.[16] Apprehension grew that the Company and its nabobs would use their wealth to subvert the delicate balance of powers between Crown and Parliament, introducing a corporate state. Ethical factors were added to the mix, driven by a genuine sense of outrage at the human costs of Company rule. Along with these points of political principle were a host of other factors, not least the sheer snobbery of the ruling aristocracy, who hated the way that mere merchants, such as Robert Clive, were able to buy themselves status, seats in Parliament and big houses in the country. And in the City, the Company's mercantile opponents were gathering once more under the leadership of the famous slave-trader and Lord Mayor, William Beckford, who raised the 'old cry for an open trade', threatening to remove the Company's charter so that all could have access to India.

Outside politics, the Company's practices in India became a central part of Britain's cultural landscape, with the corrupt 'nabob' as one of the stock literary characters of the age. An early example was the anonymous satire, *Debates in the Asiatic Assembly*, which mocked the self-serving practices of the Company's directors and shareholders – caricatured as Sir Janus Blubber, Shylock Buffaloe, Jaundice Braywell and Sir Judas Venom – along with the rapacity of Lord Vulture, a thinly disguised attack on Clive.[17] Five years later, such views had become mainstream, providing the basis for Samuel Foote's play, *The Nabob*, which opened at the Haymarket Theatre in June 1772. This poked fun at the plunderers of India in the same way as Caryl Churchill's *Serious Money* attacked the Yuppies of the 1980s. In the play, Sir Matthew Mite is cast as the nabob aiming to use his loot to marry into an ancient family and buy election to Parliament for the borough of Bribe'em. But Mite is rebuffed, 'corrupt as you may conceive this country to be, there are superior spirits living who would disdain an alliance with grandeur obtained at the expense of honour or virtue'.[18]

REDRAWING THE CHARTER

For the East India Company, state intervention was a fact of life. Its entire existence was dependent on the regular renewal of its charter. For its part, the state viewed the Company as an important source of cheap finance and a way of outsourcing the pursuit of British interests in Asia. Plassey overturned the assumptions that underlay this mutually convenient bargain. Serious questions were raised not only about the Company's right to the plunder Clive had won, but also the legality of a mercantile corporation ruling overseas territories.

The acquisition of the *diwani* merely accentuated the urgency of bringing these issues to some resolution.

For the next century, state and Company would struggle to find a settlement of this extraordinary situation. The practical and legal complexities meant that any intervention needed to be multi-dimensional, confronting the flaws in the Company's governance at home and abroad, the allocation of its Indian finances and the management of its monopoly. Money, power and principle were all at stake. Constitutionally, the state asserted its right to all conquests made by British subjects overseas. Technically, however, the *diwani* was not a conquest, but a grant from the Mughal emperor who remained the nominal sovereign of Bengal. The Company also proclaimed that its chartered status gave it autonomy from state intervention in its internal affairs. Many were concerned that any attempt to restrain the Company would mark a dangerous infringement of the property rights of a legally established corporation. More importantly, perhaps, was the ever-practical question of who should command the immensely lucrative patronage that had been opened in the East. An appointment to the Company's service in India seemed a guarantee of rapid riches, and the Company was intent on preserving the directors' right of preferment. Competing factions in the establishment feared that if either Crown or Parliament gained control of this patronage, then it would become the arbiter of British politics. For all these reasons, the efforts that were made to reform the Company over successive decades would be designed as much to retain the balance of power in Britain as resolve mismanagement in India. No wonder that the results were anachronistic and unjust.

Ultimately, it was the need for hard cash that overshadowed constitutional niceties. The Seven Years' War (1756–63) had left Britain victorious, but almost bankrupt, and the Prime Minister, William Pitt the Elder, saw the *diwani* as a godsend to fill a gaping hole in the Treasury. To pre-empt the government, the directors proposed in November 1766 that all territorial revenues (minus expenses) should go to the Crown, in return for extending the charter for 37 years and agreeing to an indefinite annual dividend of 15 per cent. But the Company's shareholders protested, rejecting the proposal as too generous to the state, and in the following May, voted for a 12.5 per cent dividend, thereby foreclosing a substantial portion of the *diwani*. The government was furious, and quickly passed the Dividend Bill, limiting payments to 10 per cent while negotiations continued.

Finally in January 1769, an agreement was reached whereby the government received £400,000 a year – in effect, a 'windfall tax' – and the Company retained the right to raise its dividend to a ceiling of 12.5 per cent. Questions of sovereignty were shelved for another day – not least in view of the fact that the Crown was wary of assuming the responsibilities for ruling India that this would entail.

The bursting of the Bengal bubble dramatically changed the situation, exposing the Company to charges of mismanagement in India. Many Members of Parliament had been shareholders and, as the stock price plummeted, a powerful body of aggrieved politicians emerged, their anger inflamed by the reports from Bengal. Seeking to forestall further intervention, the Company despatched three supervisors to remedy the situation. But their ship, the *Aurora*, was lost with all hands en route to India. When the news reached London, the Company's directors appointed Warren Hastings as Governor in Bengal in 1771, and began preparations for a new piece of legislation giving the Company additional judicial powers to tame its executives abroad. But these last-minute efforts at self-regulation were hopelessly at odds with the needs of the situation. Sulivan's Judicature Bill was thrown out by Parliament in April 1772, and in its place a Select Committee formed, chaired by John Burgoyne, to investigate the Company's affairs. As a result, the Company was already being scrutinised by Parliament before its collapse in September.

AN END TO MERCANTILE AVARICE?

Burgoyne is better known for his role as the general who later lost the Battle of Saratoga during the American War of Independence. As chair of the Select Committee, he drew a succession of high-profile witnesses to explain the Company's actions all the way back to Plassey. Clive haughtily dismissed the committee's inquiries, arguing that he was innocent of any corrupt dealings, and even if he had taken presents, he could not understand 'what good reason could be given, after risking his life so often in the Company's service, if he had neglected the only honest opportunity that ever offered the acquiring a fortune and had rested intirely [sic] upon the generosity of any set of Directors?'[19] He then turned on his former employers themselves, accusing the directors of failing to rise to the challenge of the Bengal acquisition, treating it rather 'as a South Sea bubble than anything solid and substantial', adding 'they thought of nothing but the present time, regardless of the future'.[20]

By the time Parliament reconvened in the winter, the Company's financial debacle was common knowledge. Once again the directors tried to deal with its affairs by sending out a commission of supervisors – the body which Smith had been nominated for. Yet, this was all too late and failed to recognise the 'general odium' with which the Company was now regarded. The Prime Minister, Lord North, set up his own Secret Committee, which quickly flexed its muscles by proposing legislation stopping the commission from setting sail. Advantage had passed decisively to the state, and North made clear his intentions when he declared to Parliament the following March, 'I think, Sir, it is allowed that Parliament have a right over the India Company.' Negotiations on the terms of the bail-out started in earnest in the new year. The directors made the first move, confidently requesting a loan of £1.5 million from the government, with the ability to restart dividends when half of this had been repaid. Parliament was having none of this, and proposed instead a smaller loan, much tighter caps on dividends, and all financial relief being conditional that 'at the same time due care be taken to secure by proper Regulation the future good government of the Company's affairs'.[21]

In May, Burgoyne wound up his investigations, and presented his final report. This concluded that Clive had acquired his Plassey fortune illegally. Burgoyne was supported on the floor of the house by his committee members, including William Meredith who tore into the Company's tyranny in Bengal. 'Never did such a system exist', he thundered, 'where mercantile avarice was the only principle and force the only means of carrying on government.' In full flow, Meredith cast aside the Company's attempt to win sympathy by focusing attention at the loss of life in the 'black hole' affair, declaring: 'I remember a similar accident in St. Martin's round-house'![22] Speaking to the Commons in May 1773, Burgoyne declared that 'it is the duty of the house, as guardians of the nation's honour to apply a remedy', arguing that 'our vindictive justice must go back to the origin of the evil' – in other words, to the revolution of 1757.[23] Burgoyne isolated Clive as the 'oldest, if not principal delinquent', who had set 'an evil example' to the rest of the Company's executives. Outside Parliament, Burgoyne's invective was matched by magazines and handbills full of caricatures condemning Clive for corruption: in one he recoils in horror from the ghosts of three Indian merchants who have come to demand justice. On 21 May, Burgoyne submitted his resolution to a vote: that all territorial conquests belonged to the Crown; that it was illegal for individuals to appropriate such public property for themselves; and that Clive had indeed done so. But the motion was rendered harmless through a set of amendments by Clive's allies, passed and then immediately followed by another motion praising Clive's 'great and meritorious service'. In a debate that had lasted from three o'clock in the afternoon until five o'clock the following morning, Clive had eventually escaped censure. But his reputation was broken, and he would die 18 months later in mysterious circumstances. Many believed he had committed suicide, with Dr Johnson observing that Clive had 'acquired his fortune by such crimes that his consciousness of them impelled him to cut his own throat'.[24]

Attention turned to the Company itself. North had decided not to push the constitutional argument about who owned Bengal, and also shied away from touching the Company's monopoly, realising that this was the prime mechanism for returning Indian tribute to Britain. Instead of fundamental reform, North guided through three acts to relieve the Company's financial distress and reform its practices. The first set out the terms and conditions for the government's loan of £1.4 million, notably a 6 per cent cap on dividends until the debt was cleared. In return, the Company had to swallow the second of North's pieces of legislation, the Regulating Act of 1773. This amounted to a serious intrusion into the Company's corporate independence both at home and abroad. The Company's democratic system of governance had been regarded by many as a major cause of its slide into chaos. To counter this, the Regulating Act sharply curbed shareholder rights. The threshold for voting at Company meetings was raised from £500 to £1,000. At the time of the Act, the Company had 2,153 shareholders, 1,246 of whom possessed between £500 and £1,000 worth of stock. These were all disenfranchised at a stroke. In addition, those with £3,000 got two votes, those with £6,000 three votes, and the plutocrats with £10,000 received four votes. Naively, North had hoped that cutting the numbers of active shareholders would dampen disorder and 'integrity of conduct would follow greater property'.[25] If anything the measures magnified the problems of 'cabal and corruption' by making it easier for a few rich nabobs returning from India to take over the Company. Shareholder control over the Court of Directors was curbed as well. Annual elections for the entire board were replaced with staggered ballots for a quarter of the 24 directorships each year. The aim was to give the Company's leadership a more permanent flavour, but it also cut the directors' responsiveness to their owners, without introducing accountability through other measures.

The Company's freedom to manage its own affairs in India was also curtailed. A new post of Governor-General of India was introduced, based in Calcutta and supreme over the Company's other presidencies of Bombay and Madras. The post had an impressive annual £25,000 salary – not far from what Clive had earned in a year from his exclusive Society of Trade. Awarded to the Company's existing Governor of Bengal, Warren Hastings, this new post of overlord would be part of a five-person council, three of whose members were nominated by Parliament. Crucially, this gave the state a theoretical majority over decision-making in the Company's most important subsidiary. It also laid the seeds for constant in-fighting between Parliamentary appointees and the Company's men. In addition, a Supreme Court was introduced to Bengal, with the aim of dispensing justice to British subjects living there, but with highly ill-defined powers. And the Company's privilege of commercial confidentiality was withdrawn, with the Act providing the government with the right of access to all incoming correspondence with India; this intrusion was later extended to include the right to reject outgoing letters as well.

The Company protested that all these innovations amounted to the subversion of its charter, a precedent that could be applied elsewhere 'to destroy the independence of the City of London itself'. But it was simply in no position to block the changes. For the editor of *Gentleman's Magazine*, it was clear that the Regulating Act 'will in time (and perhaps not very far removed) be the means of transferring the wealth and power of the greatest trading company in the world into the hands of government. *Sic transit gloria mundi*.'[26]

THAT WORST OF PLAGUES, THE DETESTED TEA[27]

But the Company's troubles were not yet over. Lord North's third piece of legislation was the Tea Act. Historians are now agreed that 'no bill of such momentous consequences has ever received less attention upon passage in Parliament'.[28] Bengal's pre-eminence in the Company's accounts can sometimes mask the growing importance of China tea. At the beginning of the eighteenth century, imports of this new beverage amounted to just 100,000 lb, accounting for a mere 1 per cent of the Company's trade. But this had surged to 2.5 million lb in the late 1740s, reaching over 4 million lb each year from 1760 to 1767. By this time, the Company was paying on average a shilling for each pound in Canton for tea that would later fetch more than four times as much at auction in London. In spite of freight costs and the high levels of duty the government imposed, tea was easily the Company's most profitable commodity. Mixed with slave-grown sugar from the West Indies, the afternoon cup of tea perfectly expressed Britain's emerging empire of consumption.

Like the textile trade, a large source of the Company's demand for tea came from outside the British market, notably in the Americas. As the Company's charter only extended to imports from Asia, merchants would buy tea at its quarterly auctions for re-export across the Atlantic. By 1760, America was consuming over a million pounds a year. Only a quarter of this came directly from England, however, with the rest smuggled in to avoid Britain's high tax regime. In the aftermath of the Seven Years' War, this important trade became embroiled in a new struggle, as the British Crown sought to export its powers of taxation to its American colonies. Just as the state's first raid on the Company's coffers had been driven by post-war financial necessity, so the extension of Britain's existing system of stamp duty in 1765 to America was justified by the imperative of sharing the cost of military spending with the colonists. The response was rapid and furious, with American opponents to the measure denying that Parliament had the constitutional authority to tax the colonies, and boycotts and riots forcing its prompt removal only a year later.

All this time, the Company was lobbying hard to find ways to boost its legitimate trade with the Americas. As part of its first deal with the government in 1767 to share the revenues of Bengal, it also won a five-year drawback on all of the customs duties on tea re-exported to America. Without the taxes, the price of tea was now equivalent to that paid by the smugglers in Amsterdam, and legal imports into America surged by 42 per cent into New York and 100 per cent in Philadelphia over the next 18 months. But what the government gave with one hand, it took away with the other. Simultaneous with the introduction of the duty drawback, the Chancellor of the Exchequer, Charles Townsend, introduced a revenue act imposing duties on imports of glass, lead, paper and tea into the Americas. Instead of collecting duty on tea in England, Townsend had simply transferred the tax across the Atlantic, negating the benefits the Company had just received.

Worse, tea became the focus of the colonists' opposition to the entire Townsend package. A strong anti-tea campaign arose along the eastern seaboard, with activists promoting Labradore tea from the red-root bush as an alternative. Many pledged to abstain totally from tea until the duties were removed. Legal imports of the Company's tea plummeted from a record 869,000 lb in 1768 to just 108,000 lb in 1770. When British merchants complained to the government of the disastrous effects this was having on trade, the government had second thoughts, removing all of the Townsend duties in 1770. But in spite of the Company's best efforts, Lord North kept the duty on tea. Only 1,000 lb of tea was exported to New York and Philadelphia between 1771 and 1773.

For the Company, the damage was done. Fusing with the share price crash of 1769 and mounting mismanagement in Bengal, the colonists' boycott left 18,000,000 lb of unsold tea sitting in its London warehouses. So, as part of its petition to Parliament, the Company's directors requested the right to export its tea surplus across the Atlantic. In a tactically brilliant move, the resulting Tea Act enabled the Company to sell its tea direct to America. In addition, the Act gave the Company a sizeable tax break by removing the duty paid on tea imported into England. Cutting out the middlemen and reducing the tax take would bring costs down dramatically so that Company tea could be sold cheaper than its smuggled rival. The British government thought that lower prices would allow the Americans to accept the continuing presence of the modest Townsend duty on tea. A handful of MPs protested that the government's plan would fall foul of the continuing resentment of the Townsend duty on tea. But the government stood firm. As a result, in the summer of 1773, the Company drew up plans to ship 2,000 chests of tea to four key ports – Boston, Charleston, New York and Philadelphia.

Lord North had made a strategic miscalculation. The boycott of tea had started to fizzle out in the Americas when the bulk of the Townsend duties were lifted. The Tea Act revived the campaign, and gave it a new edge – opposing corporate domination as well as unjust taxes. The patriots were also substantially aided by English merchants who had seen their business ruined by the new privileges won by the Company. According to one eye-witness, 'opposers of the measure in England wrote therefore to America, encouraging a strenuous resistance'.[29] From October onwards, newspapers and handbills provided the citizens of the 13 colonies with a barrage of analysis and polemic. The *Boston Evening Post* of 18 October 1773, for example, contained a powerful article from 'Reclusus' exposing the folly of Lord North's plan. 'Though the first Teas may be sold at a low rate to make a popular entry', he acknowledged, 'yet when this mode of receiving Tea is well-established, they, as all other Monopolists do, will meditate a greater profit on their Goods, and set them up at what price they please.'[30] Knowledge of the Company's malpractice in India provided another powerful reason for stopping it gaining a foothold in America. Writing in *The Alarm* newsletter, 'Rusticus' underlined how 'their Conduct in Asia, for some years past, has given simple Proof, how little regard they regard the Laws of Nations, the Rights, Liberties, or Lives of Men'. Clive's conquest of Bengal and the ensuing famine were all grist to the mill: 'They have levied War, excited Rebellions, dethroned lawful Princes, and sacrificed Millions for the Sake of Gain,' continued 'Rusticus', adding: 'fifteen hundred Thousands, it is said, perished by Famine in one Year, not because the Earth denied its fruits, but [because] this Company and their servants engulfed all the Necessaries of Life, and set them at so high a Rate that the poor could not purchase them'.[31]

Threats of tarring and feathering against the merchants who would handle the tea had the desired effect, and in New York and Philadelphia they wrote to the Company resigning their commission. But in Boston, three ships docked and refused to turn around. And so, on the night of 16 December 1773, patriots dressed as Mohawks dumped 90,000 lb of tea worth £9,659 into Boston harbour. The port of Boston was summarily closed by the British authorities until its citizens reimbursed the Company for its goods. The payment never came, of course, and the Boston Tea Party led inexorably to open rebellion at Lexington in April 1775. A Company that had engineered its own revolution in Bengal had unwittingly contributed to fomenting another revolution in the Americas. Looking back from the early years of the twenty-first century, Jane Anne Morris sees powerful resonance in this symbolic act of anti-corporate protest: 'The people who founded this nation didn't fight a war so that they could have a couple of "citizen representatives" sitting in on meetings of the British East India Company', she wrote in 2001. 'They carried out a revolution in order to be free of oppression: corporate, governmental, or otherwise.'[32]

RAFAEL'S REVENGE

The upsurge of revulsion against the Company was almost over. But there was one final act of reckoning still to come. When William Bolts had published his *Considerations on Indian Affairs* in early 1772, one of his greatest grievances was the failure to bring the Company's miscreants to justice. 'We behold the impotency of power to be such on this side of the ocean', he wrote, 'that not one delinquent in India is brought to justice in Europe.'[33] Bolts wrote from personal experience, feeling himself unjustly expelled from Bengal by a compromised judicial system riddled with conflicts of interest. Not content with getting rid of Bolts, the Company also broke up his joint ventures with a number of prosperous Armenian merchants. In a series of co-ordinated strikes, Clive's successor as Governor, Harry Verelst, summarily arrested Gregore Cojamaul and Melcomb Philip at Varanasi in March 1768, and a few days later imprisoned Johannes Padre Rafael and Wuscan Estephan in Faizabad. All four were eventually transferred to Murshidabad, and after more than five months in jail, were released without charge or explanation. When they regained their freedom, they found the commercial situation turned upside down: all Armenian, English and Portuguese merchants were prohibited from operating in Bengal's internal markets.

In an extraordinary move, two of the four – Cojamaul and Rafael – decided to sail all the way to England to seek redress. The arrival of these two prosperous merchants gave substance to the widespread complaints against the Company in ways that Bolts's bitter critique never could. But they faced an uphill battle: first of all to convince the British courts that they had jurisdiction over the case, and then prove Verelst's guilt thousands of miles away from the scene of the crime. It was an epic struggle that took eight years to resolve. In September 1769, Cojamaul and Rafael petitioned the directors, complaining of the 'cruel and inhuman manner' in which they had been treated, and then bewailing Verelst's arbitrary edict, which had left them 'deprived of that freedom of trade which their nation had always enjoyed in the times of the worst of the ancient Nabobs'.[34] When this was brushed aside, the two commenced legal proceedings for damages against Verelst in July 1770. Thus began a long journey through the labyrinth of British law. But in December 1774, the case eventually came before a jury at the Guildhall in the City, who found Verelst guilty of 'false imprisonment' and ordered him to pay Rafael £5,000 plus costs. Outraged, Verelst demanded a retrial. But all he managed to do was delay the inevitable, and reduce the payment by £1,000. The courts also found in favour of Cojamaul, awarding him £3,200, and in July 1777, it was all settled with another £2,500 in damages for Wuscan Estephan. In all, Verelst had to pay £9,700 – over £800,000 in 2002 money – plus the Armenians' and his own extensive legal costs.[35] It is a testimony to the British legal system that successive judges and juries were willing to put nationality aside and find Verelst guilty of 'oppression, false imprisonment and singular depredations'.[36] Verelst's career as an opulent Company director was cut short, and he would end his days in exile from his creditors.[37]

Thousands of miles away from the scene of the crime, the principle of extraterritorial liability for corporate malpractice had been established in 1770s London. Many in business regard the current upsurge of global litigation against corporations as somehow new and unjustified. Yet, Verelst's case provides a powerful precedent, demonstrating that 200 years ago one of the senior executives of the world's first multinational was tried and found guilty of what we would now consider human rights abuses. The practical implications of this breakthrough were, however, muted. Few others had the means or the determination to come all the way to England for redress.

A MOMENTARY FIT OF GOOD CONDUCT

Adam Smith hated colonies almost as much as he despised corporations, viewing them as inherently wasteful for the coloniser and usually oppressive for the colonised. He lamented that no country had ever voluntarily given up a colony, owing to the sad fact that such 'sacrifices are always mortifying to the pride of every nation'.[38] For him, the outbreak of war in America represented a huge missed opportunity for constructing an enlightened Atlantic union based on open trade and representative government. Four months after *The Wealth of Nations* was published the 13 colonies issued the Declaration of Independence, and seven years of bitter warfare were to follow. By the time Smith was turning his attention to the third edition of his masterpiece in 1783, the American war was nearing its end. But after a 'momentary fit of good conduct' immediately following the Regulating Act, the East India Company was 'in greater distress than ever'.

As his contribution to the resurgence of public and political interest into the Company's affairs, Smith wrote to his publisher, William Strahan, in May 1783, informing him that he planned to add a new section giving 'a full exposition of the Absurdity and hurtfulness of almost all our chartered trading companies'.[39] This counter-blast appeared in the final book of the new volume, dealing with 'the Public Works and Institutions which are necessary for facilitating particular Branches of Commerce'. In Smith's opinion, however, the joint stock corporation was a deeply flawed piece of public policy. A particular danger was the impetus for hazardous speculation created by the separation of ownership and management in the joint stock arrangement. By limiting the liability of shareholders to the nominal value of their investments, excessive risks would be taken. In the Company's case, investors were also drawn by the lure of patronage, acquiring 'a share, though not in the plunder, yet in the appointment of the plunderers of India'.[40] In parallel, corporate executives would never look after shareholder funds with the 'same anxious vigilance' that they would in a partnership where ownership and control were in the same hands. As a result, 'negligence and profusion must always prevail, more or less, in the management of the affairs of such a company'.[41] If this wasn't bad enough, the Company's monopoly status continued to extract an unjustified tax on both consumers and producers. Smith acknowledged that a temporary monopoly may well have been necessary in the early days of the India trade. But it had long ago outlived its usefulness, simply becoming a vehicle for the even more 'negligence, profusion and malversation' by its executives.[42] Hoping for shareholders to act with 'more dignity and steadiness' was unlikely to yield results, he felt. Instead, Smith's prescription for these dire ailments was simple: recognise that the Company would never be 'fit to govern' its possessions in India and make the trade between Britain and India 'open to all'. More generally, Smith argued that joint stocks should be strictly limited to financial services (banking and insurance) and utilities (water and canals).

A STARK UTOPIA

Reading Smith afresh and delving into his analysis of the East India Company, it is shocking how his penetrating critique of the corporation has been so comprehensively suppressed. Nothing of his scepticism of corporations, their pursuit of monopoly and their faulty system of governance, enters the speeches of today's neo-liberal advocates. Promoting his vision of free trade, they conveniently ignore that this can only be achieved with steadfast curbs on corporate power. Smith may have been a believer in open markets, but freeing the world for corporations formed no part of his vision. Smith strongly approved of the prevailing restrictions on the establishment of joint stock corporations introduced in the 1721 Bubble Act, and it took almost another century after *The Wealth of Nations* for these constraints to be removed in Britain. Across the

Atlantic, corporations would also play a highly limited role in the newly independent United States. With memories of the East India Company vivid in the public imagination, corporations were tightly circumscribed in the new republic, with time-bound charters that could be revoked for misconduct. Significantly, the writers of the US Constitution made no mention of corporations, suggesting the limited role that they expected them to play in the new Republic.[43] Future US President, Thomas Jefferson, in particular, worked tirelessly to resist concentrations of economic power, writing in 1816 that 'I hope we shall crush in its birth the aristocracy of our moneyed corporations which dare already to challenge our government in a trial of strength, and bid defiance to the laws of our country.' More recently, John Kenneth Galbraith has imagined that if Smith were to come back to earth, 'he would be appalled at a world, where, as in the United States, a thousand corporations dominate the industrial, commercial and financial landscape and are controlled by their hired management'.[44]

Smith was a penetrating analyst of the causes and consequences of corporate over-stretch. But his enlightenment faith in the 'invisible hand' blinded him to the ways in which the rule of the market would itself create injustice and instability. Not only did Smith's vision ignore the problem of what modern economists today describe as 'externalities' – the tendency of the market to deplete public goods – but his belief in the providential outcomes of the market obscured its tendency to boom and bust. In spite of his trenchant criticism of the commercial character, Smith saw no reason to temper market freedoms. As the Industrial Revolution unfolded, the 'moral sentiments' that Smith hoped would curb relentless self-interest proved to be wholly inadequate to the task of preventing shocking abuse in the workplace or the ruthless exploitation of the environment. As Karl Polanyi observed following the collapse of the liberal world order in the 1930s, Smith's self-regulating market is a 'stark utopia', which could not exist 'for any length of time without annihilating the human and natural substance of society'.[45]

Adam Smith died in July 1790, too early to see how some of his ideas would be used to justify the progressive elimination of the East India Company's trading monopoly. Rather than ushering in an era of liberty and justice, the result was colonial domination. British manufacturers were protected by high trade and tariff barriers, and the entire Indian economy progressively skewed to service the imperial interest. Smith's vindication of commercial freedom would also be used to justify often inhumane imperial policies, particularly on famine relief. In *The Wealth of Nations*, Smith had confidently stated that 'a famine has never arisen from any other cause but the violence of government attempting, by improper means, to remedy the inconveniences of a dearth'.[46] This conclusion was supported by his understanding of the terrible Bengal Famine of 1770, when 'some improper regulations, some injudicious restraints imposed by the servants of the East India Company upon the rice trade, contributed, perhaps to turn that dearth into a famine'.[47] There is a world of difference, however, between the ways that corporations manipulate the market for their own ends and the interventions that states need to make to ensure the protection of human rights, the most important of which is the right to life. Nevertheless, Smith's call for government non-intervention in times of famine would be applied with cruel effect by the British in India. As early as 1783, some of the Company's own officials would protest against attempts to offer food relief, using Smith's writings as ammunition. This was a position later strongly supported by the East Company's own resident political economist, Thomas Malthus, who taught at the Company's College at Haileybury. Famine tested Smith's benevolent market and found it wanting, unable to respond to the imperative of ultimate human need.

For the modern corporation – and the East India Company in particular – Adam Smith remains one of the most powerful enquirers into its flawed metabolism. What his world-view lacked was sufficient attention to how the 'laws of justice' could be made to work in an anarchic global marketplace. This would be the obsession of Smith's friend, Edmund Burke.

7
Justice Will be Done

THE TREES OF DESTRUCTION

Due south of Fort William in central Kolkata lies Alipur, a lush suburb that still abounds with exclusive clubs and grand mansions from the colonial era. One of the most striking of these is Belvedere House, now home to the National Library of India. Originally a summer house for the Nawab of Bengal, the site was gifted to Warren Hastings by Mir Jafar in 1763. And it was here that two of the Company's most senior executives met at dawn on 17 August 1780 to fight one of the most extraordinary boardroom battles in corporate history – a duel to the death.

On one side stood Warren Hastings, Governor-General of Bengal, and an archetypal Company man. Hastings had joined the firm in 1749 at the age of 17 and had decades of experience in India. He had been a prisoner of Siraj-ud-Daula in the build-up to Plassey, and had risen through the ranks on the basis of his evident skill and dedication. Against a backdrop of the generalised plunder in Bengal, Hastings developed a reputation for personal integrity. He was one of the very few who had tried to halt the anarchy of private trade in the 1760s, seeking a more ethical basis for British commerce. 'If our people, instead of erecting themselves into lords and oppressors of the country, confine themselves to an honest and fair trade,' he told Parliament, 'they will everywhere be respected, and the English name, instead of becoming a reproach, will be universally revered.'[1] By 1780, Hastings had been directing the Company's affairs in Bengal for eight years, juggling competing demands of trade, finance, justice and defence, often letting pragmatism trump principle. In the process, he had become embroiled in endless disputes with the Parliamentary majority on the new Bengal Council.

Opposing him was Philip Francis, the ring-leader on the Council. Perhaps the finest propagandist of his day, Francis is now known to have been the author of the anonymous 'Junius' letters, whose powerful critique rocked the corrupt government of George III between 1768 and 1771. Prior to his appointment as councillor in 1773, Francis had had a fairly unexceptional career as a junior official in the War Office. The only plausible explanation for his surprise elevation to the Bengal Council with its impressive salary of £10,000 a year was an attempt by the embattled establishment to get 'Junius' out of the country. And by sending him to Bengal, there was the added prospect that he would not come back, succumbing to disease like so many of the Company's employees. Central to Francis's identity was the need for eternal resistance to tyranny, and he quickly turned his attention from the corruption of the British court to the mismanagement of the Company. In November 1774, just one month after his arrival in Bengal, Francis was writing back to his friend John Bourke, 'the corruption is no longer confined to the stem of the tree, or to a few principal branches; every twig, every leaf is putrified'.[2]

Both of the duellists felt right was on their side. Hastings believed that Francis's constant criticisms of his policies had reached an intolerable level, challenging his authority as governor. By contrast, Francis saw Hastings as the incarnation of the Company's institutionalised corruption. But if Hastings's faults lay in his tendency to authoritarian high-handedness, Francis was crippled by his sense of superiority, mistaking vindictiveness for public virtue. Even his friends warned him of his 'reputation for haughtiness', and in Calcutta he quickly became known as 'King Francis'. After almost six years of non-stop squabbling, Hastings forced the issue on 14 August 1780, impugning his rival's character and declaring him 'void of truth and honour'. Francis had no option but to challenge Hastings to a duel. The long-running battle between principle and expedience had finally come to a head. Between 5.30 and 6.00 a.m., the two met on the western edge of the Belvedere under a clump of trees known as the 'trees of destruction'. Neither had fought a duel before, and Francis had probably never used a pistol. The two stood 14 paces apart, and after initial distractions, Francis fired and missed. Seconds later, Hastings shot, hitting Francis in the shoulder. Francis fell and cried out that he was a dead man, prompting Hastings to shout 'Good God! I hope not.' Thankfully, the wound was not life-threatening. But it did put an end to Francis's feud with Hastings, and he returned to England a year later a bitter man, vowing revenge.

The Belvedere duel was more than just an exotic skirmish between two irreconcilable individuals. It epitomised the deep-seated battle for control of the Company that was now under way – between the long-standing commercial imperatives of a joint stock corporation, and the rising interests of the British imperial state. For all to see, it exposed the utter failure of North's Regulating Act to allocate effective responsibility and so bring tranquillity to the Company's operations. Over the next 15 years, a new bargain would be struck between state and corporation, constraining and channelling the Company's power and autonomy in unprecedented ways. Running through this struggle, however, was the continuation of the ethical passion that had driven the first inquiries into the Company in the 1770s. Ultimately, the question that Edmund Burke would put before the world in his dramatic impeachment of Hastings was: can the Company and its executives be brought to justice?

SEND MORE MONEY

When Hastings took over as Governor of Bengal in 1772, his primary concern was to restore order and return the Company's operations to profitability. Corruption and spiralling military expenditure had turned the *diwani* windfall into a liability. Revenue from land taxation formed the lion's share of the *diwani*, and Hastings moved quickly to end the mirage of Clive's 'dual system' by moving the treasury from Murshidabad to Calcutta. To maximise revenues, Hastings first farmed out the task of revenue collection for a five-year period and then replaced this with a series of annual auctions. Initially, Hastings' commercialisation of the tax system paid dividends, with revenues rising almost 20 per cent between 1772 and 1776.[3] But thereafter collection tailed off once more, and cases of oppressive tax collection mounted.

In the wider economy, Hastings rigorously enforced the long-standing ban on private trade. Learning the lessons of Clive's failed Society of Trade, Hastings decided to establish corporate rather than private monopolies over opium, salt and saltpetre as a way of further increasing revenues. In the case of opium, Hastings argued that such a 'pernicious article of luxury' should be carefully regulated and only permitted 'for the purpose of foreign commerce'. So, in 1773, Hastings deprived the Company's Council in Patna of its opium privileges. In its place, the Company was given the exclusive rights to buy all opium, a function that Hastings farmed out to contractors to manage on its behalf. 'All types of compulsion and coercion were used', writes Chandra Prakash Sinha, 'to force the *ryots* [peasants] to grow opium against their will, for which they received arbitrarily low prices.'[4] Before the Company took over, opium was selling for about three rupees a *seer*. Peasants were compelled to sell their poppy to the contractor, and the price they received soon fell to between one and two rupees. The average auction price, however, was six rupees a *seer*, winning the Company a substantial profit. When Francis complained that the monopoly was producing 'universal poverty and depopulation' in Bihar, Hastings handed the opium contract to Francis's friend, John Mackenzie, thereby silencing the criticism. But Mackenzie's tenure was no better, and in 1777 a group of peasants complained that a large area of corn had been forcibly cut down and replaced with opium.[5]

Hastings introduced a similar approach for salt, imposing a Company monopoly and then farming out the actual production to contractors. But mismanagement actually reduced the Company's revenues, and so in 1780 Hastings introduced a system of direct Company management. All salt had to be sold to Company agents at a fixed price, and the agents then sold it on to wholesalers. By keeping the price it paid the producers as low as possible and the wholesale price high, the Company raised its revenues to nearly Rs3 million in the first year alone, taking this total to over Rs6 million by 1784.[6] The system would remain almost unchanged until the end of British rule in 1947.

A final source of cash for Hastings to satisfy the Company's directors was to look outside Bengal, using the Company's private army as leverage. One of his first acts was to cancel the annual tribute of Rs2.6 million to the Mughal emperor. This was followed by a series of deals with Bengal's western neighbour, Awadh. First, Hastings transferred the provinces of Allahabad and Kora to Awadh for a tidy Rs5 million, and then he hired out the Company's soldiers for a further Rs50 million to help Awadh annex Rohilkhand. All in all, Hastings had gained a much-needed £5.5 million from territory-swapping and mercenary exchanges. In 1775, Hastings took control of Varanasi (Benares) – 'a valuable acquisition to the Company', he wrote back to the directors – worth another quarter of a million pounds a year. When hostilities with France broke out in 1778 as part of the wider American War of Independence, Hastings exerted further pressure on Varanasi to squeeze out a series of extra payments.

Hastings's relentless drive for cash had dramatic human consequences, many of which were presented at his impeachment. He was by no means a cruel ruler, but he was faced by a profound dilemma, beautifully laid out by Macaulay in his 1840 essay. In essence, the Company's directors wanted Hastings to simultaneously enhance Bengal's financial performance and improve its ethical standards.

'Govern leniently and send more money', the directors urged, according to Macaulay, adding 'practice strict justice and moderation towards neighbouring powers, and send more money'.[7] Ever the practical administrator, Hastings recognised that 'it was absolutely necessary for him to disregard either the moral discourses or the pecuniary requisitions of his employers'. He chose the safest course and decided 'to neglect the sermons and to find the rupees'.[8]

FUNDAMENTAL INJUSTICE

Hastings's financial management had an air of desperation about it. What added to the stress was the dramatic change in governance brought about by the Regulating Act, all of which came to a head at the Belvedere. Traditionally, the Company's governor of each presidency had supreme powers, guided by a largely consensual council. The new Act overturned this tradition, introducing a five-person council, making decisions by majority vote. Furthermore, three of the councillors were appointed by Parliament, ostensibly to represent the public interest. Almost as soon as these three parliamentary appointees – General John Clavering, Philip Francis and George Monson – arrived in Calcutta in October 1774, tensions arose. Instead of the 21-gun salute they were expecting, Hastings had organised only 17 cannon to fire as they landed. Furthermore, Hastings had not bothered to greet them in person, and when he did meet them later in the day, he did so without the expected formality. 'Surely, Mr Hastings might have put on a ruffled shirt', wrote Alexander Macrabie, secretary to the new councillor Philip Francis. Beneath these seemingly trivial questions of protocol lay a monumental struggle for control of the Company in Bengal.

From the start, Francis along with Clavering and Monson sought to overthrow Hastings, believing him to be irretrievably corrupt, even stooping to bribe the new councillors to cease their inquiries. The first major clash came in 1775, when Francis, Clavering and Monson backed the accusations of corruption being levelled at Hastings by Rajah Nandakumar. A former Governor of Hugli under the Nawabs, Nandakumar was the most powerful local aristocrat in 1770s Bengal, and a confirmed enemy of Hastings. The Francis faction had, however, underestimated Hastings's capacity for self-preservation. Resurrecting a fraud case against Nandakumar made many years earlier, Hastings brought Nandakumar to trial at the new Supreme Court, where in accordance with English law, Hastings's ally Elijah Impey found him guilty and sentenced him to death. As Hastings's recent biographer, Jeremy Bernstein, concluded, there is 'no question that the execution of Nandakumar was a judicial murder'.[9] Beyond the savagery of the act itself lay the unfortunate comparison with Clive's infamous forgery of the treaty with Amir Chand back in 1757: Clive was ennobled and applauded for a crime that would hang Nandakumar.

Initially cowed, the parliamentary faction next tried to dislodge Hastings in June 1777 when news reached Calcutta that Hastings's agent in London had tendered his resignation. Clavering promptly declared himself the new Governor-General. Hastings stood firm, denying he had resigned and mobilising the Supreme Court, which, again, took his side. Hastings had triumphed, and Clavering's death soon afterwards left Francis isolated. Almost in despair, Francis wrote to the Prime Minister, Lord North, in September 1777, damning the Company's rule in Bengal as guilty of 'injustice in its fundamental principle', 'uniting the character of Sovereign and merchant, and exercising the power of the first for the benefit of the second'. For Francis, the only solution was to make sure that 'the government is not to be continued in the hands of a mercantile body'.[10] In the Bengal Council, Francis was in the minority, and finding his position severely weakened, he came to a truce with Hastings when war loomed with the Marathas. But peace between these two irreconcilable characters could never last long, and the result was the climactic Belvedere duel in the summer of 1780.

With Francis's departure back to England, Hastings had *carte blanche* to run affairs as he wished. In March 1781, he awarded the opium contract at a knock-down price to Stephen Sulivan, son of the Company chairman and Hastings's patron, Laurence Sulivan. The younger Sulivan promptly sold it on to John Benn for Rs350,000 (£40,000), who then made a further Rs150,000 for himself by selling it on once more to William Young.[11] Having put in place what he saw as the best mechanism for generating profit from opium production, Hastings then probed the possibility for making extra opium sales in China. Hastings ordered two ships, the *Nonsuch* and the *Betsy*, to be loaded with 3,450 chests of opium and sent undercover to China. When the directors in London heard of the escapade, they were horrified, stating categorically to Hastings that it was 'beneath the Company to be engaged in such a clandestine trade; we therefore positively forbid any more opium being sent on the Company's account'.[12] Then in January 1782 Hastings turned on his former ally,

Awadh, using the accession of a weak nawab to extort treasure said to be worth £2 million from the royal queens' (*begums*') household. After imprisoning the queens for a year and allegedly torturing the court eunuchs, Hastings's troops slunk away with a mere £5,500.

Once more, the Company seemed to be embarking on a downward spiral of corruption, conflict and desolation. In 1769, it had been news that Haidar Ali, Sultan of Mysore, had attacked Madras that pricked the 'Bengal Bubble'. In July 1780, he invaded the Carnatic, smashing the Company's forces at Polilur. In Bengal, droughts struck in 1781 and 1782. And rebellion finally exploded against the extortions of the Company's system of land revenue. In June 1782, peasants from Dinajpur travelled to Calcutta with a petition against the oppressive behaviour of Debi Singh, the Company's agent in the region. The *ryot*s wanted relief from unpayable levels of tax, the removal of unauthorised levies and an end to the forcible sale of property to pay tax arrears, as well as redress for the violence of the Company's agents. But the Company rejected the complaint as 'frivolous' and 'fabricated'. By November, *ryot*s were refusing to pay their rents, and in January, full-scale revolt broke out in Dinajpur and Rangpur.[13] Peasant grievances merged with the holy war of the *sannyasin* led by Shah Munju and Shah Musa. This rebellion was, however, quickly suppressed by the Company's troops. But neighbouring Awadh also rose up in revolt against Hastings's mounting demands for tribute, which had resulted in those unable to pay being 'confined in open cages'. Again, the uprising was easily crushed, only to be followed by a vicious famine in 1784, thankfully not on the scale of the 1770 disaster.

Bankim Chandra Chattopadhyaya would later base his groundbreaking novel, *Anandamath*, on the story of *sannyasin* uprisings against the Company during Hastings's tenure. Central to the story of Mahatma Satya, Mahendra, Bhavan and Kalyani is the inclusion of the nationalist anthem, 'Bande Mataram' (Hail to the Mother) as the song of the rebels. What was striking about the novel was the emphasis that the main characters placed on armed rebellion as the only way to rid India of the British, a strategy that was later adopted by Bengal's revolutionary movement at the beginning of the twentieth century. In the novel, the radical Bhavan attempts to convince Mahendra of the need for revolt: 'the British are shipping our wealth to their treasuries in Calcutta', he says, 'and from there that wealth is to be shipped again to England. There is no hope for India until we drive the British out ... by sheer force of arms.'[14]

By the time Hastings left Calcutta in February 1785 to return home, peace had been restored with the Marathas, Hyder Ali was dead and Madras regained. But back in England, his reputation had been shattered. William Cowper captured the mood in his 1782 poem, 'Expostulation'. A one-time school-mate of Hastings, Cowper turned on him in a highly personal rebuke:

> Hast thou, though suckled at fair freedom's breast,
> Exported slav'ry to the conquer'd East
> Pull'd down the tyrants India serv'd with dread,
> And rais'd thyself, a greater, in their stead?
> Gone thither arm'd and hungry, return'd full,
> Fed with the richest veins of the Mogul,
> A despot big with pow'r obtain'd by wealth
> And that obtain'd by rapine and by stealth?
> With Asiatic vices stor'd thy mind,
> But left their virtues and thine own behind;
> And, having truck'd thy soul, brought home the fee,
> To tempt the poor to sell himself to thee?[15]

NIBBLING AT THE CHARTER

After the crash of 1772, the overwhelming priority for the Company's directors back in London was to pay off the £1.4 million loan from the government and regain financial freedom. Their task was hampered by the rumours of civil war in the Bengal Council that filtered back to England. Scandalised by Nandakumar's judicial murder and the in-fighting it exposed in the Council, the directors had voted to recall Hastings in the summer of 1776, but they were overruled at a meeting of the Company's shareholders. However, Hastings's representative in London had used this occasion to tender Hastings's resignation in an attempt to secure good terms, which the directors accepted. Of course, when Hastings himself heard of his departure from office the following year, he refused to budge. This stubbornness enflamed passions in London even more, exposing the failure of the Regulating Act to give the state the right to recall the governor-general. King George III demanded that Hastings should be dismissed, and some talked of his impeachment. But war in the Americas took precedence and events in India were allowed to drift. In the meantime the Company successfully paid off its debt in 1776, cut its debt and triumphantly raised its dividend from 6 to 8 per cent.

When news of Haidar Ali's invasion of the Carnatic reached London in April 1781, this happy situation was quickly overturned. The Company was already in the middle of negotiations with Lord North's embattled administration for a renewal of its charter, and this powerful reminder of the Company's incompetence strengthened the government's hand. North demanded that the Company should hand over three-quarters of its net profits over what was required to pay the annual 8 per cent dividend, amounting to £600,000 a year. Speaking for the opposition Whigs, Edmund Burke sprung to the Company's defence, arguing that this was no more than 'a violent and shameless attempt to rob the Company in order to pursue the purposes of the most lavish waste and the most profligate corruption'.[16] But the Company was desperate for its charter, and in return for another ten years' monopoly it agreed to pay £400,000 up front, as well as three-quarters of the surplus going forward.

This was not the end of the matter. In February, Burke had been appointed to a Parliamentary Select Committee investigating the administration of justice in Bengal. Two months later, Henry Dundas, the 39-year-old rising star of the Scottish elite, was charged with leading a parallel Secret Committee into the Carnatic affair. Just as in 1773, the Company was facing a two-pronged parliamentary assault. Over the next two years, these twin investigations would make 17 reports to Parliament, exposing the Company and laying the foundations for its subordination to the state. Although they were political adversaries, Burke and Dundas shared much of the same analysis concerning the roots of the problem. Where they differed was over which institution should have the whip-hand. For Dundas, the Crown should be in the driving seat, but for Burke, it was clear that the Company should be accountable to Parliament. What complicated matters even further was the mounting political instability at Westminster as the British establishment struggled to come to terms with the loss of the Americas. North finally fell in March 1782, and there followed three short-lived administrations before Pitt the Younger took office in December 1784, driving through Dundas's vision of reform.

For Dundas, the problem lay in the chronic inability of the Company to act any longer as a commercial concern and avoid the lure of military conquest. 'I wish every servant of the Company', he told Parliament, 'to consider that it is and ought to be the first aim of his life to prove himself a faithful steward of the Company, and that he has no right to fancy he is an Alexander or an Aurangzeb and prefer frantic military exploits to the trade and commerce of the country.'[17] To demonstrate Parliament's authority over the Company, Dundas sought to discipline all three of the Company's governors in India – Rumbold in Madras, Hornby in Bombay and Hastings in Calcutta. Rumbold was renowned for corruption, which many blamed for the failure of Madras to withstand Hyder Ali's assaults. Between 1778 and 1780, he had managed to send home £160,000, three times his salary for the period. But Hastings was the main prize, and, in May 1782, Dundas presented a resolution that he had 'acted in a manner repugnant to the honour and policy of this nation and thereby brought great calamities on India and great expense on the East India Company'. Parliament agreed and voted to recall Hastings. But the Company's shareholders vetoed the decision by 428 to 75, just as they had overturned the directors' recall order in 1776. For one leading shareholder, this was just another example of a 'settled design to nibble away the charter rights of the Company'.[18] Frustrated by the shareholders, in the following spring Dundas presented a fully fledged bill to force the Company's shareholders to respect 'the sense of parliament'. But nine days before, the short-lived Shelburne coalition that Dundas served had fallen. There followed the extraordinary nine-month government of Lord North and Charles James Fox, an alliance of inveterate enemies. For the East India Company, the parliamentary initiative passed from Dundas to Burke.

THIS CONTINUAL DRAIN

Born in Dublin in 1729, Edmund Burke is widely seen as the father of modern conservatism for his passionate defence of the *ancien régime* during the French Revolution. His *Reflections on the Revolution in France* quickly became the handbook of reactionaries across Europe in their battle for the 'rights of property' against the 'rights of man'. Yet Burke was by no means a natural supporter of unchecked monarchical power. Indeed, for much of his political career with the Whigs, Burke sought to check tyranny and uphold the balance of powers between Crown and Parliament that had been achieved at the Glorious Revolution. In 1779–80, for example, he launched a campaign for 'economical reform', seeking to curb the corrupt use of public money by the royal court. Burke also took a resolutely pro-American line in Britain's struggles with the 13 colonies, and backed religious toleration for Catholics in his native Ireland. His stance towards the East India Company was also consistent with his philosophy of respect and duty. As long as the Company could demonstrate that it had fulfilled the terms of its charter, Burke would support its independence. But as soon as he had concluded that it had become a tool of oppression, he would press for root-and-branch remedies.

Initially, Burke had opposed the efforts taken by Lord North to regulate the Company, seeing these as unjustified infringements of the Company's chartered status. This hostility to North's policies towards the Company also chimed with the political expediency of the opposition Whigs. But this all changed with the fall of North in 1782. Burke's own position was also shifting as the conclusions of his intensive Indian investigations became clear. In the south, leading Company executives in Madras had abused their position to make a series of private loans to local rulers, notably the Nawab of Arcot and the Rajah of Tanjore. Burke's close friend and namesake, William Burke, had become the agent for the Rajah of Tanjore in 1778, and the two Burkes collaborated in a 1779 pamphlet revealing the scandal of these odious debts, amounting to more than £3 million. In the east, Burke's knowledge of Bengal had been enhanced by a close collaboration with Philip Francis on his return from Calcutta. These two streams came together in the summer of 1783 with the publication of the Select Committee's Ninth Report, a masterpiece of political economy, largely authored by Burke.

The reason why the Regulating Act had so catastrophically failed, according to Burke, was its inability to 'follow the Tracks of the Abuse' and apply 'an appropriate Remedy to a particulare Distemper'.[19] The Bengal Revolution had broken 'the commercial circle', which had ensured that trade between Britain and India had brought mutual benefit. Using his words with precision, Burke described this model of exchange as 'Intercourse – for it is not Commerce', with India suffering 'what is tantamount to an Annual Plunder of its Manufactures and its Produce to the Value of Twelve hundred thousand Pounds'. In effect, India was being screwed.

Not only was Burke indignant at the way in which the Company's revolution had harmed the traditional rights of Indian traders and producers, but he also revealed how it had failed in providing any long-term benefit for the corporation either. A business model that rested on such unequal exchange inevitably reduced the productive capacity of Bengal, requiring increasingly 'casual and extraordinary' measures to extract financial resources. And on the expenditure side, the Company's involvement in 'an endless Chain of Wars' substantially increased the amount that Hastings needed to raise through trade and taxation. In December 1780, Hastings was confidentially telling the directors that the gap was too great and there would have to be a 'total Suspension of their Investment' in the year ahead. The Company's commercial system lay in ruins. The only way it could send back any goods for sale at the Company's quarterly auctions was to let out space on its East Indiamen to its own executives, who purchased Bengal goods on their own account. This was a trading mirage, with no hope of any profit for the Company once costs were deducted.

> By this extraordinary scheme, [Burke wrote] the Company is totally overturned, and all its Relations inverted. From being a body concerned in Trade on their own account, and employing their Servants as Factors, the Servants have at One Stroke taken the whole Trade into their own Hands, on their own Capital, at their own Risque; and the Company are become Agents and Factors to them, to sell by Commission *their* Goods for *their* Profit.[20]

The only solution to this crisis was to re-establish the Company on 'a Bottom truly Commercial',[21] ending the pretence that it could undertake public responsibilities with any form of justice. More than this, the Company's systems of governance needed fundamental restructuring, going beyond the temporary palliatives of the Regulating Act. Rather than acting as any restraint on executive misconduct in Bengal, 'the Negligence of the Court of Directors has kept pace with, and must naturally have quickened, the Growth of the Practices which they have condemned'.[22] With the formation of the Fox–North coalition, Burke had an opportunity to put his conclusions into practice. Here, his hand was considerably strengthened by the parlous state of the Company's finances. In March 1783, the directors had sent a grovelling petition to Parliament begging for 'relief and effectual aid' from the state, and by the autumn, it was clear that the Company could no longer honour its debts.

The Company had become financially and institutionally bankrupt, breaching the implicit terms of its Georgian 'licence to operate'. Drawing from the rich Whig tradition of legitimate resistance to tyrannical government, Charles James Fox argued that corporations, like kings, owed duties to the people. The Company's charter was not to be seen as a sacrosanct grant of rights, but rather as an expression of a mutual trust between company and people. 'If this trust be abused', argued Fox, and 'its failure arises from palpable guilt, ignorance or mismanagement, will any man say that trust should not be returned and delivered to other hands?' Burke took up the same theme, arguing that 'every description of commercial privilege [is] all in the strictest sense a trust, and it is of the very essence of every trust to be rendered accountable'.[23] Burke continued with a rhetorical flourish: 'to whom then would I make the East India Company accountable?', he mused. 'Why, to Parliament, to be sure.' The East India Bill framed by Fox aimed to enforce this accountability by replacing the Court of Directors with a body of seven commissioners appointed by parliament. In effect, the Company would be decapitated, its shareholders remaining as nominal owners, but disenfranchised of any voice in the management of their assets. It is said that when Sir William James, one of the Company's oldest directors, read the bill, he died of shock. The Company's shares also suffered, falling some 13 per cent on the news of the bill, reaching a lowly £120 at the end of November.

Proposing the India Bill before the Commons in December 1783, Burke was clear that 'the remedy is demanded of us by humanity, by justice and by every principle of true policy'. The broad-based sense of outrage against the Company in the Commons meant that sizeable majorities were quickly achieved. But the Company was not giving up easily, and counter-attacked with a propaganda assault that upheld the sanctity of its chartered privileges, warned the nation of the concentration of patronage that the bill would place in Fox's hands, and played on the King's deep personal hatred of Fox. To counter Fox's apparently unstoppable progress in Parliament, James Sayers produced a string of anti-Fox caricatures, the most successful of which was published on 5 December, depicting 'Carlo Khan's Triumphal Entry into Leadenhall Street'. Fox is shown as the 'Great Mogul', sitting astride an elephant which bears the face of the Prime Minister, Lord North. The elephant is led by Edmund Burke dressed as a herald with a map of Bengal hanging from his trumpet. Crucially, Fox carries a banner stating in Greek, 'King of Kings'. No longer a man of the people, Fox had become a tyrant. Reflecting on this dramatic turnaround, Lord North later admitted that 'the idle nonsense about Carlo Khan had misled the weak part of the country so strangely'.[24]

This shift in public mood provided a cloak for King George to strike at the coalition. The King despised Fox for meddling in his household affairs and saw the India Bill as a perfect opportunity to rid himself of a government he resented. In a move that breached the constitutional principle that the King should not interfere in the affairs of Parliament, George let it be known that any peer voting for the bill in the House of Lords would be regarded as his enemy. The ploy worked to perfection, and the bill was defeated. Refusing to budge, Fox and North were forced to relinquish their seals of office, just days after their apparent triumph in the Commons. William Pitt the Younger was made Prime Minister, and Burke would never again hold public office.

DIRECT AND CONTROL

In place of Burke's decapitation strategy, Pitt introduced a far more subtle plan for exerting state control over the Company. In March 1784, Parliament was dissolved, and a new one elected that was much more conducive to Pitt's cause. The Whigs were crushed, blaming their defeat on the extensive use of bribery by the Company's nabobs on Pitt's behalf. Their suspicions were justified the following year when Pitt arranged for the private loans of Company executives to the Nawab of Arcot to be paid off, without first investigating the legitimacy of the claims. Between 1784 and 1804, an average of £480,000 was transferred each year. But by then a new mountain of loans totalling some £30 million had been contracted, only one-twentieth of which turned out to be genuine. In a scandalous form of eighteenth-century debt relief, the British state had backed the corrupt claims of the Company's nabobs in exchange for political favours, paying them off with the revenues of India.

Pitt's first priority was to stabilise the Company's finances. Bailiffs had entered East India House a few days after the election was called in March to claim the Company's properties in lieu of over £100,000 it owed to the government. New ways had to be found to boost its trading revenues and restore the confidence of the financial markets. Just as in 1773, the government turned to tea. But in place of the disastrous Tea Act, which had retained an unjust tax, Pitt cut the hated taxation on tea from 119 to 12.5 per cent, replacing the initial loss of revenue with the peculiar Window Tax. It was a brilliant move, reducing the price of legal tea, putting many of the smugglers out of business, and driving up the Company's imports of tea from just 5 million lb in 1784 to 13 million lb the following year. Pitt then turned his attention to the markets. Once again, the Company was financially embarrassed, lacking the wherewithal to pay its dividend. In June 1784, the Company's chairman, Nathaniel Smith, pleaded to Parliament for temporary assistance, warning that another Europe-

Illustration 7.1 Unknown, *East India House*, late eighteenth century

wide financial meltdown could take place if a bail-out was not forthcoming. If he had 'to go in to the Court of Proprietors and tell them they were to have no dividend', Smith told the Commons, he 'would not be answerable for the consequences. The news would soon reach Holland and the government need not be told what would follow.'[25] To avoid a run on the stock, Pitt pushed through legislation extending the Company's ability to raise debt, and so pay its regular dividend at 8 per cent. Of course, this measure made little financial sense as the Company was paying dividends out of debt. But it helped to stabilise the situation.

To crown his achievements, Pitt presented to the house his bill for the 'Better Regulation of the Government' of India on 6 July 1784. Drafted by his firm ally, Henry Dundas, the bill respected the 'sacred' character of the Company's charter. But a five-man Board of Control appointed by the King was established in Whitehall. The board was given full powers to 'superintend, direct and control' the civil and military affairs of the Company's territorial possessions. In addition, the proprietors' right to veto decisions taken by the directors was removed, and the Crown gained the power to recall any of the Company's executives in India, solving the problem that Hastings had posed for London throughout the previous decade. As one wise historian observed, 'it was a clever, dishonest bill, which successfully concealed the Ministry's intention of effectively subordinating the

Court of Directors'.[26] Pitt had managed to take control because he understood that the Company's main concerns were pre-eminently financial and not political. By leaving the directors with the power of patronage and propping up the dividend, he successfully seduced the Company into the state's embrace. As one government official observed with some satisfaction after the Act had been passed, the directors had been reduced to 'mere clerks'.[27]

GEOGRAPHICAL MORALITY

Edmund Burke was not one to call an end to his pursuit of justice simply because of a lost election. What depressed Burke most was his belief that 'all the tyranny, robbery and destruction of mankind practised by the Company and their servants in the East is popular and pleasing to the country'.[28] Indeed, even his closest friends were baffled at Burke's concern for the 'black primates' of India.[29] Burke was also fully aware of the futility of pursuing the cause of India in the face of Pitt's supremacy. In February 1785, he savaged Pitt's policy on the Arcot debt, describing Paul Benfield and his gang of creditors as 'those inexpugnable tape-worms which eat up the bowels of India'. But four hours of high-flown rhetoric failed to move Pitt and Dundas, no doubt partly because of their election dealings with the 'Arcot interest'. Still, four months later, shortly after Hastings landed at Plymouth, Burke tried again, starting a process that would last for another decade in an epic impeachment trial.

What hampered Burke was the poverty of legal instruments he had at his disposal to bring the Company's executives to account. He could try for a vote of censure, as Burgoyne had done in 1773, or revive the ancient practice of impeachment. Neither of these could be considered effective judicial procedures. In an impeachment proceeding, for example, the House of Commons first had to vote on charges to be judged by the House of Lords, which would then sit as a court rather than a legislative body. The flaws in such a process are obvious. Majority voting rather than evidence or law would decide the matter, with party loyalties likely to have greater sway than the merits of the case. Furthermore, as Macaulay would observe many years later, 'ordinary criminal justice knows nothing of the set-off. The greatest desert cannot be pleaded to a charge of the slightest transgression.'[30] Yet, in the system of political justice represented first by Burgoyne's motion against Clive and then by Burke's impeachment of Hastings, off-setting is exactly what took place. Hastings's strongest defence was not that he was innocent, but that 'extraordinary means were necessary, and those exerted with a strong hand, to preserve the Company's interests from sinking'.[31] In such a situation, the possibility of a fair trial – for either side – vanished almost immediately.

Yet impeachment was the only tool at Burke's disposal. Writing to his ally, Philip Francis, Burke was clear that 'my business is not to consider what will convict Mr Hastings (a thing we all know to be impracticable) but what will acquit and justify myself to those few persons and to those distant times, which may take a concern in these affairs'.[32] It is testament to Burke's mastery of his brief that he not only swung the Commons around to his argument, but also managed to sustain the trial long after many had given it up as a lost cause. Pitt could easily have blocked the whole proceedings. Indeed, when Burke's first charge against Hastings for his complicity in hiring out the Company's troops to suppress the Rohillas, Pitt's overwhelming majority carried the day. In their hearts, however, the government's leading lights knew that 'the force of evidence' – in Dundas's words – meant that Hastings simply had to face justice.[33] Dundas, of course, had led the parliamentary struggle for Hastings's recall in 1782. And, by backing Burke's motion for impeachment, Pitt and Dundas could free themselves of the stain of being mere tools of the nabobs. So, when the charge against Hastings's conduct towards Varanasi came to a vote in June 1786, Pitt signalled his consent.

In all, 20 charges were voted through by the Commons. The full trial opened on 13 February 1788 in Westminster Hall, with the cream of the British establishment looking on. The drama of the case and the fabulous Enlightenment language employed by Burke and his ally, the playwright/politician Richard Brinsley Sheridan, are enough to give Hastings's impeachment a prominent place in eighteenth-century English history. Bringing the charges against Hastings for his abuse of the *begums* of Awadh, Sheridan compared Hastings to 'the writhing obliquity of the serpent' and damned him for a character that was all 'shuffling, ambiguous, dark, insidious, and little'. And as for the Company, it combined 'the meanness of a pedlar and the profligacy of pirates ... wielding a truncheon with one hand, and picking a pocket with the other'.[34]

This was all good knock-about stuff. But what makes the trial so significant for the accountability of corporations are the principles upon which Burke based his case. For him, natural law meant that all humans should be accorded equal rights to justice, wherever they may be. 'The laws of morality', he declared on the third day of the trial, 'are the same everywhere, and that there is no action which would pass for an act of extortion, of peculation, of bribery, and oppression in England, that is not an act of extortion, of peculation, of bribery, and oppression in Europe, Asia, Africa and the world over.'[35] Against the corrosive relativism that was increasingly viewing India as an inferior land in which different standards of justice should be applied, Burke unfurled the standard of absolute values. 'I must do justice to the East', he declared, for 'I assert that their morality is equal to ours.' Full of contempt for what he saw as Hastings's 'geographical morality', Burke denounced the view that 'the duties of men are not to be governed by their relations to the great governor of the universe, or by their relations to men, but by climates, degrees of longitude and latitude, parallels not of life but of latitudes', adding in a wonderful image: 'as if, when you have crossed the equinoctial line, all the virtues die'. For someone who would become so opposed to Tom Paine's *Rights of Man* in the heat of the French Revolution, the peculiar thing is that in his contest with Hastings Burke propounded the case for universal human rights.

A SOFT IMPEACHMENT

For Burke, what best ensured that these 'laws of morality' were upheld was respect for organic systems of governance. The Company, however, had engineered a revolution in India overturning an established order for which Burke had an abiding reverence. In his Ninth Report, he had even compared the *zamindars* of Bengal to the landed aristocracy of France, whom he would later defend with such passion following the fall of the Bastille.[36] In the words of the nineteenth-century Liberal politician John Morley, Burke demonstrated 'a reasoned and philosophic veneration for all old and settled order, whether in the free Parliament of Great Britain, in the ancient absolutism of Versailles, or in the secular pomp of Oudh [Awadh]'.[37] The puzzle for later generations of radicals opposing the British Empire in India was that it was the conservative Burke who demonstrated far the greatest sympathy for people cast aside by the Company conquest. In comparison, with later generations of liberals (notably the father-and-son pair, John and James Stuart Mill), and even socialists, such as Karl Marx, Burke was the real champion of India's identity. Rather than viewing history as a civilisational contest between primitive and progressive nations, Burke believed that each society had its own intrinsic value, which should not be sacrificed to the interests of profit or power.[38] 'The first step to empire is revolution', Burke argued as he opened his assault on Hastings in February 1788. For him, it was the Company's revolutionary character, the way its pursuit of market dominion led it to overturn both prince and peasant that was its most serious flaw. Against the arrogance of an England that saw only 'Oriental despotism' when it looked to the East, Burke presented a picture of a complex society of rights and responsibilities, underpinned by 'a law interwoven with the wisest, the most learned, and the most enlightened jurisprudence that perhaps ever existed in the world'.[39] If the trial demonstrated anything, it was 'the great lesson that Asiatics have rights, and that Europeans have obligations'.[40]

Burke and Sheridan certainly had rhetoric on their side. Burke's opening speech was four days long, and lashed Hastings with a verbal assault:

> It is with confidence that, ordered by the Commons, I impeach Warren Hastings Esquire, of high crimes and misdemeanours.
>
> I impeach him in the name of the people of India, whose laws, rights and liberties, he has subverted, whose properties he has destroyed, whose country he has laid waste and desolate.
>
> I impeach him in the name and by virtue of those eternal laws of justice which he has violated.
>
> I impeach him in the name of human nature himself, which he has cruelly outraged, injured, and oppressed, in both sexes, in very age, rank, situation and condition of life.

Women were carried out fainting, and even the Speaker was rendered speechless. When Sheridan presented the *begums*'s charge, he took a whole week to complete his case, with spectators paying £50 a seat to soak up his rhetorical extravagance. And, when the marathon came to an end in April 1795, Burke completed the prosecution case with a nine-day closing address.

Yet, for all the sophistication of their analysis and the extent of their verbal prowess, the prosecution case was a muddle and a mess – a 'soft impeachment' to use the phraseology of Sheridan's great theatrical character, Mrs Malaprop.[41] The articles of impeachment were poorly drafted and lacked legal detail. The trial itself was interrupted by huge gaps in the proceedings, caused not least by the madness of King George III and the onset of the French Revolution. Even though the trial lasted a full seven years, the Lords only sat for 149 days, often for less than a few hours a day. To no-one's surprise, Hastings was acquitted of all charges in April 1795.

The injustice of the judgment still cries out to be answered. Looking across Hastings's actions as Governor-General, there is little doubt that many of the means he employed to promote the Company's interests were dubious to say the least, notably the conduct of the Rohilla war and the execution of Nandakumar – neither of which were included in the impeachment. His treatment of the Rajah of Varanasi and the *begums* of Awadh also were also deeply suspect, even by the standards of eighteenth-century foreign policy. And his fiscal policies generated real oppression in Bengal and Awadh. Hastings certainly needed to be censured for these failures of judgement and the suffering they caused. But impeachment proved to be a blunt and obsolete tool for reining in such policy abuses. Furthermore, the broad-brush prosecution brought by Burke meant that Hastings escaped conviction for some clear breaches of corporate rules. It is incontestable that Hastings accepted a series of 'presents', thereby breaking the covenant he had signed with the Company. In addition, the charge brought against him for corruption in his handling of the opium contract – giving it to the son of the Company chairman – is simply 'unanswerable'.[42] The tragedy was that these unambiguous crimes were not separated out from the unwieldy impeachment case and pursued in the criminal courts to their logical conclusion.

THE SKULKING POWER

Where Burke was all passion and principle, the Tory duo of Pitt and Dundas were single-minded in their utterly pragmatic pursuit of power. The 1784 India Act had introduced a two-tier system – a 'double government' – with the Company maintaining a façade of authority, behind which the state pulled the strings.

Outwardly, the Company still seemed supreme. In the second half of the eighteenth century, its total trade with Asia had amounted to well over £200 million, earning a sizeable average profit of 17 per cent each year. It had a fleet of 70 ships in 1784, which would rise to over a hundred by the end of the Napoleonic wars, ranging in size from some 500 to 1,200 tonnes. From the dire days of bailiffs and plummeting share prices, its finances showed strong signs of recovery in the 1780s and 1790s. The Company's capital stock was increased for the first time since 1709, first with an injection of £800,000 at

£155 in 1786 and then another £1,000,000 at £174 in 1789. This took the paid-in capital to £5 million. And, in February 1792, the Company shares hit £200 for the first time since 1770.

It was the Board of Control, however, that was directing the Company's management of India. The first symbol of this shift was Dundas's decision to appoint Charles, Lord Cornwallis, as Governor-General of Bengal in 1785. He could not have been more different than his predecessor, Hastings. He was a soldier – defeated at Yorktown – and a landed aristocrat with extensive estates in Suffolk. But he was free from the taint of corruption, describing what he found in India as 'a system of the dirtiest jobbing'.[43] He separated the Company's civil and commercial branches to put a stop to the structural embezzlement of corporate revenues. More profoundly still, Cornwallis decided to insulate the Company's administrative machine from India by reserving all senior posts for Europeans. Unlike generations of Company merchants who had intermingled with local society, Cornwallis had a deep disdain for trade and particularly trade with Indians, famously declaring that 'every native of India, I verily believe, is corrupt'.[44]

Cornwallis's main task was to bring some order to the Company's ad hoc system of tax collection. Taxes had certainly risen under Company rule in Bengal. One estimate suggests that the annual taxes collected in Bengal during Mir Kasim's reign in the early 1760s amounted to about £646,000, rising to £1,470,000 in the first year of the Company's *diwani*. During the 1770s, the collection had advanced to £2,577,000 and by 1790–1 to £2,680,000, a four-fold increase in 30 years.[45] But the revenue system remained forever temporary, with frequent changes to the rates and management methods. Starting with Philip Francis, a growing number within the Company believed that the only way to resolve the situation was to fix the system of tax collection in perpetuity. In a case of tragic misperception, the Company's analysts came to see the *zamindari* class of Mughal tax-farmers as equivalent to the propertied landed gentry of England, with the *ryots* as their tenant farmers. But self-interest was at work as well. The Company wanted to build up a political class of landholders who would support their presence. In place of complex systems of ownership, with intersecting rights and responsibilities, the Company introduced the English model of landlordship.

For Cornwallis, a 'permanent settlement' was 'the only effectual mode to render the proprietors of the lands economical landlords and the prudent trustees of the public interest'.[46] And so on 22 March

1793, a proclamation was made fixing the *jumma* at £3 million 'for ever'. For this, Bengal's peasantry were sacrificed in the same way as the rights of England's commoners had been smashed by the enclosure movement.[47] The *zamindars* were given exclusive rights over their lands and, in Ranajit Guha's phrase, a 'rule of property' was introduced, bringing a total rupture with previous systems of landholding and governance.[48] According to John Capper, writing in the 1850s, the result was that '20 million small landholders were dispossessed of their rights, and handed over, bound hand and foot to the tender mercies of a set of exacting rack-renters'.[49] From an imperial perspective, this was Cornwallis's greatest achievement – absorbing the Company's territories in Bengal into a legal and administrative system that was fully aligned to the wider needs of the British Empire. On his return to England, the grateful merchants of London made Cornwallis an honorary freeman of the City, awarding him a gold medal in a gilded box. But back in Bengal, large numbers of *zamindars* were unable to pay the new levy, with the result that their lands were forcibly auctioned off. By 1796 perhaps one-tenth of the whole of Bengal, Bihar and Orissa was advertised for sale, and 163,000 lawsuits over arrears remained outstanding in 1812.

Dundas's ambitions did not stop there, however. As discussions opened for the renewal of the Company's charter in 1793, he turned his attentions to the Company's commercial operations. Its exclusive trading position had always been resented by Britain's provincial ports. Now it was challenged by the rising industrial interest, which saw its monopoly as a major barrier to successful export to Asia. Ever the pragmatist, Dundas recognised that the Company's import monopoly was still essential as a means of returning tribute. But its right of exclusive export no longer served the national interest. Sweetening the pill for the Company and its shareholders by supporting an increase of its guaranteed dividend from 8 to 10 per cent, Dundas breached its monopoly by requiring the Company to offer at least 3,000 tonnes a year to private exporters, around one-third of the total. 'My plan is to engraft an open trade upon the exclusive privilege of the Company,' he told the House of Commons.[50] War had broken out with France, and the 1793 Charter Act passed almost unnoticed. The Company was given authorisation to increase its capital stock by another £1,000,000, taking it to £6 million, while Dundas's behind-the-scenes' role was formalised with the creation of a new post of President of the Board of Control. From the back-benches, Philip Francis was one of the few MPs either to bother with the proceedings or to recognise their importance, accusing his old foe Dundas of 'holding up the name of the Company as a mask and a stalking horse to shelter the operation of a real power which skulks behind it'.[51]

THE ROAD NOT TAKEN

By the middle of the 1790s, it was clear that in the harsh battle between the imperatives of power and principle, justice had been the loser. Fox's unpopularity at court and his apparent attempt to monopolise the Company's patronage shattered the Whig bid for corporate reform in 1783. Pitt and Dundas played the system far more effectively, gaining the reality of power in all essential matters, without any associated responsibility. To the surprise of many, they had supported Burke's impassioned attempt to impeach Hastings. But Pitt and Dundas had little to lose, realising that allowing the proceedings to go ahead would help them draw a line under the Company's disreputable past. More importantly, they knew that Burke could never succeed. By the time the impeachment verdict was given in April 1795, the political mood in Britain had been transformed. Instead of restoring the nation's honour in India, defending the country against the revolutionary ambitions of France was the order of the day. Burke's effort to overthrow the principle of 'geographical morality' had ended in glorious failure.

As Adam Smith had warned in the midst of the American War of Independence, pride and patriotism would always interfere in efforts to resolve the ethical imperatives of empire. Few, if any, of those who challenged the Company's practices questioned British rule in India. Burke, for example, was insistent that Britain had been given control of Bengal by 'the Sovereign Disposer'. For both Burke and Francis, the Company's incompetence was not just an ethical disaster, but also risked losing valuable acquisitions in India. Almost alone among his contemporaries, George Dempster (1732–1818) argued that Britain should cease ruling India. A friend of the poet Robert Burns, Dempster became a shareholder of the Company in 1763 and was elected a director in the dark days of 1769 and 1772. Perturbed by the direction the Company was taking, Dempster angered his fellow directors by urging that the Company should relinquish its territorial acquisitions and return to its trading roots. Unable to make any progress in the Company, Dempster resigned and entered Parliament to pursue the case against empire by state or corporation. Speaking in the debate on Fox's India Bill in November 1783, Dempster was profound in his critique, arguing that the Company's excesses now meant that its charter 'ought to be destroyed, for the sake of the country, for the sake of India, and for the sake of humanity'.[52] But dealing with the Company was insufficient: Britain as a whole should renounce control. 'I for my part lament that the navigation to India had ever been discovered,' Dempster concluded, adding 'I now conjure ministers to abandon all ideas of sovereignty in that quarter of the world: for it would be wiser to make some one of the native princes king of the country, and leave India to itself.'

Dempster's pleas fell on deaf ears. The Company's commercial and imperial position was central to the British state's global struggle with revolutionary France. The loss of Britain's American colonies reinforced this process, placing ever-greater emphasis on retaining the Company's Indian possessions. For all the high-flown critique of the Company's behaviour, the deal that emerged was limited, tawdry and unworthy of the Enlightenment. One of the great 'might have beens' of history is to imagine the application of the ideals of the American Revolution to that other problem province of the British Empire, India. But India was not modern, European or Christian, and so was ultimately subjected to a second-class settlement, treated as a piece of property rather than a living community of people.

This epic struggle is still on display at London's National Portrait Gallery. Up the stairs to the second floor are the galleries charting Britain's rise to imperial dominance in the eighteenth century. On one side of the room hangs Joshua Reynolds's joyous portrait of 1766–68 showing Warren Hastings as a young Company executive, a few years away from his appointment as governor-general. On the other side, Philip Francis looks down from the wall, his face full of disappointment. Painted by James Lonsdale between 1806 and 1810, Francis had not only failed to overthrow Hastings, but had failed to become governor-general himself, winning the Order of the Bath as a consolation prize. In an unconscious reconstruction of the duel that exploded between these two on the lawns of Belvedere, the space that separates these portraits is almost exactly the 14 paces that divided the two men one dawn in August 1780. Yet the captions say nothing about the duel they fought over the future of one of the world's most powerful corporations. The Company's hotly disputed rise to imperial pre-eminence is hidden once more.

8
A Mercantile Sovereign

ON McDRUGGY'S TRAIL

The crossroads at Bank marks the centre-point of London's financial world. To the north lies the Bank of England, the 'Old Lady of Threadneedle Street', who once vied with the East India Company for the position as the most influential corporation of the eighteenth century. On the eastern edge stands the Royal Exchange in whose cellars the Company often stored pepper. Just across the road is 'Change Alley where the Bank's and the Company's shares were traded with such exquisite zeal. Further east along Cornhill is Leadenhall Street, the site of East India House. And under a modest archway to the south is 3 Lombard Street, the offices of Matheson & Co., a London outpost of Jardine Matheson, the giant Hong Kong-based conglomerate. Founded in July 1832, Jardine Matheson headed a new generation of aggressive enterprises that aimed to replace the Company in the Asia trade. William Jardine had been a doctor on the Company's ships, but left to pursue a business career in 1817 at the age of 33. Eight years his junior, James Matheson was also from Scotland and had gone straight into private trading in 1815.

The two brought together a winning combination of commercial wisdom and political verve, which they deployed with great skill as the Company lumbered dinosaur-like towards commercial extinction. Matheson was the Firm's propagandist, founding *The Canton Register* to act as a mouthpiece for his aggressive free trade views, urging the end to the Company's monopoly. When Parliament finally laid the China trade open to all in 1833, Jardine Matheson was well prepared, shipping out the first private consignments of tea to Britain the following year. Soon, the Firm, as the partnership was known, had the biggest share of a booming market, 'the safest and most gentlemanlike speculation I am aware of',[1] Jardine told a friend interested in investing in the business. By the end of the decade, the company had a fleet of a dozen ships operating along the China coast, sending out tea and silk and importing thousands of chests of opium in return.

The Firm was quite frank about its trade. Writing to a potential business partner in 1831, Jardine stated 'we have no hesitation in stating to you openly that our principal reliance is on opium'.[2] The Firm knew full well that the import of opium into China was illegal. But the reality of deeply porous borders and ever-present corruption meant that the tide of 'foreign mud' had grown steadily higher through the 1820s. While it is easy to criticise the ethics of the Firm's early business model, Jardine Matheson and other free traders did little more than intensify a poisonous exchange that had been progressing under Company guidance for half a century. For the private traders, the profits were high; for the Company, the trade provided a valuable outlet for opium grown under its monopoly licence in Bihar; and for the British government back in London, it offered the only means of paying for the country's passion for tea, which in turn contributed a large slice of the Exchequer's taxation base through import duties. In the words of 'A British Merchant' – most likely either Jardine or Matheson – 'this illicit commerce is so interwoven with our financial system in India, as well as with our commerce, that it is not inferior in importance to revenue obtained from tea at home'.[3] This easy defiance of law did not appeal to everyone, and Dr Jardine was lampooned by the up-and-coming Benjamin Disraeli in his 1837 novel, *Sybil*, as 'a dreadful man! A Scotchman richer than Croesus, one McDruggy fresh from Canton, with a million of opium in each pocket, denouncing corruption and bellowing free trade.'[4]

This 'bellowing' included urging the British government to use force to make China accept the enlightened logic of free trade in all goods, even opium. Two wars later, China's ports had been prised open, Hong Kong transferred to Britain and opium legalised. The Firm had got its way. Having made its fortune, it smartly diversified out of opium in the 1870s. By then, William Jardine was dead. But Matheson would live on to 1887. Like so many nabobs before him, Matheson used his Asian treasure to buy his way into the British landed aristocracy, purchasing the Hebridean island of Lewis for over half a million pounds in 1844. Back in China, however, the scourge of opium addiction rolled on. In all, millions of Chinese died during the nineteenth century as a result of opium, a 'crime which no one even today acknowledges as the man-made catastrophe it was'.[5] Not surprisingly, perhaps, there's no place for opium in the corporate timeline displayed on the modern Jardine's website, even though it matched tea as the Company's principal product in its early years.

The Keswick family, descendants of the founding partners, continue to control the Firm, and remain one of the wealthiest families in Britain.[6] The group now straddles a diverse range of interests from property through insurance to hotels and retail. Opium might have disappeared from Jardine Matheson's contemporary public image, but the Firm remains one of the clearest links with the dying days of the East India Company.

For by the beginning of the nineteenth century, the Company was in inexorable decline as a commercial concern. The reforms of the 1770s, 1780s and 1790s had punctured the Company's autonomy as a business and breached its monopoly of the Asia trade. The fish was now hooked, and successive Whitehall ministers would reel in the Company's remaining privileges one by one until it was a mere corporate husk and could be safely wound up. There was no grand plan in this decades-long process of liquidation, and during the process, the Company's outward appearance looked mightier than ever, with unprecedented trade, revenues and military might. Yet as a free-standing corporation, the Company's trajectory was remorselessly downhill, so that it became little more than an implementing agency for imperial expansion, its commercial character peeled away until it traded in little but paper.

THE MALABAR ITCH

Instead of merchants and traders, a succession of soldiers and aristocrats ruled the Company's possessions, accentuating the burgeoning militarisation of its operations in India. Clive and Hastings had shown how the successful deployment of the Company's private army could reap corporate and private benefits – additional taxes for the Company's exchequer and the spoils of war for the officer class. Between 1763 and 1805, the Company's army had grown almost ten-fold from 18,000 to 154,500, far beyond the needs of self-defence. This created a powerful dynamic in favour of further aggression. Indeed, with the end of the private trade era, military adventurism was the only avenue left open for aspiring individuals to make their fortune in India. Nominally, this was at odds with the legal requirements of the 1784 East India Act which had ruled that 'to pursue schemes of conquest and extension of dominion in India are measures repugnant to the wish, the honour and policy of this nation'. But after Cornwallis's relatively restrained administration, the reopening of conflict with France gave a perfect cover for a new phase of aggression under Richard Wellesley, the Governor-General from 1798 to 1805.

In south-west India, Wellesley brought the 30-year conflict with Mysore to a crushing close. Known as 'the terror of Leadenhall Street', the small principality of Mysore under first Hyder Ali and then his son, Tipu the Tiger, had rattled the security of the Madras Presidency for decades. Fondly seen by subsequent nationalists as a modernising Indian ruler, Tipu sought to match the Company's institutional and technological advantages by investing heavily in agricultural improvement and naval expansion. He also spread his diplomatic net in the hope of forging alliances against the British. Tipu certainly had strong connections with revolutionary France, earning the title of 'Citizen Tipu' in the process. He also invoked the Islamic notion of holy war (*ghazwa*) to mobilise support for his repeated conflicts with the Company. But the bid for alliances with France and the Ottomans failed to protect him from the Company's encirclement. In 1792, he was defeated by Cornwallis and forced to cede Malabar. Seven years later, in April 1799, Seringapatam was finally sacked and Tipu killed. Writing in triumph to Dundas at the Board of Control, Wellesley hoped that his conquest would 'enable me to gratify your voracious appetite for lands and fortresses'.[7] The booty for the victorious Company forces was immense, and Seringapatam's treasures were scattered across the museums and country houses of England. The loot included Tipu's infamous 'Man-Tyger-Organ', a life-size model of a tiger chewing out the neck of a Company soldier, which growled when wound up. This was shipped back to the Company's own in-house museum of oriental curiosities on Leadenhall Street, and later transferred across London to where it now stands on display at the Victoria and Albert Museum.

Conquest also provided the Company with the opportunity to deploy its well-tried techniques of monopoly extraction in new territories. Malabar's experience highlights the economic trauma so often brought by Company rule. Land taxes were tightened, and monopolies introduced over the production and sale of salt, tobacco and timber – the latter to secure a vital supply of teak for the Royal Navy in the war against Napoleon.[8] The Company also established a massive 1,000-acre spice plantation at Anjarakandi to produce cinnamon, coffee, pepper and nutmeg. But the land for the plantation was usurped, and its labourers effectively kidnapped to work as little more than slaves. Children were taken from their families in the middle of the night, with clothes stuffed in their mouths to keep them quiet and all caste marks removed.[9] Not surprisingly, perhaps, the local people refused to sell pepper vines to the new plantation manager, Murdoch Brown, to stock his spice garden. But this was only the beginning on the backlash.

In the first decade of Company rule, Malabar rose up twice in rebellion, led by a local nobleman, the Pazhassi Rajah. The Anjarakandi plantation was a particular focus of hatred and was laid waste by the rebels. Avoiding open combat with the Company's troops, the Pazhassi Rajah took to the Wynad jungles and waged guerrilla war. The younger brother of the Governor-General, Arthur Wellesley, commanded the Company's troops in the area and responded with terror. 'The more deserted villages you burn and the more cattle and other property that are carried off the better', Wellesley wrote to one of his officers, adding to another that 'the people of Malabar are not to be coaxed into submission: terror, however, will induce them to give up their arms'.[10] The Company's remorseless tactics bore fruit and in 1805, the Pazhassi Rajah was eventually surrounded in the hills. Local tradition tells that he then committed suicide by swallowing an immense diamond.

As Company rule became entrenched, the situation of the local people deteriorated sharply. In 1819, the inhabitants of Kadatanad petitioned the Company to relieve the burden of tax and other oppressions.

> Instances have occurred [they wrote] of some respectable persons having put a voluntary end to their life, so as not to survive the cruel necessity of not being able to afford relief to their dying children. Neither in the time of the Rajahs nor Tippoo, have our ancestors and ourselves experienced such grievances and been reduced to such cruel necessities. We are no longer able to endure them.[11]

In the hills, low-level conflict continued for decades as the Kurichiar tribals resisted Company attempts to stop their practices of shifting cultivation. For his pains, Wellesley picked up the 'Malabar itch', a virulent skin infection that proved resistant to the normal lard and sulphur treatment, and could only be removed by frequent baths in diluted nitric acid.[12] Wellesley would later be known as the 'sepoy general' for his Indian exploits, winning the title Duke of Wellington for his wars against Napoleon. The Anjarakandi estate still operates more than 200 years on, a prototype for the plantation economy that came to dominate the hills of Kerala in the nineteenth and twentieth centuries.

Governor-General Wellesley would next turn his attention to the Marathas, winning Agra, Delhi and Gujarat in 1803; conflict with the confederation would only be conclusively resolved in 1818. In the process, however, he consumed £2.5 million in bullion shipped to India by the Company to pay for its trading operations, and plunged into chronic deficit. As a result, the Company's debts soared from just £9 million in 1792 to £30 million in 1809, adding the extra burden of interest repayment to the load that the Indian taxpayer had to support. Eventually, Wellesley was recalled. But the impulse for invasion would remain primary. Military action had now become 'the master, not the servant of business opportunity'.[13] Not only did this breach the terms of the 1784 Act, but broke just about every treaty with Indian rulers, causing immense human suffering in the process. Unable and unwilling to stop the slide, the directors were simply guilty of 'cant and whining about the accession of territory', wrote Randle Jackson and Joseph Hume in February 1819, adding that 'the regular system for the last thirty to forty years has been to lament deeply over the act and to pocket the income'.[14] Wars large and small continued to be the focus of attention for the next 40 years from Afghanistan, Punjab and Sind in the west to Nepal and Burma in the north and east.

THE DHAKA EARTHQUAKE

The decade-long war with France that followed the 1793 charter severely disrupted the Company's operations, depressing trade and playing havoc with its finances. In the City of London, its share price languished long after the Battle of Waterloo had decided the contest, and only exceeded £200 with any confidence from 1817 onwards. By then, the Company's 200-year monopoly of trade with India had been broken. Industrial interests had forced the initial breach in 1793, and by the time the Company's 20-year charter came up for review once more in 1813, they had gathered sufficient strength to open the Indian trade to all.

Throughout the eighteenth century, the competitiveness of Indian textiles had prompted the introduction of extensive protectionist barriers in England to protect domestic producers. It was behind these walls that Britain's infant textile sector could grow, responding to India's entrenched labour cost advantage with mechanisation. This early modern strategy of import-substitution proved remarkably successful. Imitation 'calicoes' were manufactured in Britain from the early 1770s, and in 1781, mass production of British 'muslins' commenced. Only five years later, the first Lancashire cottons were being exported to India, a small fraction of the 500,000 pieces of industrial muslin being churned out annually. Industrial muscle had done the job: by 1793, a Lancashire mill operative had become 400 times more productive than the average Indian weaver.

In the run-up to the 1793 charter renewal, Manchester cotton manufacturers had petitioned the government that their goods should be received duty-free in India, while the wearing of Indian cottons should be banned in Britain. The government sensibly rejected this self-serving nonsense – for the time being. Underneath the surface, however, the Company's well-established import–export business was being eaten away. Mill-made cottons took increasing slices of the Company's market share of textiles in both Britain and its key re-export markets in Africa. Simultaneously, Napoleon's 'continental system' had eliminated the important re-export trade with the rest of Europe. From £3 million worth of Indian textiles brought back to England in 1798, the Company imported just £433,000 in 1807. Worse still, the goods it did import could no longer be sold at a profit, resulting in over £7 million of unwanted Bengal cottons piling up in the Company's London warehouses. This time the government could not ignore the mass of petitions that flooded into Westminster calling for an end to the Company's exclusive position. In addition, mounting Indian debts forced the Company to request a loan of £2,500,000 from the government in April 1812. This combination of industrial lobbying and financial distress left the Company in no position to resist the push for greater liberalisation. As a result, its commercial monopoly was removed for all except the China trade, which was extended for another 20 years. For many, notably the evangelical William Wilberforce, trade was no longer the main issue where the Company was concerned, but rather the promotion of Christianity. After years of campaigning, Wilberforce and others managed to include in the 1813 Charter Act provisions for the establishment of a Church of England bishopric in India, as well as the removal of the Company's longstanding ban on missionary activity.

As Smith had predicted, the Company was soon unable to compete against the surge of new entrepreneurs, and it ceased exporting merchandise to India in 1824, largely because there was little it could buy in India for sale back in Britain. For India's producers, this so-called opening of trade brought little relief. In the wake of the Bengal Revolution, the East India Company had used its political position to establish monopoly control over Bengal's weavers. Its hunger for the weavers' output was still as strong, if not stronger, than ever before as it looked for new ways of returning the wealth of Bengal to Britain through increased exports of cloth. Exploitation certainly followed in the most cruel form, and for the weavers the result was dislocation and impoverishment. Paradoxically, however, it was the end of the Company's trading monopoly in 1813 that would turn this terrible situation into one of complete destitution. A 20 per cent increase in import duties on Indian goods was added in 1813 to ensure that open competition did not challenge the British producer. This took the tariff wall to a huge 78 per cent on calicoes and 31 per cent on muslins. 'Had not such prohibitory duties and decrees existed,' wrote Henry Wilson in 1858, 'the mills of Paisley and Manchester would have stopped in their outset and could scarcely have been set in motion, even by the powers of steam.'[15] In place of its earlier position as the monopoly purchaser of Indian cloth, the Company's new role was simply to prevent the introduction of any countervailing measures to 'level the playing field'.

The earthquake that struck Dhaka in 1812 – demolishing the Company's agency building in Tejgaon – was only a portent of a far more savage economic disaster that was about to strike. In 1753, just before Plassey, Dhaka exported Rs2,850,000 in textiles to Britain; by the end of the century, this had already fallen to Rs1,362,000. But it took only four years following the removal of the Company's monopoly for exports to cease altogether, and in 1818, the Company's cloth 'factory' at Dhaka was wound up. The city imploded upon itself, and by 1840, its population had fallen from 150,000 to just 20,000, with jungle and malaria 'fast encroaching upon the town'. Once again, horrific acts of mutilation are said to have accompanied this upheaval. In a grisly repeat of earlier cruelties, when machine-made yarns were first introduced into Dhaka in 1821, the 'thumb and index finger of some of the renowned artisans began to be chopped off in order to disable them from twisting finer yarns', according to Syed Muhammed Taifoor.[16] Taifoor adds that some reputed artisans also 'chopped off their own finger-ends in order to avoid the tyranny of the middlemen'.

Until 1813, India had a strongly positive balance of trade, operating as it had done for centuries as 'the great workshop of cotton manufacture for the world'.[17] But in the next 20 years, exports to India of British cotton rose more than fifty-fold, while textile imports from India fell by three-quarters. The deliberate manipulation of trade and industrial policy resulted in the elimination of India's handloom weavers; English weavers were also being driven to extinction by the same remorseless forces. In India, the Company's role was simply passive – to observe, but to do nothing. By 1834, the Governor-General, William Bentinck, was reporting that 'the misery hardly finds parallel in the history of commerce', adding that 'the bones of the cotton-weavers are bleaching the plains of India'.[18] This was not the free trade that Adam Smith had called for – even though his name was invoked repeatedly by the mill-owners in their quest to dominate India's markets. Observing what Britain did rather than what its philosophers wrote, the German economist Friedrich List cited the cotton trade as a case study of the successful use of protectionism to build up national industrial strength.[19]

COMMERCIAL SWANSONG

The loss of the India trade marked the pinnacle of the Company's commercial operations, with sales at auction yielding over £8 million in 1814, four times the level in 1757. Thereafter, sales steadily declined to less than £4 million in 1833.[20] Throughout, however, one commodity remained steady: tea.

Indeed, tea had started to eclipse the India trade since the middle of the eighteenth century, a position boosted by Pitt's Commutation Act of 1784. By undercutting the smugglers, the Act provided a huge fiscal stimulus for increased tea consumption. Over the next half-century, the Company's tea sales doubled from 15,931,193 lb in 1786 to 32,913,840 lb in 1833. This represented a slow, but steady annual growth of some 1.5 per cent, making the Company more than £1 million a year in profits. For decades, the Company's quarterly auctions were dominated by the four main black teas – Bohea, Congo, Souchon and Pekoe – along with the three key green teas – Singlo, Heyson and Bing. At its September 1798 sale, the tea catalogue ran to 635 pages and the auction took six days. Each chest was finely graded according to its character, all the way from 'Good Ordinary to But Middling' through 'But Middling to Middling' and on to 'Good Middling to Middling Good'. And despite the inevitable squabbles with the tea brokers that erupted, the Company enjoyed a reputation for consistent high quality. Unlike the violence and corruption that overtook its business interests in India, the Company's tea trade was rarely charged with malpractice.

A clue to this apparent oasis of good conduct lay in the special circumstances of the tea trade. On one side was the Celestial Empire of

Qing China, dismissive of all things foreign, and accepting trade only on sufferance. The Chinese authorities refused to establish normal diplomatic relations with the Company – or any other European nation – for the simple reason that this would have implied some equality of status. The Company was allowed to trade through the single port of Canton on the Pearl river, and could only operate from temporary facilities that were open for just a few months of the year. Moreover, the Company had to deal with a cartel of Chinese merchants, the Co-Hong. The Company put up with all these indignities and more for the simple reason that China was the world's only source of tea. Here monopoly came face to face with monopoly – and found a highly effective *modus vivendi*. Mutual trust became an essential element of the trade, with the Co-Hong accepting the Company's word when it reported each year the number of chests that had failed London's quality control. Sub-standard tea was either dumped in the Thames and the Co-Hong's account was debited accordingly, or, extraordinarily, sent all the way back to Canton. Equally, the directors were quite willing to reimburse a Chinese merchant whose goods had been undervalued by the Company's agents, the Supercargoes. 'In their eyes,' observed two experts on the tea trade, 'long-term considerations were more important than temporary profit.'[21]

This healthy commercial exchange, however, masked a 'dirty little secret' that belied the integrity of the trade. Just like Mughal India, the Company was unable to interest Imperial China in British-made commodities in exchange for tea. This meant massive exports of silver bullion to balance the books. And just as in India, the Company ended the flow of bullion through criminal means. In India, territorial conquest had been the answer; in China, the solution was the contraband trade in opium. Throughout the East, the opium of the Bihar region around Patna was famed for its excellence. Long known for its medicinal properties, opium was also used at the Mughal court as a narcotic. In Britain, opium was also consumed in liquid form, mixed with alcohol to create laudanum. But it was in China that demand for this by-product of the oriental poppy became the most intense. In 1729, the Chinese authorities banned its import, except under licence for medical purposes. The Company was then in one of its 'quiett' phases, and its traders in Canton respected the imperial decision. Access to the Chinese market was exceedingly precarious, and the Company's agents did not want to engage in any practices that might threaten their core business. The Company had achieved pre-eminence in Canton, giving it control over the tea trade, and the Company was anxious to retain this position.

Winning market dominance in Bengal, however, enabled the Company to move upstream and monopolise the source of opium supply. As we have seen, in 1781, Warren Hastings sent two ships, the *Nonsuch* and the *Betsy,* to smuggle opium into China. Hastings's escapade proved to be a failure. But opium would subsequently become a central part of the Company's commercial strategy. Using its market power to compel Bengali *ryot*s to cultivate opium at below the cost of production, the Company harnessed its monopoly position in such a way that it was making 2,000 per cent profit by the time each chest of 63 kg was sold in China. A vast system of bribes was put in place to encourage the Chinese customs (*hoppo*) to turn a blind eye to endemic drug smuggling. Periodically, the imperial authorities in Beijing tried to enforce the law. In 1811, the Company was even told that it must show special co-operation as opium was known to originate in British India. But the Company agents were sanguine about this latest effort, writing to the directors that 'we are perfectly satisfied that it is merely made pro forma, and without the least intention of taking any effectual steps for the suppression of a trade which the officers of the government have so long and so notoriously found it in their interests to connive at'.[22]

For all this, the Company was keen to disown any direct responsibility and ensured that the drug was shipped into China by independent agency houses. But everyone knew that its role was fundamental, that opium was grown under Company monopoly in India, sold at Company auction and had the Company's distinctive *chop* mark stamped on each chest as an essential guarantee of quality. The Company also intervened with military force to protect its dominant position. In the early nineteenth century, increasing volumes of so-called Malwa opium grown in the Maratha lands were being exported to Macao. This depressed the price for the Company's Bengal brand, prompting Governor-General Wellesley to call in 1803 for action to prevent further growth and achieve 'its ultimate annihilation'.[23] Many factors contributed to the Company's incessant wars with the Marathas, and controlling the opium trade was certainly among them. 'The revenue from Bengal opium was being used to finance a war to secure the revenue from Malwa opium', observed Brian Inglis in his history of the opium wars.[24] But the anarchic nature of Malwa production meant that the Company was unable to suppress the trade, and so was forced to buy up the entire crop if it was to establish control. This massive boost to supply further cut the price of Bengal opium. As the downward spiral in Company revenues continued, the Company decided it had to break its long-standing policy of restricting production to keep prices high. Instead, it ordered increased production of Bengal opium to make up the loss of revenues. This crucial decision dramatically increased the export of opium, which surged from 5,000 chests in 1820 to 12,000 in 1824 and 19,000 in 1831. But when Parliament questioned a former member of the China Council in 1832 about the Company's involvement in the opium trade, the answer was legalistic and straightforward: as the opium was no longer its property when it left India, the Company 'could scarcely be said to trade in it'.[25]

A stench of hypocrisy hung over the Company's final years of trade with China, an exchange that was nominally legal but ultimately dependent on structural complicity with drug smuggling. For all this, the economics of the trade were deeply compelling. Sales of opium provided the Company with one in seven of its tax rupees in India. Its export to China grew ten-fold in the first three decades of the nineteenth century, matching the parallel growth in tea consumption (see Table 8.1). This turned China's solid trade surplus of some $26 million between 1800 and 1810 into a deficit of $38 million between 1828 and 1836. Crucially, by 1828, the Company was generating enough revenue from its sales of opium at auction in Calcutta to pay for its entire purchase of tea, a truly unrequited trade. And, with a tenth of government revenues back in Britain derived from tea duties, the entire imperial edifice rested on a mountain of opium.

Table 8.1 The opium trade with China 1800–1879

Year	Chests (63.5 kg)
1800	2 000
1820	5 000
1824	12 000
1831	19 000
1833	24 000
1839	40 000
1844	48 000
1859	58 000
1879	105 000

Sources: Robert Blake, *Jardine Matheson*, London: Weidenfeld & Nicolson, 1999; Brian Inglis, *The Opium War*, London: Hodder & Stoughton, 1976; W. Travis Hanes and Frank Sanello, *The Opium Wars*, London: Robson Books, 2003.

The success of the Company's tea and opium trading model was not enough, however, to protect it from the clamour for total free trade. Extensive parliamentary inquiries into the China trade in the early 1830s found few faults in the Company's conduct; most agreed that the imperial benefit of the opium trade justified its blatant illegality. But it was a foregone conclusion that the Company would be stripped of its monopoly privileges: in 1829–30, 257 free trade petitions were presented to Parliament, almost double the amount during the 1813 charter debates. Sensing that the end was near, the Company decided in 1825 to award only short-term shipping contracts. The real issue was whether the Company should retain its status as the licensed administrator of India. More and more, its position seemed out of step with the spirit of the age. Somewhat unwisely, the Company confirmed its reputation as a leftover of the past by joining a petition of merchants and bankers opposed to the Reform Bill of 1832, which was designed to increase the proportion of the population entitled to vote. When the first general election under new rules took place in December 1832, the representation of Company interests in the House of Commons was cut by half. Company supporters had usually entered Parliament by purchasing seats in the country's 'rotten boroughs', many of which had now been eliminated in the reforms.

The obvious solution would have been to open the China trade to all, let the Company sink or swim against real competition, and for the Crown to take over the administration of India. The Secretary of the Board of Control, Thomas Babington Macaulay, acknowledged the peculiarity of a situation where a commercial body was 'exercising sovereignty over more people, with a larger revenue and a larger army' than the British state.[26] For him, there was little doubt that 'the Company is an anomaly' and 'part of a system where everything is anomaly'. James Silk Buckingham, MP, went further pointing to the sheer absurdity of a group of shareholders having ultimate control over an entire people – 'a body so changeable that it was never composed of the same materials for any two days following, some selling out their stock, and some buying in, every day of the week, and no other qualification than being a stockholder being required to form part of this governing body'.[27] For these stockholders, uncertainty over the Company's future earnings had translated in a precipitate fall in value, from almost £300 in April 1824 to £194 at the beginning of 1832. A resolution was needed if for no other reason than to calm the market.

Macaulay, however, decided to persist with Dundas's strategy of giving the state control without responsibility, letting the Company rule India on its behalf with all the risks this entailed. Won over by the government's decision to raise the guaranteed dividend from 10 to 10.5 per cent the Company's shareholders voted overwhelmingly in favour of commercial surrender on 3 May 1833 by 477 votes to 52. Importantly, both the annual dividend and the interest on the Company's by now extensive debts were to be paid out of the tax revenues of India. In return for surrendering its extensive commercial assets to the state, Parliament pledged to extend the Company's charter for another 20 years and guarantee the dividend for a further 20. Thereafter, each £100 of Company stock would receive a £200 pay-off. The Charter Act was passed in August, stating in stark terms that 'the said Company shall, with all convenient speed close their commercial business, and make sale of all their merchandize, stores and effects at home and abroad'. The Blackwell docks were sold off, and the Company's warehouses put up for auction. Two hundred and thirty-three years after starting trading operations, the Company had moved into a twilight existence as the profit-making agent of the British state in India, a kind of early public–private partnership. For its shareholders, the decision to exchange its commercial gene for what amounted to a state-backed pension was the right one: shares rose some 30 per cent from the beginning of 1833 to the end of 1834.

AN EMPIRE OF SCORN

The Company had been fortunate that its case before Parliament had been handled by one of the leading intellectuals of the day. James Mill, the Scottish utilitarian activist, had joined the Company in 1819 as an assistant examiner, charged with preparing directives for India. The previous year, Mill had published his immense *History of British India*, whose arguments would come to dominate the Company's thinking, not least as a set text at its in-house training establishment, East India College at Haileybury. Mill had never visited India – indeed, he took some pride in his detachment from his subject-matter. And his analysis took few prisoners. He tore into the corruption and criminality that had underpinned so much of the Company's operations from Clive to Wellesley. He savaged the Company's monopoly status, impatient for the benefits of free trade to be introduced. And he attacked the inequity of the 'permanent settlement', exposing instead the 'permanent deficit' that the Company was running in India.

Most importantly, Mill launched an all-out assault on Hindu civilisation, criticising earlier observers, such as William Jones, for believing that it had a value equal to ancient Greece and Rome. Mill introduced a fundamentally modern perspective, arguing that societies could be graded along a spectrum of social progress. For Mill, there was no doubt that Hindustan languished in a state of utter barbarism. Its history was mere fable, its government despotic, its religion superstition and its caste system fundamentally degraded. According to Mill, Hindus were 'the most enslaved portion of the human race', with a 'general disposition to deceit and perfidy'.[28] In Mill's progressive view of history, Hindu dominance had been replaced by a more advanced Muslim rule and then by modern British administration. Crucially, Mill argued that Hindu society was incapable of achieving social progress on its own, requiring the helping hand of imperial rule to achieve the greatest happiness of the greatest number. In an earlier review article for the *Edinburgh Review* published in 1810, Mill made his views crystal clear: 'whatever may be our sense of the difficulties into which we have brought ourselves by the improvident assumption of such a dominion, we earnestly hope, for the sake of the natives, that it will not be found necessary to leave them to their own direction'.[29]

Perhaps in an unconscious bid for employment, Mill's views of early nineteenth-century Company were more favourable. 'I know of no government,' he wrote, 'either in past or present times, that can be placed equally high with that of the East India Company', concluding that it deserved 'the highest applause.'[30] In the crisis of the early 1830s, Mill amply repaid the trust that the Company's directors had placed on him, appearing before Parliament on numerous occasions to fight its case. Putting his free trade beliefs to one side, Mill argued that only the principle of *caveat emptor* ('buyer beware') should apply to the opium trade, urging the retention of the Company's monopoly in Bengal as the financial burden fell primarily upon foreign – Chinese – consumers. And when he was questioned by MPs in the newly reformed Parliament about his views on whether some form of democracy should be applied to India as well, he responded firmly that this was 'utterly out of the question', not least because of the 'total absence of moral feeling' in the country.[31]

Through his *History* and his career at East India House, Mill profoundly shaped British views towards India. His intellectual assertion of the superiority of Western modernity was a perfect match for the arrogance of power that the Company increasingly displayed in India. In a warning full of foresight, one of the Company's leading executives, Thomas Munro, protested in 1817 against the Company's refusal to employ Indians in all but the most menial positions, arguing that 'there is perhaps no example of any country in which the natives have been so completely excluded from all share of the government of their country as in British India'. For Munro, 'the consequence of the conquest of India by British arms would be, in place of raising, to debase the whole people'.[32] But like Burke's views before him, Munro's concerns were cast aside by those who asserted that Anglo-Saxon values and institutions should prevail. Certainly, there were many aspects of Indian society that needed to be changed, as home-grown reformers such as Ram Mohun Roy would argue, not least the caste system and practices such as *sati* (widow-burning).

Supremely confident in their superiority, some British officials almost revelled in the contempt with which they held India. This attitude was perhaps most forcefully expressed by Macaulay in his 1835 Minute on Education, where he held that 'a single shelf of a good European library was worth the whole native literature of India and Arabia'.[33] Scorn was translated into a host of practical measures that increasingly separated the Company from its Indian hinterland. By the 1830s, the Company's Governor-General William Bentinck would admit that 'we are in fact strangers in the land'.[34] Verbal abuse mounted, with 'nigger' becoming a common expression for Indians in the 1840s and 1850s.

Social uplift might well have been paraded as the rationale for the Company's continued presence in India. But the twin pillars of late Company rule remained constant: commercial and military conquest. Technology and trade barriers had transformed India into a vital market for Britain's industrial output, taking 23 per cent of its cotton exports in 1850, by far the biggest share. In return, de-industrialisation had transformed India into a producer of agricultural inputs for the imperial economy. Before the opening of trade in 1811, textiles had formed the largest part of India's exports at 33 per cent, followed by opium (24 per cent), indigo (19 per cent), raw silk (8 per cent) and raw cotton (5 per cent). By 1850, however, textile exports had been eliminated, and opium had surged to 30 per cent, followed by cotton (19 per cent), indigo (11 per cent) and sugar (10 per cent).[35] Alongside this, the Company's 'permanent deficit' provided another valuable source of income for imperial Britain as tax revenues were diverted to pay the interest on the ballooning Indian debt, growing from £27 million in 1836 to an immense £51 million in 1857. The Company's army also played its part, taking the area under British control from just over 7 per cent of the subcontinent at the time of the 1784 East India Act with its nominal ban on expansion to 62 per cent in 1856 following the annexations of Jhansi, Nagpur, Hyderabad and Awadh.

ENFORCING THE POISON TRADE

Just five years after the Company closed its factory in Canton, full-scale war broke out between Britain and China. Tensions started almost immediately, with the Royal Navy bombarding the forts that guarded the entrance to Canton in August 1834. The new generation of free traders led by Jardine Matheson openly defied the Chinese authorities. The Firm was also in the vanguard of a highly effective lobbying campaign back in Britain to mobilise the government in favour of armed intervention. The break came in 1839 when the Chinese authorities sent Commissioner Lin Tse-hsu to suppress the opium trade. By now, there were an estimated 12.5 million opium smokers in China, draining the health and wealth of the nation. In a powerful letter sent to Queen Victoria to explain his actions, Commissioner Lin placed ethics at the heart. 'Even though the barbarians may not necessarily intend to do us harm, yet in coveting profit to an extreme, they have no regard for injuring others', he argued, continuing, 'let us ask, where is your conscience?' Intriguingly, Lin's views were shared by many in Britain. Translating the situation into imagery that the British could understand, Williams Storr Fry, a leading Quaker and cocoa magnate, suggested that the situation was comparable to Britain deciding to ban the import of wine for health reasons, and the French responding by bribing the British customs authorities to smuggle in contraband wine, and when intercepted, employing armed vessels to fight their way in.[36]

Tragically, Lin's letter never reached Victoria. After surrounding the foreign trading quarters in Canton, Lin confiscated and destroyed 20,000 chests of opium – 7,000 of which belonged to the Firm. The reaction of the free traders was one of somewhat staged fury, bitterly denouncing this assault on property when everyone knew that opium was contraband. Nevertheless, the British government was easily won over by Jardine's arguments that it should use force to extract compensation from China for the loss. In Parliament, the future

Prime Minister William Ewart Gladstone denounced the opium trade as unjust, a crime that would bring 'permanent disgrace' on Britain. After two years of coastal warfare, the Chinese were bombarded into submission. In August 1842, the Treaty of Nanking forced China to pay $21 million in reparations to the merchants and open the ports of Amoy, Canton, Fuzhou, Ningbo and Shanghai to foreign trade. The one-time base of the opium smugglers at Hong Kong was formally transferred to Britain as a colony. The Company had had a shadowy role in the whole affair: enforcing the monopoly production of opium in India, and providing military support, sending four armed steamers, the 49th Bengal Volunteers, a corps of Bengal engineers and a corps of Madras sappers to join the British forces. Technically, opium was still illegal, and the British authorities temporarily banned the traffic at Hong Kong. Matheson was unmoved, viewing the proclamation as 'meaning nothing', while the Company's Governor-General in India, Lord Ellenborough, remonstrated that 'Her Majesty's Government should do nothing to place in peril our Opium Revenue.'[37] The Government quickly backtracked, and opium imports resumed their upward course.

The Company maintained its covetous attitude towards opium up to the end. In spite of its control over the Maratha lands, non-Company opium was still reaching China via the ports of Sind. Following the humiliating retreat from Afghanistan in 1841, Ellenborough sought to restore the reputation of the *Company Bahadur* ('Brave Company'). The conquest of Sind in 1843 went ahead on the flimsiest of grounds, an act of aggression described by the social reformer Lord Ashley as a 'foul stain' on the nation's honour.[38] *Punch* magazine tried to satirise the crime with its conqueror Major-General Sir Charles Napier exclaiming, 'Peccavi' – Latin for 'I have sinned'. To this day, Napier's triumphant statue stands in London's Trafalgar Square. With Sind in its possession, the Company had complete control of India's opium outlets, and could have decided to retrench and cut production. But the addiction to opium revenues was simply too great.

THE LAST CHARTER

When the Company's charter came up for renewal once more in June 1853, the coalition government of William Gladstone and John Russell aimed to make a few administrative changes and extend a largely satisfactory arrangement for a further 20 years. Presenting his case to Parliament, the President of the Board of Control, Charles

Wood, urged his listeners to understand the difficulties Britain faced. 'In India', he declared, 'you have a race of people slow to change, bound up by religious prejudices and antiquated customs. There are in fact, all obstacles to rapid progress.'[39] To address these obstacles, Wood proposed to cut the number of directors from 24 to 18 and simultaneously raise the director's salary from £300 to £500. For the Young India campaign led by Liberal MPs Richard Cobden and John Bright, the Company's anachronistic position cried out for resolution. The time had come to abolish the Company and refocus British rule from plunder to public works.

Outside Parliament, the charter debates caught the eye of the European correspondent of the *New York Daily Tribune*, then the world's best-selling newspaper. In the autumn of 1851, the paper had chosen the émigré German communist, Karl Marx, to provide twice-weekly reports from the capital of the world's imperial superpower. Marx had fled to London in 1849 following the defeat of the 1848 revolutions across the continent, and journalism gave him a much-needed source of income. Under its founding editor, Horace Greeley, the *Tribune* took a strong reforming line, giving Marx a platform for his emerging critique of capitalism. Over the summer of 1853, Marx produced a string of articles that dissected the Company's affairs for his American readers. In his eyes, the Company's charter could be boiled down to five simple points: 'a permanent financial deficit, a regular over-supply of wars, and no supply at all of public works, an abominable system of taxation, and a no less abominable system of justice and law'.[40] Digging beneath the façade of Company rule, Marx argued that it 'no longer existed but in name and on sufferance'. He mocked the Court of Directors, only one of whom been to India, and this was by accident. He lampooned the Company's famed administrative system, arguing that 'there exists no government by which so much is written and so little done'. For Marx, 'we have thus a Corporation ruling over an immense Empire, not formed, as in Venice, by eminent patricians, but by old obstinate clerks and the like odd fellows'.[41]

But Marx's interest in the Company went deeper than biting commentary. Drawing on his analysis of class society, Marx positioned the Company as tool of Britain's elite interests in India: 'the aristocracy wanted to conquer it, the moneyocracy to plunder it and the millocracy to undersell it'.[42] Like Burke before him, Marx argued that the Company had brought about a revolution in India. But where Burke protested against the disruption of Indian culture,

Marx's almost mystical view of the logic of history led him to believe that this destruction would ultimately yield positive results. Sharing many of the same beliefs in the march of progress as James Mill before him, Marx saw Asia as burdened by an unchanging reign of oriental despotism. India was thus sunk in a state of stagnant, vegetative barbarism characterised by caste and superstition. Marx was certainly sickened by the way in which the Company had first plundered India, and then dismantled its economy, destroying the textile industry in the process. There was no doubt in his mind that 'the misery inflicted by the British on Hindostan is of an essentially different and infinitely more intensive kind than all of Hindostan had to suffer before'.[43] Yet Marx believed that Western intervention was essential if India was to achieve any form of regeneration. Motivated by the 'vilest interests' it may have been, but Marx saw British domination producing all the conditions for modernisation: political unification, a well-equipped army, a free press and rapid communications, along with the creation of a new class 'imbued with European science'.[44]

Two things are remarkable about Marx's analysis of the Company. The first is how little he is interested in the Company as a corporation. Unlike Smith, Marx had no time for evaluating the comparative merits of partnerships and joint stock companies. Marx's fascination was with large-scale, factory-based, industrial production. As a result, the great trading companies would later be relegated, in the first volume of *Capital*, to the zone of 'primitive accumulation'. Readers look in vain for Marx's insights into the speculative dynamics of the shareholder-owned company or how the corporation's drive for monopoly fits with the wider concentration of capital. The other notable aspect of his attitudes to India is their underlying alignment with those of his friend, John Stuart Mill. Remembered today for his two liberal masterpieces, *On Liberty* and *The Subjection of Women*, as a corporate executive, Mill was extremely hesitant in promoting freedom in India. Mill had followed in his father's footsteps and joined the Company aged 17 in 1823, and would stay in its service for 35 years as a loyal, if somewhat unconventional, employee. One account describes how 'when particularly inspired, he used, before sitting down to his desk, to not only strip himself of his coat and waistcoat, but of his trousers, and so set to work, alternately striding up and down the room and writing at great speed'.[45] Mill wrote widely on political and economic issues, but very little about India, suggesting that his career at East India House made little impression on his wider philosophical interests. What he did express suggests that he saw the Company's undemocratic rule in India as 'a legitimate mode of government in dealing with barbarians'.[46] This great apostle of liberty in Britain upheld the Company's position largely because it provided a bulwark against the populism of Parliament. Like a child, India needed to be guided with 'leading strings' by a paternal, but authoritarian British parent.[47]

Mill was one of Marx's few friends in London in the early 1850s, and the two shared a passion for economic theory.[48] Mill had published his own *Principles of Political Economy* in 1848, the same year as the *Communist Manifesto* and a decade before Marx's first volume of *Capital* appeared. It is an extraordinary pairing. On one side, we have John Stuart Mill, the intellectual insider, earning his living as a corporate executive managing an overseas empire, while retaining an eye to a utopian future beyond the office. On the other, there is Karl Marx, the outsider in exile, divining the seeds of revolution in the ruins of imperial rule, and paradoxically admiring the capacity of capitalism to overthrow the old order. Mill's great failure was to accept the deceptive rationalisation of the Company's role in India as an educative force. As Edward Said remarked in *Culture and Imperialism*, 'it is genuinely troubling to see how little Britain's great humanistic ideas, institutions and monuments, which we still celebrate as having the power ahistorically to command our approval, how little they stand in the way of the accelerating imperial process'.[49] It is no surprise that James and John Stuart Mill's works have been approvingly referenced as the model for 'democratic imperialism' in present-day occupied Iraq.[50]

In August 1853, Parliament passed an extension to the Company's charter after some perfunctory debates. One of the last areas of corporate privilege – the right of patronage over appointments in India – was replaced by selection by competitive exams; the proposed increase in director salaries was clawed back. But this was not the end to Marx's coverage of Asian affairs. Over the next seven years, he became increasingly interested in the series of interlinked conflicts that were shaking the East, starting with the far-reaching Taiping rebellion, which targeted both the Qing dynasty and foreign intruders in China. Once again, Marx saw the Company as the cause of revolution in the East – this time through its involvement in the opium trade with China.[51] When the uneasy truce between Britain and China after the Treaty of Nanking broke down in October 1856, Marx used the opportunity to investigate the deeper causes of the second opium war. What lay before him was an exceptional struggle between 'the Celestial Emperor, [who] in order to check the suicide of his people prohibited at once the import of the poison by the foreigner' and 'the East India Company [who] was rapidly converting the cultivation of opium in India and its contraband sale to China into internal parts of its own financial system'.[52] With his characteristic knack for getting to the nub, Marx revealed the hypocrisy at the heart of British strategy. 'While openly preaching free trade in poison,' he wrote, 'it secretly defends the monopoly of its manufacture. Whenever we look closely into the nature of British free trade, monopoly is pretty generally found to lie at the bottom of its "freedom".'[53]

British gunboats were sent in once more, and the British government despatched another punitive force. But when it reached Singapore in June 1857, terrible news was waiting: the Company's sepoys had mutinied across northern India. The bulk of the force headed for China was diverted immediately to Calcutta to help turn back the mutineers. By the time the second opium war was over in October 1860, the Company's presence in Asia was no more.

A REBELLION FORETOLD

The Great Rebellion of 1857 is often seen as a one-off event, a revolt that came out of the blue against a backdrop of an otherwise peaceful acceptance of Company rule. But powerful warning signs had been ignored. Many explanations have been given for this uprising against the Company, but its increasing racial and administrative arrogance lay at the root. The seeds of racism had always been there. As long before as the Company's botched evacuation of Calcutta in 1756, Maria Carey, the Anglo-Indian wife of an English soldier, had been refused entry on one of the departing ships because of her mixed race. But it was from the beginning of the nineteenth century that the slide into separatism became unstoppable. One by one the traditional ties between the army and local communities were cut. Hindu and Muslim holy men were barred from blessing sepoy regimental colours, and troops were stopped from participating in festival parades. As missionary presence grew, fears mounted that the Company was planning a wholesale forcible conversion to Christianity.

The first sign of what was to follow came as early as July 1806, when sepoys belonging to the army of the Madras Presidency mutinied against new rules that introduced a uniform dress code. The rules removed many of the distinguishing marks of caste and religion that defined the sepoys' identity. Egged on by the exiled family of the Tipu Sultan, the sepoys in Vellore rose up and killed or wounded over 200 of the 370-strong British garrison. Although the mutiny was quickly suppressed, an investigation into the affair pointed to the increasing distance between the Company's officials and the people. A commission of Indians was proposed as a way of channelling popular complaints, along with a recommendation to send additional British troops as a precautionary measure. Neither step was taken, however. The warnings were intensified in the debates over missionary activity in 1813. In his last public engagement, Warren Hastings came out of retirement to testify for three hours before a parliamentary committee examining the Company's charter. His advice was clear: 'a Surmise had gone abroad that there was an intention of forcing our Religion on the Natives. Such an Opinion, propagated among the Native Infantry might be attended by dangerous consequences', indeed it 'might create a religious war'.[54]

All these sleights and apprehensions came to a head when sepoys in northern India rejected a new type of rifle cartridge said to be greased with cow and/or pig fat. What turned a mutiny into a rebellion, however, was the Company's crass behaviour towards local rulers in Awadh, Kanpur and Jhansi, who all turned against the Company when the soldiers mutinied. Called the 'First War of Indian Independence' by Veer Savarkar, the rebellion may have been limited in geographic scope, but the goal of ousting the British, regarded by many as 'trespassers', was clear. Symbolically, the first act of the mutineers at Meerut was to march the 36 miles to Delhi to claim the puppet Emperor Bahadur Shah as their leader. The war lasted for almost two years, and was characterised by extreme savagery on both sides. When the Company retook Kanpur (Cawnpore), where rebel troops had slaughtered European women and children, captured sepoys were made to lick the blood from the floors before being hanged. Summary executions became the norm. According to one officer, 'we hold court-martials on horseback, and every nigger we meet with we either string up or shoot'.[55] The Company's recapture of Delhi was followed by systematic sacking, and the surviving inhabitants were turned out of its gates to starve. At the end of this third and final Company–Mughal war, Bahadur Shah's two sons and grandson were killed in cold blood, and the old emperor sent into exile in Rangoon.

The Company that had grown in a symbiotic relationship with the Mughal Empire could not long survive its passing. The rebellion had generated a ferocious bloodlust in British society, and the anomalous Company was an easy scapegoat for the nation's fury. *Punch* magazine summed up the feelings of many when it published its cartoon of the 'Execution of the East India Company' on 15 August 1857 (see Illustration 8.1). Mimicking the Company's practice of blasting captured rebels from the mouths of its cannon, the cartoon shows the 'blowing up (there ought to be) in Leadenhall Street', with the classical grandeur of East India House flying through the air with all charges of 'avarice', 'blundering', 'nepotism', 'misgovernment' and 'supineness'. Even the mild-mannered Charles Dickens wished that he was the commander-in-chief in India so that he would able to 'do my utmost to exterminate the Race upon whom the stain of the late cruelties rested' – a chilling foretaste of Kurtz's crazed call to 'exterminate the brutes' in Joseph Conrad's novella *Heart of Darkness*.[56]

Like failed corporations before and since, the only solution was nationalisation. But the Company put up a last-ditch fight to forestall the inevitable. Promoted to chief examiner in March 1858, John Stuart Mill presented a lengthy petition to Parliament. In perhaps the longest corporate whinge in history, Mill first of all argued that the Company had at its 'own expense, and by the agency of their own civil and military servants, originally acquired for this country its magnificent empire in the East' – as if it was doing the nation a favour. The language became richer still, with Mill claiming that it was 'the most beneficent [government] ever known among mankind'. In the debates that followed, George Cornewall Lewis MP exposed the vacuity of Mill's claims, asserting that 'no civilised government ever existed on the face of this earth which was more corrupt, more perfidious, and more rapacious' than the East India Company between 1757 and 1784. For Lewis, the Company had become an 'accidental body' of shareholders with no relation to the affairs of India. The rest of Parliament agreed, and legislation was passed stripping the Company of all its administrative powers in India, and transferring these to the Crown. On 1 November 1858, a proclamation was read from every military cantonment in India: the East India Company was abolished and direct rule by Queen and Parliament was introduced. Firework displays followed the proclamation.

Illustration 8.1 Punch, The Execution of 'John Company', 1857

The Company is often regarded as an inevitable stepping-stone to the British Raj. Instead, the British Empire in India is better thought of as the product of the Company's failure. Observing the Company's fall with some glee, Marx told his American readers that the directors 'do not die like heroes': 'they commenced by buying sovereignty and they have ended by selling it'.[57]

THE LAST LAUGH

Yet the Company was not quite dead. Many histories of the Company stop either with the removal of commercial privileges in 1833 or in 1858 with its expulsion from Indian affairs. But the Company continued on for another 16 years, a corporate zombie, reduced to the most basic corporate task of all: the distribution of the annual dividend. With all its administrative functions transferred across town to the India Office in Whitehall, the Company sold its impressive headquarters on Leadenhall Street, and pensioned off most of its employees: John Stuart Mill received an annual £1,500, along with an inlaid inkstand. The Company kept a clerk and its directors continued to meet, first in the boardroom of the Red Sea Telegraph Company at 62 Moorgate, and then at 11 Pancras Lane, north of the City.

The Company's archives stretch for miles at the British Library. But the account of its activities after 1858 is contained in a single volume, the Treasury Court Minutes. With the Company's crest stamped on the back, this leather-bound book is only half-full. It describes a desultory existence of empty meetings and routine payments. The cycle started to come to a close in the summer of 1873. In May, Parliament rubber-stamped the government's proposals for redeeming the remaining £6 million of Company stock. The Act of 1833 had not only guaranteed investors a 10.5 per cent dividend until 1874, but it had also laid down generous terms for any eventual buy-out. In the East India Stock Redemption Act, the government offered shareholders either £200 of 3 per cent government annuities, £200 of 4 per cent India debt or £200 in cash for every £100 of Company stock. In effect, another £12 million of debt was added to the India account, its interest to be covered by the Indian taxpayer, equivalent to over £650 million today.[58] After the transfer of the stock, shareholders met for the last time in December, and the final dividend was paid on 30 April 1874. Among their number were Corpus Christi College, Oxford, holding £145, Richard Benyon de Beauvoir with some £4,000, Deeble Boger at £10,000 and Joseph Dobree with £11,700 in shares.

A final clear-out of the Company's affairs was now required, and on 13 May 1874, the clerk sent a rather pathetic letter to the Secretary of State for India asking whether he would 'take charge of the Charters, Seals, Documents etc'. On Wednesday 20 May at 1.30 p.m., the Company's Court of Directors gathered for the last time. There was some £32,000 in the accounts, matching almost exactly the £30,000 raised by investors back in 1599, a nice piece of historical symmetry. After paying the directors' fees, the housekeeper, clerk and accountant, the chairman 'ordered the Court adjourn'. It never met again, and the Company was officially dissolved on 1 June 1874.

Its actions lived on, however. In a government report on the 'moral and material progress and condition of India', published the same year, tax revenues of some £50 million were recorded, including £8 million from salt and £6 million from opium, both measures that had been introduced under Hastings's campaign to 'send more money'. Jardine Matheson had by then diversified away from opium, which had become a low-margin commodity following its legalisation at the Convention of Peking in 1860. Nonetheless, the trade continued to grow, reaching 105,000 chests in 1879, four times the size at the end of the Company's China trade in 1833. China's dependency deepened ever further, and by 1895, 80 per cent of the external trade of China was with the British Empire.[59] Only in 1907 did Britain finally agree to stop the export of Indian opium, and in 1911 its manufacture was abandoned in Bihar owing to the 'loss of the Chinese market'. The salt tax, of course, continued right up to the end of British rule in India, and became the focus of Gandhi's famous march to Dandi in 1930, where he defiantly broke the imperial state's monopoly on salt production.

The Company's financial footprint extended equally deep into the twentieth century. Writing in 1908, Romesh Chander Dutt was furious at the way in which the people of India had not only supplied the troops for their own conquest, and financed the Company's acquisition of the subcontinent through heavy taxation, but had also paid for the Company's nationalisation. 'And the Indian people are virtually paying dividends to this day', he wrote, 'on the stock on an extinct Company in the shape of interest on Debt!'[60] This ghostly drain eventually ended in the depths of the Second World War when Britain's massive expenditure in India finally extinguished the historic debts of both Company and Raj. Long after its demise, the Company continued to shape the economies and societies it had left behind.

9
Unfinished Business

STATUES TO A SHEEP-STEALER

If you walk to the Foreign and Commonwealth Office in London from St James's Park, you will climb up 'Clive's steps', named after the larger-than-life statue of Robert Clive that stands outside the old India Office building (see Illustration 9.1). It was here that the governance of India passed after the Company's demise in 1858. But it took another 60 years for this monument to the great 'nabob-maker' to be erected. The reasons for this delay say much about his contested record. From the early 1750s, his triumph at Arcot had made Clive Britain's 'heaven-born general' in the eyes of Prime Minister William Pitt the Elder. The Plassey Revolution brought him even greater fame as a much-needed national hero during the bitter Seven Years' War. For this, Clive was made Baron of Plassey – a title that carried a sting, however, as it was only an Irish baronetcy, with a distinctly second-class status. Praise soon turned to loathing when the size of his fortune and the means by which he had acquired it became known. Even King George III protested at Clive's 'fleecing' of India. Hauled before Parliament to explain his actions, Clive declared his resentment at being treated like 'a common sheep-stealer'. Cleared he may have been in the vote that followed, but his reputation was ruined. At the time of his death, there is little doubt that he had become 'the most hated man in England', according to a recent biographer.[1]

For decades thereafter, Clive's military exploits would be praised in imperial literature, but his corruption would be equally denounced as somehow un-British, not least by Macaulay in his celebrated essay of 1840. It was only in the run-up to the 150th anniversary of Plassey in 1906–7 that a former Viceroy of India, Lord Curzon, proposed rehabilitating Clive's memory in the twin imperial cities of London and Calcutta. The reception was frosty. In India, the British authorities feared that such a celebration might exacerbate the rising nationalist tension in Bengal. Back in London, the Liberal Secretary of State for India, John Morley, retorted that it would have been better for Britain if Clive had lost the battle. Instead of a statue to Clive, Morley suggested erecting a monument to the Italian nationalist, Garibaldi.

Illustration 9.1 Statue of Robert Clive, London

But Curzon's idea tapped into the rising mood of imperial jingoism, and drawing subscriptions from the public – as well as some reluctant Indian princes – two rather bombastic statues of Clive were installed in 1911, the year of the British imperial *durbar* in Delhi.

In Kolkata, Curzon's white marble statue of Clive still stands in the lobby of the Victoria Memorial, passed by thousands of visitors who come each day to look at the historical curiosities contained within. Across the world in London, Clive's statue has a more formal and elevated place in the heart of Whitehall (see Map 3). His left hand rests on the pommel of his sword, underlining the critical role of military force in the Company's rise to power. In his right hand, he clasps a bundle of documents, perhaps the forged agreement with Amir Chand that paved the way for the takeover of Bengal. Panels around the base of the statue tell how Clive made his name at the siege of Arcot, portray him poised for victory on the eve of Plassey, and show him enjoying the fruits of his acquisition of the *diwani*.

Facing west, the statue looks towards the numerous properties that Clive acquired with his Indian loot. Less than a mile away in Berkeley Square is the house where he died in November 1774, with a plaque commemorating him as 'soldier and administrator' – not businessman. Outside London in Surrey's stockbroker belt stands Claremont, which Clive had bought from the penniless Duke of Newcastle. Clive was not able to implement his grand plans he had for the place before his untimely death, but Macaulay describes how 'the peasantry of Surrey looked with mysterious horror on the stately house which was rising at Claremont, and whispered that the great wicked lord had ordered the walls to be made so thick in order to keep out the devil'. Clive's former mansion has been converted into a private boys' school, while its landscaped gardens are owned by the National Trust, where green parrots fly between the beech trees, as if they were among the *gumbads* of Delhi's Lodi Gardens. Further west still, Clive's mansion at Walcot Hall in his native Shropshire today boasts a number of holiday apartments, bearing such evocative names as 'Arcot' and 'Plassey', while his Plassey estate outside Limerick in Ireland has been recycled as the home for the town's university.

Public statues reflect the values of the ruling elite. In many countries, not least India, the heroes of previous regimes have been removed from their places of honour to mark changing perspectives on the past. The fact that one of Britain's greatest corporate rogues continues to have pride of place at the heart of government suggests that the British elite has not yet confronted its corporate and imperial

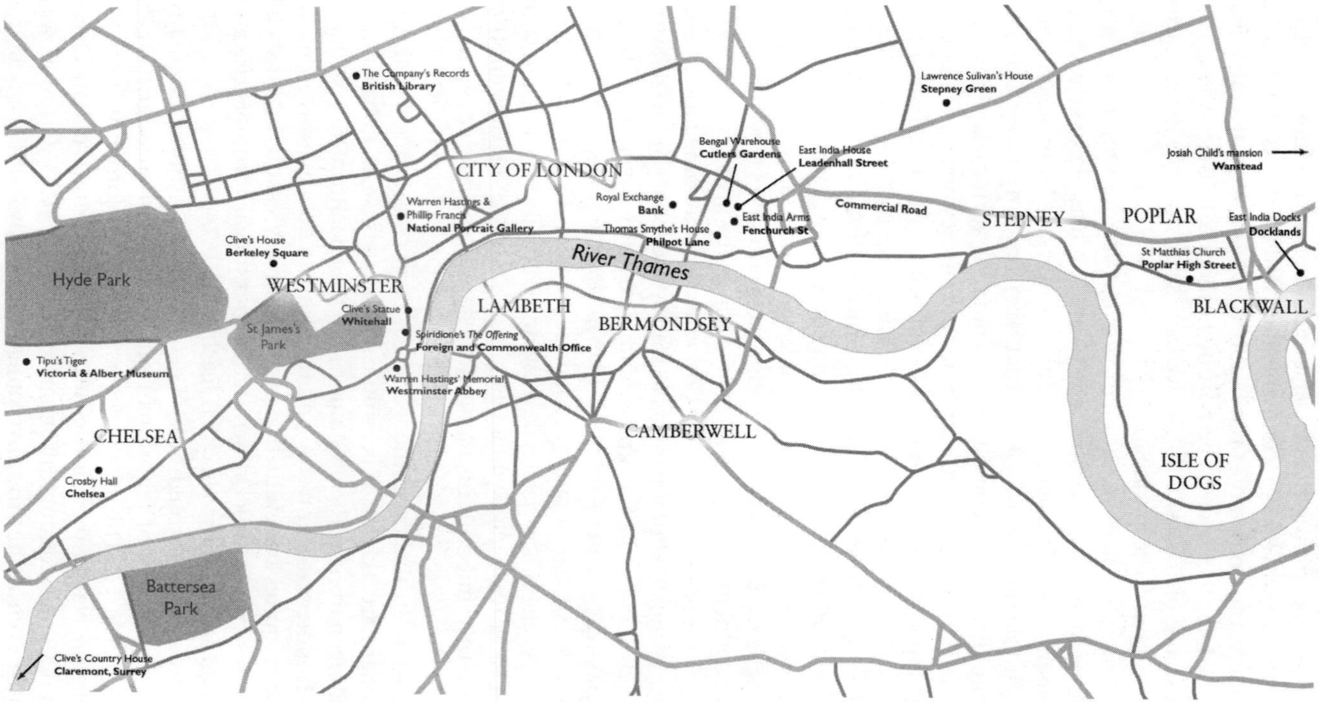

Map 3 The Company's London

past. Equally curious is the fact that the statue is in Whitehall rather than the City. Clive was a 'company man' and made his acquisitions to promote the Company's (as well as his own) interests. If a memorial is needed at all, it should be outside Leadenhall Street where East India House once stood. But, as we have seen, the City is curiously evasive about its corporate history.

Intriguingly, Clive's elevation is strikingly at odds with how many of the Company's contemporaries wished its leading executives to be remembered. The leading utilitarian thinker, Jeremy Bentham, for example, proposed in 1822 that the Company's directors and shareholders should commission a statue to Warren Hastings with the following inscription: 'Let it but put money into our pockets, no tyranny too flagitious to be worshipped by us.' Bentham added that the statue should be twinned with 'a long-robed accomplice ... lodging the bribe in the hand of the other'.[2] A memorial to Hastings was eventually erected, but with a very different inscription. Installed by his widow just inside the north transept of nearby Westminster Abbey, the sculpture is modest, stating that Hastings had been 'selected for his eminent talents and integrity'. Across the aisle, in what could be called the Abbey's 'Company Corner' are eye-catching monuments to two of the chief protagonists at Plassey: Admiral Charles Watson and Eyre Coote, then a captain, but eventually a general. Mixing the classical with the oriental, like Spiridione's *The Offering*, the monuments speak of pure corporate supremacy. Under a palm tree, Watson's celebration has a naked Indian slumped at the bottom with his head in his hands, while Eyre Coote's tableau displays another Indian, this time with his hands tied behind his back.

A century has passed since Curzon decided to rebuild Clive's reputation. In this time, the world has been transformed, with the end of empire, the fall of communism and the rise of globalisation. Standing in front of Clive's statue today, the anachronism is striking. One hundred years on, the approach of the 250th anniversary of Plassey requires a re-evaluation of the Company's status in our social memory – not to knock down statues, but to learn from its rise and fall, and act upon the lessons it teaches us.

Consistently throughout its career, the East India Company generated a mix of emotions from admiration through fear to outright hatred. This clash of perspectives was brought out with particular clarity during the heated parliamentary debates over Robert Clive's conduct in Bengal on 10 May 1773. Opinion was divided even within the government of the day, with the Solicitor

General Alexander Wedderburn coming out strongly in favour of the Company, arguing that

> the recording pen of a candid historian will relate these transactions as they were – and he will not fail to hold forth for the admiration of posterity that in a revolution which acquired to the Company a dominion larger, wealthier and more populous than ever Athens possessed or than Rome itself … so few actions are to be discovered by the most inquisitive examiner, so few that reflect dishonour on individuals, none that tarnish the British name.

Almost immediately, the Attorney General Edward Thurlow stood to contradict his learned friend, remonstrating that 'to what but the rapacity of the Company's servants is it owing that Bengal under its own government so flourishing, under ours be brought to the brink of ruin?'[3]

What is clear from its 275-year-long life is that there was not one Company, but many. In institutional terms, the original corporation with its joint stock limited to a single voyage was an entirely different beast from the global 'blue chip' multinational of the 1750s, let alone the administrative agent of empire in the 1850s. Its progress was also anything but smooth. It was almost wound up in 1657, and 30 years later, its arrogance and adventurism cost the company its trading privileges, which it only won back by exploiting legal loopholes and forging a merger with its enemies to form the United Company in 1709. And then when the Bengal Revolution turned the world upside down, the Company's status as an autonomous business enterprise was progressively stripped away – first, the independence of its governance systems, then its trading privileges and finally all of its remaining functions, until all that was left was a financial shell, paying out dividends. From this continual metamorphosis, four sides to the East India Company emerge most clearly: the Company as entrepreneur, its role as a revolutionary force in world history, its tendency to imperial dominion, and its accountability as a corporation for its actions. These four faces are examined in turn.

AN AGENT OF ENTERPRISE

The Company's demise in 1874 ended the era of the chartered corporation. These leviathans of mercantilism were no longer suited to the new empire of free trade that Britain was establishing across the globe. Where the Company and other chartered companies had once married the functions of overseas sovereign and trader, these were now prised apart, with the Royal Navy taking up the role of commercial enforcer, as it had done in the opium wars. The decline of the slave trade had brought the end of the Royal Africa Company in 1821, and two years later, the ancient Levant Company was wound up. Strangely enough, the South Sea Company that had caused such panic in 1721 had lingered on for another century, and was only closed in 1853. The Hudson Bay Company continues to this day, but surrendered its territorial rights in 1869 for a future in retail. In parallel, the long-standing restrictions on corporate expansion were progressively removed, with the repeal of the 1721 Bubble Act in 1825, and the passing of the Joint Stock Act in 1844 allowing companies to be set up through simple registration. Finally, in 1862, a year after the demolition of East India House, the comprehensive Company Act was placed on the statute book, swiftly followed by a stock market bubble and the collapse of Overend & Gurney, a major bank in 1866.[4]

The precise legal form embodied by the East India Company may well have died, but its systems of administration and governance live on in the modern multinational. Indeed, the Company's management of information – through its countless writers and clerks – makes it one of the pioneers of the knowledge-based corporation.[5] Its success at matching supply and demand along lengthy supply chains whether for textiles or tea proved to be one of the secrets of its enduring commercial success. In its twin 'golden ages', first in the 1670s and early 1680s, and then in the 1720s and 1730s, the Company demonstrated a sophisticated and focused approach to sourcing, marketing and finance that brought the consumer quality goods, earned the investor regular dividends and yielded healthy tax revenues. Yet, in each case, boom was not just followed by bust, but by a deliberate attempt to achieve unwarranted wealth and power. For Philip Francis, newly arrived as the public's champion in Bengal in the 1770s, instead of securing a 'moderate but permanent profit', the Company seemed hell-bent on producing 'immediate and excessive returns'.[6]

Part of the problem lay in the way monopoly formed an essential part of the Company's commercial identity, driving it to achieve dominion at both ends of the chain. More fundamental, according to Adam Smith, was the way in which the design of the joint-stock company created a predisposition to 'negligence and profusion' on behalf of both executives and investors. For Smith, this separation of ownership and management brought a dual danger, of executives turning the corporation to their own ends, and of shareholders investing with an absence of responsibility that direct involvement brings. Perhaps not as spectacular as the South Sea Bubble of 1720, the Company's own Bengal Bubble still bears witness to the inherent propensity of the joint stock corporation to managerial capture, insider trading, over-optimistic projections of future earnings and the irrational exuberance of financial markets. The crash and share price implosion that followed revealed to a stunned English establishment both the financial and human consequences of allowing corporations free rein.

John Company's example shows us that open markets and corporations do not necessarily mix – that economic diversity and enterprise often flourish best where corporations are kept in check. From Smith's contemporary analysis of the rising commercial economy of eighteenth-century Britain, it emerges that the truly entrepreneurial company is likely to be locally rooted, limited in size and liable for the costs it imposes on others. Although he is frequently cited as the theoretical inspiration for globalisation, Smith would be horrified at the way that the unlimited corporation now dominates economic and political life, seeing dangers not just for the achievement of world prosperity, but also for ethical practice in society at large.

THE CORPORATE REVOLUTIONARY

The acquisition of trading preferences and commercial property was second nature to the Company. What set it apart is the way that it acquired whole regions, and then managed them as profit-making estates. The British Company was not alone in this. Much earlier, the Dutch VOC had showed how to establish corporate rule in its conquest of Indonesia. And it was in southern India that the French had pioneered the practice of 'nabob-making', which Clive would transfer so successfully to Bengal. Where John Company's revolution differed was in the way it overturned the world's existing commercial order.

Bengal was the richest province of one of the two great Asian economies – India and China – and had become central to the Company's trading strategy from the late seventeenth century. But the Company's quest for personal and corporate profit was not satisfied by the confirmation of its duty-free status in the famous *firman* of 1717. Almost immediately, its officers in Bengal began to use it as a cover for their own private trade. Not only did this break the letter of a legally binding agreement, but it represented tax evasion on a huge scale, depriving the Bengal treasury of revenues. The road to Plassey would be marked by repeated efforts by the local nawab to make the Company obey the terms of its trade agreement. For years, the Company's executives on the spot as well as its directors in London recognised that this constituted a 'gross abuse', yet did nothing to root out the problem.[7] The contempt of local law was just too profitable and too deeply embedded.

Clive's triumphant takeover effectively enabled the Company to divert Bengal's surplus from the courts of the Mughal emperor and the provincial nawab to the mansions and country estates of Britain. In addition, the acquisition provided the Company with the platform for its next round of adventurism in China. Hesitantly at first, and then increasingly insistent, the Company brought Bihar's opium production under its monopoly control and actively encouraged its smuggling into China as a way of funding the burgeoning trade in tea. Once again, the Company at home and abroad were fully conscious of the illegality of its actions. But the prize was simply too great. When the Chinese authorities eventually intervened to suppress the trade, gunboat diplomacy was the joint response of Company and Crown.

It was the Company's persistence in the use of both political and economic means to achieve its financial ends that lay behind the breaking of these world empires. The Mughal Empire was already in decline by the 1750s. The European companies still played a marginal role, their territories confined to the coastal edges, and their trade accounted for only a fraction of the empire's external commerce. Following Plassey and thereafter the transfer of the *diwani* in 1765, a profit-making institution was established at the heart of the tottering Mughal regime, progressively draining its resources and influence. The bid to control China's markets took much longer to achieve, and the Company's role is certainly secondary to the wider imperial impetus of the British state. But its remorseless promotion of opium provided the lever with which to prise open the self-sustaining Qing economy. It was the British East India Company that broke the regulatory authority of first the Mughals and then the Qing; the industrial production of Manchester merely delivered the economic *coup de grâce*.

There was no doubt in the minds of Robert Clive, Edmund Burke or much later Karl Marx that what the Company had achieved was revolutionary. Clive's reaction was one of sheer delight, seeing an endless flow of treasure from East to West. Initially, Burke also revelled in Clive's successes. But as he learned more, and delved deeper into the Company's practices, he became increasingly horrified at the way this commercial body had illegitimately overturned the established order in India. And for Marx, ever the dialectician, the revolution engineered by the Company was both a human disaster and the spur to modernisation. Even Burke's great empathy with the people of India, however, would not allow him to touch the reality of imperial rule.

THE IMPERIAL GENE

For the last 20 years of its operational life, the Company ruled purely as an agent of the British Empire. Going further back, it is possible to see in the momentous India Act of 1784 its steady transformation from a purely commercial body into an imperial administrator. The business of empire – to use Huw Bowen's phrase – was therefore central to the Company's identity for at least the final third of its existence. Yet, it is possible to identify an 'imperial gene' influencing the Company's actions far earlier, most notably in the disastrous bid for power under Josiah Child in the 1680s. The constant jostling with the state over who should benefit from regulatory and fiscal regimes was inherent in the corporate form. What made this tension imperial was the peculiar nature of the Company's chartered existence whereby it took on certain attributes of a sovereign state in its dealing with foreign powers. More fundamental than this, however, was the perpetual corporate drive for maximising returns for its executives and its investors. This could be achieved most effectively by placing both state and society in a subordinate role, extracting wealth without accountability – the operating style of empires through the ages.

The result was, of course, the great drain of India, a subject of heated controversy ever since Burke first coined the phrase back in the 1780s. Two problems have bedevilled analysis of the Company's economic impacts on India: statistics and implications. The fragmentary nature of corporate and national accounting in the eighteenth and nineteenth centuries makes any estimate of the Company's financial impact open to critique. Considerable judgement is also required in defining what should be incorporated in the drain, which at its broadest would encompass the value of the Company's unrequited trade with India and the value of its executives' private trade. Despite their incessant squabbling over the issue, the estimates of modern academics do not differ greatly from the annual £1.2 million that Burke calculated in 1783. In the 1960s, Professor N.K. Sinha derived a somewhat higher figure of £1.6 million averaged between 1757 and 1780, while Rajat Datta more recently cut the amount drained to £1 million in the years between Plassey and 1794.[8] These are likely to be significant underestimates as they fail to account for the significant value the Company's monopoly position gave it in extracting below-market rates for commodities such as textiles and opium, and the resulting subsidy this provided to the China trade. The drain, of course, changed its character radically in the nineteenth century, when the Company ceased trading. For Montgomery Martin, writing in 1838, the average transfer of the previous 30 years had amounted to some £3 million, which he calculated as equivalent to £723,997,917 at a 12 per cent compound rate of interest.[9] In terms of twenty-first-century purchasing power, this represents a tribute of well over £40 billion.[10]

The more substantive issue is what difference these flows made to the rise of Britain and the decline of India and, subsequently, China. Contemporaries were clear. 'We may date the commencement of the decline', wrote Alexander Dow in 1772, 'from the day on which Bengal fell under the domination of the foreigners.'[11] Turning to Britain, controversy rages over the links between the Company's conquest of India in the financing of the Industrial Revolution. For Brooks Adams, writing at the end of the nineteenth century, the coincidence of the influx of Bengal plunder with the deployment of new industrial technologies was compelling. Without the resources provided by the Indian drain, Adams argued that the spinning jenny, Crompton's mule and Watts's steam engine would have lain dormant. 'Possibly since the world began,' Adams concluded, 'no investment has ever yielded the profit reaped from the Indian plunder.'[12] Adams's conclusions were deployed extensively by Indian nationalists in the struggle for independence. But modern Indian historians have been more cautious, arguing, for example, that 'it is highly unlikely that these private fortunes constituted an element of any importance in the financing of the Industrial Revolution'.[13]

To get to the heart of the matter, a more granular analysis is required. Markets move at the margin, and the key to the drain lies in its impact on relative patterns of consumption and capital formation. In India, the drain depressed consumption and diverted its already small savings rate, while enabling Britain to live beyond its means, to consume, trade and invest at a greater rate than its own internal economy would allow. The great secret of the drain lay in its capacity not to support the extravagant lifestyles of a few hundred nabobs, but to furnish the commodities for an extensive re-export trade of Asian goods to Europe, the Americas and beyond. The Company's unrequited import surplus with Asia was already £1.4 million by 1770 and surged to £4.8 million in 1800. This raw statistic hides the true significance of the shift, however. Drawing on recent analysis carried out by Utsa Patnaik, the Asian drain grew as a proportion of Britain's gross domestic product from 1.7 per cent in 1770 to 3.5 per cent in 1800.[14] Crucially, from 1800 onwards the Asian drain began to match the enormous extraction of wealth that Britain had historically achieved from the slave-based sugar plantations of the West Indies. Together, the combined surplus in 1801 was equivalent to over 86 per cent of Britain's entire capital formation from domestic savings.[15]

For Jawarhalal Nehru, the most powerful indicator of the harm done by the combined impact of the Company and British Raj was that 'those parts of India which have been longest under British rule are the poorest today', picking out Bengal, Bihar and Orissa for particular mention.[16] More fundamentally, expert estimates suggest that India's already waning per capita income levels fell from $540 in the year of Plassey to $520 on the outbreak of the Great Rebellion in 1857; over the same period, Britain's per capita income leapt from $1,424 to $2,717.[17]

MAKING THE COMPANY ACCOUNTABLE

As Edmund Burke observed at first hand, corporations are not self-correcting. There is nothing in their design to call a halt to further market expansion, or desist from political interventions that rig the market in their favour. In Burke's age and ours, the need for external mechanisms to bring corporate malpractice to account is therefore essential. But when the Company's extensive network of bribes came to light in the 1690s, and Parliament tried to impeach the President of the Privy Council, the King simply dismissed Parliament. When Clive's crimes of the 'blackest dye' were presented to the Commons 70 years later, his misdeeds were offset against his contribution to imperial expansion, and he escaped without censure. And when Burke used the impeachment process once more to make Hastings accountable for his actions in Bengal, the House of Lords found him not guilty. In the face of Hastings's evident malpractice, Burke's mismanagement of the case makes the outcome even more frustrating.

The Company did have in place a series of rules and covenants to direct the behaviour of its employees. After the corruption of the 1690s, the Company managed to operate a reasonably ethical standard of conduct. But when presented with the windfall profits generated by its acquisitions in India, these controls simply crumbled in a frenzy of greed. The introduction of a ban on the receipt of bribes in 1764 was simply too little, too late. Lawrence Sulivan did try to rein in the more extreme aspects of Clive's adventurism. But when he was in dire need of cash in the 1770s, Sulivan was only too happy to send his son, Stephen, to Bengal to regain the family fortune in opium and contracting. Monopoly power, Adam Smith warned, does not just damage the market, but it also gives licence to managerial negligence. The Company's practices did not just result in economic losses for English consumers and Indian producers, but in social dislocation and the corrosion of the public realm. The Bengal Famine of 1770 continues to stare down the centuries as a shocking reminder of where corporate negligence can lead. Writing over a hundred years after the event, George Chesney, a civil servant at the India Office in London, was forced to admit in 1877 that the Bengal Famine had caused a 'desolation ... the marks of which have not wholly ceased'.[18]

For Burke, the only way to confront this impunity was to recast the Company's charter so that it became accountable once more. Speaking to Parliament in defence of his India Bill in December 1783, Burke made a clear distinction between political and commercial rights. The 'Magna Charta is a charter to restrain power and to destroy monopoly'; but 'the East India charter is a charter to establish monopoly and to create power'. Burke believed that he had a strong case for making the Company and its executives accountable for their actions: 'they themselves are responsible – their body as a corporate body, themselves as individuals – and the whole body and train of their servants are responsible to the high justice of this kingdom'. The grant of a corporate charter carried with it intrinsic duties, according to Burke, since 'this nation never did give a power without imposing a proportionable degree of responsibility'.[19] Yet Burke's passionate rhetoric was insufficient to make these principles of natural law overturn the vested interests and imperial pride that dominated eighteenth-century Britain.

For centuries, states pursued the imperial interests of monarchs against their own and other peoples. Reform and revolution have ensured that most states are bounded by constitutions at home and international law abroad, and charged with promoting the wider public interest within the community of nations. When states still act in an imperial manner – pursuing their self-interest to the disregard of others – it is now transparent that this breaks established norms of behaviour. The international opposition to the US and British invasion of Iraq in 2003 drew much of its passion from this powerful sense that well-established standards of law and ethics were being flagrantly violated.

Somewhat surprisingly, this process of democratisation has passed by the gates of the corporation. Just as the state was tamed through democracy and law, so corporations need to be retuned so that they work in harmony with the rest of society. 'It wasn't necessary to throw out government to do away with monarchy,' argues business ethics writer Marjorie Kelly, 'instead we changed the basis of sovereignty on which government rested.'[20] For this exercise, the Company's history offers fragments of hope, principles that can be used in our own times – most notably Smith's analysis of the corporation's agency problem and its monopolising tendencies, as well as Burke's dual recognition that all people, whatever their culture, have equal rights to justice, and that corporations are public institutions accountable to Parliament.

INSERTING THE ETHICS GENE

Both theory and practice teach us that the conditions under which the corporation can contribute to human welfare are clear and precise. First of all, its market power and political influence must be limited. If its sway in the marketplace grows too great, it will deny choice and invariably use its position to narrow the opportunities for others, squeezing suppliers and gouging consumers. And if the corporation becomes a powerful political force then it can rig the rules of regulation so that it enjoys unjustified public subsidy or protection. Next, stringent rules are needed to ensure that management and investors do not use the corporation as a tool for their short-term interests at the expense of others. And, finally, clear and enforceable systems of justice have to be in place to hold the corporation to account for damage to society and the environment. The road to legal remedy must be accessible and with effective measures to level the playing field between the individual and the institution.

If the creative energies of enterprise are to be realised, then the ethic of trust between the corporation and society needs to be re-established. The issue is how to encode ethical conduct into corporate design. Advocates of corporate reform have generally focused on introducing regulations to tackle specific issues, such as workplace safety, equal opportunities or environmental management. Others have seen state ownership as the solution to the corporate abuse of power, a process now being reversed worldwide through privatisation. Yet, the in-built pursuit of institutional and individual self-interest – which forms the foundation of the British and American model of the firm – has been left untouched in company law. As if blinded with awe at the imperial might of the corporation, politicians have not only extended the legal rights of the modern firm, but deliberately disarmed the state of its countervailing powers. In many ways, the global economy is currently living through the worst of both worlds: the removal of government restraints on economic activity without the introduction of compensating restraints on the power of corporations.

In many countries, such as Britain and India, the sole duty of company directors remains to the company's shareholders. In spite of the best intentions of many corporate executives, this legal imperative has a deeply corrosive effect on the way in which companies approach their social responsibilities. In most cases, corporate responsibility becomes another term for enlightened self-interest – that good conduct towards customers, regulators and communities helps to generate a 'licence to operate'. The problem comes, of course, when the interests of company and society conflict. At this point, corporate responsibility slips into the shadows and the supremacy of shareholder value reasserts itself. Equally, there are no codes or regulations to ensure that shareholders place their demands for returns within a broader framework of respect for the long-term interests of the corporation or the rights of others. In the fine words of Adam Smith, special measures are required to bring more 'dignity and steadiness' to the conduct of both executives and investors.

Central to this effort is a rebalancing of corporate rights and privileges, so that the current protection of limited liability does not screen executives and investors from the consequences of their actions. For one of the pioneers of socially responsible investment in the UK, the argument is clear: 'society gives companies the privilege of limited liability; such a privilege should have social responsibility associated with it'.[21] For this to happen, an 'ethics gene' needs to be inserted into company law. The first rule of ethics is to 'do no harm'. To realise this in the corporate context, company directors need to be given a legal duty of care to ensure that their actions do not damage society or the environment; investors equally need to have a parallel duty to ensure that their demand for financial returns does no harm. Generate a profit by all means, but this cannot be at the expense of others.

Moves in this direction are under way. After years of consultation, Britain's system of company law is being updated, with the result that directors will need to 'have regard to the interests of employees' and 'consider the impact on the community and the environment'. This gives directors a 'duty to think', but not a 'duty to act'. The broad-based Corporate Responsibility (CORE) coalition argues that the law needs further refinement so that directors would not only have to consider the negative impacts on other stakeholders, but have to take steps to reduce and eliminate these burdens.[22] Establishing a legal requirement would just be the first step. Companies would need to review their operations to check for compliance. Transition periods could be considered to manage the shift from harmful industries to those that truly added value through their products and processes. And ultimately, these statutory duties would need to be matched by sanctions that were visible and dissuasive, including the removal of a company's licence for gross misconduct. As Burke declared more than two hundred years ago, 'if the abuse is proved, the contract is broken'.

Through this simple, yet profound alteration in the corporation's genetic code, its inner dynamics would be reshaped to match its social obligations. Shareholders would also become aware of the wider implications of their investments, stimulating a search for companies that take a proactive approach to reducing their harmful impacts on others. Not just corporations, but capital itself would start becoming accountable.

DOWNSIZING THE CORPORATION[23]

Corporate scale serves to magnify an underlying problem of behaviour. When it was small, the damage that the Company could inflict was relatively limited. When it grew in size to dominate whole markets and territories, its potential for harm grew correspondingly large. Twenty-first century corporations rarely enjoy the chartered monopolies that the East India Company fought so hard to sustain. But there is little doubt that the corporation's dual focus on 'widening the market and narrowing the competition' that Smith observed continues to prevail. Tragically, global deregulation has not been accompanied by assertive antitrust and competition policies, and so concentration in key markets has climbed to economically destructive and politically dangerous levels. In this drive for monopoly, the contemporary corporation is rewarded by its investors, who favour those who can demonstrate strong 'barriers to entry' and extensive 'pricing power' since these will generate excess profits for shareholders.

In sector after sector – banking, energy, food processing and retail, media and telecoms – the remorseless search for profits is leading companies to close down competition through mergers and acquisitions. The global media industry is a case in point. In the early 1980s, the US market was dominated by 50 firms; by the turn of the millennium, this had fallen to fewer than ten. Speaking on World Press Freedom Day 2002, Czech President Vaclav Havel declared that 'fifty years from now, the globalisation process may be the biggest threat to freedom of expression'.[24] Privatisation and deregulation have, perversely, contributed to this trend. In the European power sector, a recent study concluded that 'market concentration in the field of power generation has to be seen as endangering fair, competitive and sustainable energy markets'.[25] Just as the East India Company monopolised the textile production of India to force down prices and exert greater control, so many of today's major commodity chains have become highly concentrated, generating powerful downward pressure on the prices of goods exported by developing countries. Three companies control 45 per cent of all of the world's coffee roasting, for example, while four companies account for 40 per cent of cocoa grinding.[26] Diversity in global retailing has also shrunk dramatically in recent years, with the top 30 companies accounting for around one-third of all grocery sales. This retail concentration helps to explain why successive rounds of trade liberalisation have not led to improved prosperity for poor nations. As Jean Ziegler concluded for the UN Commission on Human Rights in early 2004, 'global commodity markets are increasingly dominated by fewer global transnational corporations that have the power to demand low producer prices, while keeping consumer prices high, thus, increasing their profit margins'.[27] The great drain is being repeated once more, with supermarkets able to deploy their market power to 'drain the wealth from farming communities and marginalised small-scale producers'.[28] And, as the Company showed in its relations with European and Asian states, corporate power is as much a political as an economic problem.

Whether it is trade agreements that bias development towards business interests, or successive reductions in the share of tax levied from corporations (a proportion that has halved in the USA since the 1950s), the East India Company casts a long shadow over a process of globalisation that so many of its supporters claim is new to the world.[29]

Antitrust and competition policies are supposedly designed to deal with these threats to market diversity. But these have largely failed to 'have much bearing on the concentration of economic activity'.[30] Although market dominance by a few key firms (oligopoly) breaches the tenets of neo-classical theory, it has been increasingly accepted in practice across the world. Writing in the 1970s, John Kenneth Galbraith acknowledged somewhat despairingly that 'King Canute looks down on those who administer our antitrust laws with the utmost understanding and sympathy'.[31] Since then, 30 years of privatisation, deregulation and trade liberalisation have undone many of these modest gains, and created new global combinations to replace the national champions of an earlier age. The result is a crisis of control that demands a similarly robust approach to global antitrust as inspired reformers in the last century. Not only is such a global antitrust approach economically urgent, but it also offers the prospect of a powerful new alliance between those supporting open markets and those aiming to curb corporate power.

In Adam Smith's economic vision, monopoly corporations were simply 'nuisances in every respect'. Urgent action is needed to reverse the process of corporate concentration. Targeted global antitrust investigations are needed to redress the balance, for example, in highly concentrated commodity chains on which developing countries are dependent. These investigations could help to build the mandate for the establishment of a global competition authority that would be charged with breaking up the most damaging cartels and combinations of corporate power. Importantly, this authority would need to be wholly independent of the World Trade Organisation. Alongside this, national action has to be intensified, first by implementing the 'standstill' principle to prevent any further corporate concentration, and then introducing the 'rollback' principle to break open markets to enable economic diversity to flourish once more.

RAFAEL'S LAW

The absence of a world competition authority is certainly a major gap in the architecture of global governance. But it is not the only thing that is missing. As Burke's struggle to remove the impunity of Hastings and others demonstrated, the legal accountability of corporations and their executives is equally an essential element of an effective international order. Then, as now, human rights are universal entitlements, subject to the rule of law in spite of convenient appeals to special circumstances or 'geographical morality'. Legal victories for human rights abuse were rare in the age of Enlightenment – as they are, sadly, still today. But Gregore Cojamaul and Johannes Rafael's stunning victory in winning damages from the Company's Governor of Bengal, Harry Verelst, demonstrates that the principle of extraterritorial liability has been long established in British law at least.

From the same era, a tool has endured that is now being used to enable today's victims of corporate abuse to seek civil redress. In 1789, the new American Republic passed the Alien Tort Claims Act (ATCA) to allow foreigners to bring violations of international law to trial in US courts.[32] Originally designed to combat the scourge of piracy, in late 1970s legal experts revived ATCA to bring those accused of international human rights abuses to justice in the USA. In 1979, Dolly Filartiga won a landmark judgment in New York against the police inspector who had supervised the torture and killing of her brother in her native Paraguay. Summing up the sentence, Justice Irving Kaufman concluded that 'the torturer has become – like the pirate and slave trader before him – *hostis humanis generis*, an enemy of mankind'. Subsequently, both Ferdinand Marcos, the former dictator of the Philippines, and Radovan Karadzic of the breakaway Serb republic in Bosnia have been charged under ATCA. From the mid-1990s, the use of ATCA has been expanded to address the complicity of US and other corporations in human rights abuses across the developing world. From Chevron and Shell in Nigeria to Exxon and Freeport in Indonesia and Unocal in Burma, about two dozen cases have been filed in US courts on behalf of individuals and communities alleging killing, torture, arbitrary arrest and forced labour.

Just as Cojamaul and Rafael faced huge legal obstacles to achieving justice in the 1770s, so today's victims have faced an uphill struggle to gain recognition in the courts. About half of the ATCA cases against corporations have been dismissed. But in December 2004, a major breakthrough was achieved when Unocal reached an out-of-court settlement with 15 Burmese plaintiffs in an eight-year-long ATCA case. The lawsuit had alleged that California-based energy company Unocal was complicit in forced labour, rape and murder committed by the Burmese military during the construction of the Yadana gas pipeline from Burma to Thailand. Even though the final settlement was out of court, a number of powerful legal precedents had already been set demonstrating that corporations can be held liable for civil damages in the US for aiding and abetting human rights abuse by oppressive regimes overseas.[33] But the Unocal case also highlights the limits of existing international mechanisms for corporate accountability. Just as the Armenians in 1770s London could only win financial damages for Verelst's actions, so ACTA only involves civil law, leaving aside the frequent need to bring criminal prosecutions for corporate abuse. Even this modest relief is under threat from the Bush Administration seeking to free business of any form of redress for their actions overseas.

In this latest attempt to make corporations above the rule of law, inspiration can be drawn from the case of Cojamaul and Rafael. Instruments of justice need to be as international as business. The liability of corporations for harm they do needs to be clarified and access to justice facilitated. All countries, Britain and India included, need to ensure that effective legal remedies are in place to enable those affected by corporations to bring legal action either in the company's place of registration or in an international court. The realistic prospect of judicial intervention to penalise malpractice – wherever it may occur – would be a powerful deterrent, further encouraging business to adopt responsible practices that prevent problems in the first place.

CORPORATE KARMA

In the closing pages of his *The Discovery of India*, Nehru examined the consequences of 200 years of domination of India by England in terms of karma, the Hindu law of cause and effect. 'Entangled in its meshes', he wrote from his cell in Ahmadnagar Fort in 1944, 'we have thus struggled in vain to rid ourselves of this past inheritance and start afresh on a different basis.'[34] Independence of course was a necessary starting point for release, but one that needed to be supplemented by further action to deal with the bitter lessons of empire. For Edward Thompson, friend of Nehru and supporter of independence, England needed to make atonement (*prayaschitta*) – particularly for the barbarities that followed the rebellion of 1857–58 – if relations between the two countries were to flourish.[35] At the time, this was a step too far. But perhaps with greater distance from events, it is possible for an honest cultural reckoning to be attempted to enable both societies to 'start afresh'.

The first step in atonement is acknowledgement, and in the case of the East India Company – and other historical corporations – this requires visibility. The Company's practices, its legacy and historical debt need to be brought into the open. Its physical remains can become the starting point for a vigorous programme of challenge and interpretation. This should not be limited to rather superficial questions about whether Clive's statue should remain outside the Foreign Office – although it might well be a good idea to replace it with one to China's anti-opium champion, Commissioner Lin. More importantly, the question is how the Company's remains can become living symbols of renewal. In Kolkata, the Belvedere, Hastings's mansion and scene of his duel with Francis, is now home to India's National Library, while in London, the mansion of a former Company director has been transformed into a Muslim educational foundation. Most inspiring perhaps is the way that the Company's former chapel in Poplar has now become a centre of community efforts to reconcile the diverse communities in London's Docklands.

There are also growing signs of public interest in a historical reckoning with the East India Company. Over recent years, I have been working with the London-based arts and environmental group, Platform, on a programme of activities to reveal the Company's hidden history and make the links with contemporary corporate activities. It has hosted a series of guided walks around the site of the Company's headquarters, warehouses and docks, which have stimulated broad public discussion and debate. Building on the success of these walks, Platform has launched a project to establish the Museum of the Corporation, which would provide a focal point for public reflection on this most powerful institution of our time.[36] Aiming to inform and intrigue, the museum could combine exhibitions, education and other activities to engage the public on the role of corporations in their lives, the strengths and the weaknesses. The museum would range through the history of the corporation, showing the commonalities and discontinuities between contemporary business and forerunners such as the East India Company. The museum would also balance physical artefacts and the best of electronic media, acting in a network with like-minded institutions across the globe. In London, the museum could be hosted in one of the East India Company's former warehouses, for example, at Cutlers Gardens, one part of which was set aside for public use as part of the redevelopment exercise in the 1970s. In Kolkata, Clive's former house at Dum-Dum would be an equally symbolic site for such a place of reflection in India.

The partial view of the Company in existing museums also needs to be addressed. Wonderful artefacts remain, but often lie mute in their glass display cabinets. The need for new ways of revealing the Company's past was highlighted in the 'Encounters' exhibition hosted by London's Victoria and Albert Museum at the end of 2004. Examining the economic and aesthetic exchanges between Europe and Asia in the 300 years up to 1800, the exhibition portrayed the interaction as generally one of mutual benefit and fascination. Yet there appeared to be little attempt to look at the human realities that lay behind luxury goods on display, to examine how trade was conducted, as well as what was exchanged. A simple, neo-classical gown on show in the exhibition, for example, could have told a deeper and more tragic story. Woven of Bengali muslin, most probably in Dhaka, around 1800, the gown at first glance was just a thing of beauty. No reference was made, however, to the fact that this gown was part of a dying generation, coming from an industry that was just about to be eliminated through industrial technology, tariff walls and the Company's imperial management. A mere 18 years after the gown was woven, the Company had shut its factory in Dhaka and ceased all imports of Indian muslin. Simply looking at this and other artefacts through the lens of culture fails to tell the whole story.

FUTURE FLOWERINGS

If there is to be hope of creating a positive future, the Company's role in the shared pasts of Europe and Asia need to be confronted. For the writer Ben Okri, 'nations and peoples are largely the stories they feed themselves', and 'if they tell themselves lies, they will suffer the future consequences of those lies'. But, continues Okri, 'if they tell themselves stories that face their own truths, they will free their histories for future flowerings'.[37] It is with a view to these 'future flowerings' that the East India Company has to be examined in the twenty-first century.

The East India Company's story is ultimately a tragedy, the tale of an institution that generated great wealth, but also great harm, an institution that was ultimately doomed by the flaws in its corporate design. This story has much to teach the twenty-first century about the dangers of unchecked corporate power and the enduring capacity of people to press for justice. As interest in the Company's relevance for today's world grows, a full reckoning is long overdue. An honest confrontation with the corporate origins of the modern age can help both to illuminate both our history and stimulate renewed action to align corporations with the wider public interest.

Knowing the Company's story, the obligation is to remember and then to act. This is what motivated those like Edmund Burke who championed the cause of justice in the eighteenth century, without hope of either personal reward or, indeed, of success. At the end of his life, Burke wrote to his young friend and literary executor, French Laurence, to communicate what he still valued in his long political and literary career. Known today for his conservative defence of social hierarchy during the French Revolution, Burke told Laurence that everything apart from his work to bring justice to India should be forgotten. His outrage burning once more, Burke damned the way that the Company had turned its relations with India into 'nothing more than an opportunity of gratifying the lowest of their purposes, the lowest of their passions'. Unlike Macaulay, with his bitter scorn for all things Asian, Burke continued to argue for an ethical equality between East and West. But this had been violated through the Company's acquisition and subsequent oppression of India. In the process, Europe had incurred an enormous moral deficit. 'If ever Europe recovers its civilisation', Burke concluded, then his 'work will be useful'. And summoning his own generation and those to come to face the full reality of the East India Company, Burke calls out from the eighteenth century, 'Remember! Remember! Remember![38]

Notes

INTRODUCTION

1. Edmund Burke, Speech to Parliament, 1 December 1783.
2. Karl Marx, 'The British Rule in India', *New York Daily Tribune*, 25 June 1853.

1: THE HIDDEN WOUND

1. Edward Edwards, *Anecdotes of Painters*, quoted in William Foster, *Catalogue of Paintings, Statues etc. in the India Office*, London, 1921, p. 57.
2. Accounts differ whether the river god is the Thames or Ganges.
3. See Kees Zandvliet, *The Dutch Encounter with Asia, 1600–1650*, Amsterdam: Rijksmuseum, 2002.
4. Using the retail price index, 'In 2002, £2,500,000 from 1757 is worth £232,673,621 and £234,000 from 1757 is worth £21,778,251': see <www.eh.net> [last consulted 30/10/05].
5. Alexander Dow, *History of Hindostan*, 1773, quoted in Sushil Chaudhury, *The Prelude to Empire: Plassey Revolution of 1757*, New Delhi: Manohar, 2000, p. 18.
6. Ninth Report of the Select Committee, July 1783, in P.J. Marshall, ed., *Writings and Speeches of Edmund Burke*, V, Oxford: Clarendon Press, 1981, p. 232.
7. Adam Smith, *Inquiry into the Wealth of Nations*, book I, chap. VIII, New York: The Modern Library, 1994 [1776], p. 84.
8. 'To the Tradesmen and Mechanics of Pennsylvania', 4 December 1773.
9. Ninth Report, in Marshall, *Writings and Speeches of Burke*, V, p. 226.
10. Lawrence Norfolk, *Lemprière's Dictionary*, London: Minerva, 1996.
11. John Keay, *The Honourable Company*, London: HarperCollins, 1993, p. 219.
12. James Noorthouck, *New History of London*, quoted in William Foster, *The East India House*, London, 1924, p. 133.
13. Quoted in Anthony Sampson, *Company Man: The Rise and Fall of Corporate Life*, London: HarperCollins, 1996, p. 21.
14. Olwen Campbell, *Thomas Love Peacock*, London: Arthur Barker, 1953, p. 54.
15. Prior to the construction of the new building, there was a plaque, which stated 'Site of East India House, 1726–1861'.
16. Romesh Chunder Dutt, *The Economic History of India under Early British Rule (1757–1837)*, London: Kegan Paul, Trench, Trubner & Co., 1908, p. xii.
17. Jawaharlal Nehru, *The Discovery of India*, London: Meridian Books, 1946, p. 248.
18. Gurcharan Das, *India Unbound*, New Delhi: Penguin India, 2002.

19. Quoted in 'Enron's Abuse of Power', *Multinational Monitor*, vol. 18, no. 9, September 1997.
20. Arundhati Roy, *The Algebra of Infinite Justice*, London: Flamingo, 2002, p. 146.
21. Sandip Roy, 'Enron in India: the Giant's First Fall', Pacific News Service, 8 February 2002.
22. See *Rediff Business Special*, 26 May 2000 or *Tehelka*, 14 February 2004.
23. Sowmya Sundar and Suresh Krishnamurthy, 'Foreigners hold 30pc shares in nifty cos', *Business Line*, 28 March 2004.
24. Arvind Virmani, 'Economic Reforms: Policy and Institutions – Some Lessons from Indian Reforms', ICRIER, New Delhi, January 2004.
25. See the speech of Shri Shankar Roy Chowdhury on patent reform, Rajya Sabha debates, 23 March 2005.
26. Patrick Gillam and Mervyn Davies, Sponsor's Foreword in Antony Farrington, 'Trading Places', London: The British Library, 2002.
27. Rod Eddington, 'Only the world's favourite empires last', *Financial Times*, 14 July 2003.
28. See <www.theeastindicacompany.com> [visited 23/02/2001]
29. See <www.metrojayaonline.com>.
30. William Dalrymple, quoted in Archie Baron, *An Indian Affair*, London: Channel 4 Books, 2001, p. 110.
31. William Dalrymple, *White Mughals*, London: HarperCollins, 2003, p. 501.
32. See Baron, *An Indian Affair*.
33. See <http://www.thetruthabouttradingplaces.org.uk> [last referenced 24/06/02].
34. *Gentleman's Magazine*, March 1767, pp. 100–1.
35. *Gentleman's Magazine*, April 1767, p. 152.
36. Nehru, *The Discovery of India*, p. 266.
37. Richard Clarke, 'The Nabob' (1773), quoted in *Arenas of Asiatic Plunder*, Jack p. Greene, 2003, see <www.uga.edu/colonialseminar/AsiaticPlunders.pdf> [last referenced 24/10/2005].

2: THIS IMPERIOUS COMPANY

1. Quoted in Rozina Visram, *Asians in Britain: 400 Years of History*, London: Pluto Press, 2002, p. 19.
2. Thomas Babington Macaulay, *The History of England in the 18th Century* [1849], London: Folio Society, 1980, p. 183.
3. Kirti N. Chaudhuri, *The Trading World of Asia and the East India Company 1660–1760*, Cambridge: Cambridge University Press, 1978, p. 21.
4. Fernand Braudel, *Civilization and Capitalism*, vol. 2: *The Wheels of Commerce*, London: Collins, 1982, p. 436.
5. See Ron Harris, *Institutional Innovations: Theories of the Firm and the Formation of the East India Company*, Berkeley Program in Law and Economics Working Paper no. 161, 2004, p. 49.
6. Philip Lawson, *The East India Company*, London: Longman, 1993, p. 21.

7. *Gentleman's Magazine*, July 1767, p. 348.
8. Thomas Friedman, *New York Times*, 28 March 1999.
9. Chaudhuri, *The Trading World of Asia*, p. 13.
10. Quoted in Huw Bowen, *Revenue and Reform*, Cambridge: Cambridge University Press, 1991, p. 39.
11. See Santhi Hejeebu, 'Contract Enforcement in the English East India Company', Cornell College, July 2004; also in *Journal of Economic History*, vol. 65, no. 2, 2005, pp. 1–27.
12. See Ann M. Carlos and Stephen Nicholas, 'Giants of an Earlier Capitalism: The Chartered Trading Companies as Modern Multinational corporations', *Business History Review*, vol. 62, no. 3, Autumn 1988.
13. Timothy Alborn, *Conceiving Companies*, London: Routledge, 1998, p. 2.
14. Adam Smith, *Inquiry into the Wealth of Nations*, book IV, chap. VIII, pp. 692–3.
15. Ibid., book IV, chap. III, p. 527.
16. George Miller, 'Everyday Low Wages', US House of Representatives, 16 February 2004.
17. Center for Community and Corporate Ethics, *Wal-Mart Watch Annual Report 2005*, <www.walmartwatch.com>
18. Frank Partnoy, *Infectious Greed: How Deceit and Risk Corrupted the Financial Markets*, London: Profile Books, 2004, p. 4.
19. William Bolts, *Considerations on Indian Affairs* [1772], in *The East India Company: 1600–1858*, ed. Patrick Tuck, London: Routledge, 1998, pp. iv–v.
20. Amnesty International, *Clouds of Injustice – Bhopal disaster 20 years on*, London: Amnesty International Publications, 2004.
21. *Gentleman's Magazine*, April 1767, p. 152.
22. P.J. Marshall, *Problems of Empire: Britain and India 1757–1813*, London: George Allen & Unwin, 1968, p. 17.
23. Karl Marx, 'The Government of India', *New York Tribune*, 20 July 1853.

3: OUT OF THE SHADOWS

1. Willke Jeeninga, *The East Indies House and St Jorishof*, Utrecht: Wanders Uitgevers, 1995.
2. Els M. Jacobs, *In Pursuit of Pepper and Tea: The Story of the Dutch East India Company*, Amsterdam: Netherlands Maritime Museum, 1991, p. 16.
3. Jeeninga, *The East Indies House*, p. 38.
4. David Landes, *The Wealth and Poverty of Nations*, London: Little, Brown and Company, 1998, p. 143.
5. Henry Hobhouse, *Seeds of Change: Six Plants that Transformed Mankind*, London: Papermac, 1999, p. xiii.
6. Holden Furber, 'Rival Empires of Trade 1600–1800', in *Maritime India*, New Delhi: Oxford University Press, 2004 [1976], p. 231.
7. Richard Hall, *Empires of the Monsoon*, London: HarperCollins, 1996, p. 172.
8. Hall, ibid., p. 190, quotes Joao de Barros's justification of this policy: 'It is true that there does exist a common right to all to navigate the seas, and

in Europe we acknowledge the right which others hold against us, but that right does not extend beyond Europe, and therefore the Portuguese by the strengths of her fleets are justified in compelling all Moors to take out safe-conducts under pain of confiscation or death. The Moors and the Gentiles are outside the law of Jesus Christ, which is the true law which everyone has to keep under pain of damnation to eternal fire. If then the soul be so condemned, what right has the body to the privileges of our laws?'

9. Described by Gaspar Correa in *The Three Voyages of Vasco da Gama* and quoted in Hall, *Empires of the Monsoon*, p. 198.
10. Quoted in Om Prakash, *European Commercial Enterprise in Pre-Colonial India*, New Delhi: Cambridge University Press, 2000, p. 139.
11. Ibid., p. 48.
12. William Logan, *Malabar Manual*, New Delhi: Asian Educational Services, 2000, p. 308.
13. Giles Milton, *Nathaniel's Nutmeg*, London: Hodder & Stoughton, London, p. 70.
14. Quoted in Furber, 'Rival Empires of Trade', p. 32.
15. Logan, *Malabar Manual*, p. 70.
16. See Ramkrishna Mukherjee, *The Rise and Fall of the East India Company*, New York: Monthly Review Press, 1974, p. 393.
17. Keay, *The Honourable Company*, p. 113.
18. Quoted in Mukherjee, *Rise and Fall of the East India Company*, p. 73.
19. See Furber, 'Rival Empires of Trade', p. 91.
20. Keay, *The Honourable Company*, p. 150.
21. Thomas Babington Macaulay, *History of England Since the Accession of James II*, 1848–60, chap. XVIII.
22. Chaudhuri, *The Trading World of Asia*, p. 77.
23. Daniel Defoe, *Anatomy of Exchange Alley*, quoted in Maureen Waller, *1700: Scenes from London Life*, London: Hodder & Stoughton, 2000, p. 243.
24. See Stephen Pincus's *Whigs, Political Economy and the Revolution of 1688–89* (2002) for a fascinating account of Child's political economy.
25. Quoted in John E. Wills, *1688 – A Global History*, London: Granta, 2002, p. 285.
26. East India Company to Fort St George, 9 June 1686, quoted in Pincus, *Whigs*, p. 12.
27. East India Company to Fort St George, quoted in Chaudhury, *The Prelude to Empire*, p. 68.
28. Newsletter from London, 14 August 1688, quoted in Pincus, *Whigs*, p. 14.
29. Macaulay, *History of England*, chap. XVIII
30. Quoted in Lawson, *The East India Company*, p. 53.
31. Report of Sir Thomas Cooke's Examination, *House of Lords Journal*, vol. 15, 24 April 1695.
32. Sir Basil Firebrace's Examination, *House of Lords Journal*, vol.15, 27 April 1695.
33. Edward Chancellor, *Devil Take the Hindmost*, London: Macmillan, 1999, p. 50.
34. Smith, *Wealth of Nations*, book v, chap. I, art. 1, p. 808.

35. Lucy Sutherland, *The East India Company in Eighteenth-Century Politics*, Oxford: Clarendon Press, 1952, p. 17.
36. Letter to an MP, 1708, published in *Gentleman's Magazine*, 1781, p. 1018.
37. Smith, *Wealth of Nations*, book V, chap. I, art. 1.
38. 'In 2002, £200,000 from 1699 is worth £18,786,836 using the retail price index.' See <www.eh.net> [last consulted 30/10/2005].
39. Quoted in Gardner, *The East India Company*, p. 53.
40. Quoted by Chaudhury, *From Prosperity to Decline: 18th Century Bengal*, New Delhi: Manohar, 1999, p. 24.
41. J.H. Plumb, *England in the 18th Century*, Harmondsworth: Penguin, 1990, p. 171.
42. 31 January 1708, *Weekly Review*, quoted in Prasannan Parthasarathi, 'Rethinking Wages and Competitiveness in the 18th Century: Britain and South India', *Past and Present*, no. 158, February 1998.
43. Robert J. Allen, ed., *Addison and Steele*, Orlando: Rinehart, 1974, p. 212.
44. Furber, 'Rival Empires of Trade', p. 130.
45. Quoted in James Mill, *History of British India* [1858 edn, 10 vols], vol. III, book IV, chap. 1, London: Routledge/Thoemes Press, 1997, p. 30.

4: THE BENGAL REVOLUTION

1. William Bolts, *Considerations on Indian Affairs* [1772], in *The East India Company: 1600–1858*, ed. Patrick Tuck, London: Routledge, 1998, p. 84.
2. Krishna Dutta, *Calcutta*, Northampton, MA: Interlink Books 2003, p. 55.
3. 'In 2002, £1,000,000 from 1797 is worth £70,725603 using the retail price index.' See <www.eh.net> [last consulted 30/10/05].
4. Fernand Braudel, *Civilization and Capitalism*, vol. 3: *The Perspective of the World*, London: Collins, 1984, p. 489.
5. See, for example, the March 1767 issue of *Gentleman's Magazine*, p. 99.
6. Philip Francis, quoted in Joseph Parkes and Herman Merivale, *Memoirs of Sir Philip Francis*, London: Longman, Green & Co., 1867, II, p. 18.
7. Quoted in Mike Davis, *Late Victorian Holocausts*, London: Verso, 2002, p. 294.
8. Uzramma, *A Brief History of Cotton in India*, Hyderabad: Independent Handloom Research Group, 2002.
9. P.J. Marshall, *East Indian Fortunes: the British in Bengal in the Eighteenth Century*, Oxford: Clarendon Press, 1976, p. 33.
10. Prakash, *European Commercial Enterprise*, p. 121.
11. Chaudhury, *From Prosperity to Decline*, p. 206.
12. Sudipta Sen, *Empire of Free Trade: the East India Company and the Making of the Colonial Marketplace*, Philadelphia: University of Pennsylvania Press, 1998, p. 13.
13. Quoted in Chaudhury, *From Prosperity to Decline*, p. 35.
14. Marshall, *East Indian Fortunes*, p. 43.
15. Quoted in Chaudhury, *From Prosperity to Decline*, p. 316.

16. Quoted in Chaudhury, *The Prelude to Empire*, p. 69.
17. Smith, *Wealth of Nations*, book V, chap. 3, art. 1, p. 809.
18. Quoted in Keay, *The Honourable Company*, p. 299.
19. Quoted in Chaudhury, *The Prelude to Empire*, p. 42.
20. Sen, *Empire of Free Trade*, p. 74.
21. Ibid., p. 74.
22. *Gentleman's Magazine*, July 1757, p. 309.
23. Quoted in Chaudhury, *The Prelude to Empire*, p. 111.
24. Quoted in Chaudhury, *From Prosperity to Decline*, p. 322.
25. Gardner, *The East India Company*, p. 84.
26. Chaudhury, *The Prelude to Empire*, p. 86.
27. Robert Clive, Letter to Directors, 26 July 1757.
28. Jean Law, quoted in Chaudhury, *The Prelude to Empire*, p. 119.
29. Chaudhuri, *The Trading World of Asia*, p. 109.
30. Robert Clive to the Secret Committee of the Directors, 26 July 1757, <www.mssc.edu/project southasia/history>.
31. Robert Harvey, *Clive: Life and Death of a British Emperor*, London: Hodder & Stoughton, 1998, p. 193.
32. Clive, quoted in ibid., p. 251.
33. Clive Mathieson, 'Vodafone chastised by vote over bonus', *The Times*, London, 28 July 2000.
34. Philip Mason, *The Men Who Ruled India*, London: Jonathan Cape, 1985, p. 37.
35. Thomas Macaulay, 'Essay on Lord Clive', January 1840.
36. Chaudhury, *The Prelude to Empire*, p. 166.
37. Luke Scrafton, *Reflections on the Government of Indostan* [1763], quoted in R. Palme Dutt, *India Today*, London: Victor Gollancz, 1940, p. 113.
38. R.C. Dutt, *Economic History of India*, p. 23.
39. Smith, *Wealth of Nations*, book IV, chap. VII, p. 687.
40. 'In 2002, £300,000 from 1759 is worth £34,150,824, using the retail price index.' See <www.eh.net> [last consulted 30/10/2005].
41. 'In 2002, £1,650,900 from 1765 is worth £152,072,698 using the retail price index.' See <www.eh.net> [last consulted 30/10/05].
42. Robert Clive, Letter to the Directors, September 1765, quoted in Bolts, *Considerations*, p.154.
43. <http://banglapedia.search.bd/HT/C_0290.HTM>.
44. James Mill, *History of British India*, vol. III, book IV, chap. IX, p. 359.
45. Braudel, *Civilization and Capitalism*, vol. 3, p. 496.
46. Parthasarathi, 'Rethinking Wages and Competitiveness in the 18th Century'.
47. 'Of the mode of providing the Company's Investment', quoted in Guha, *A Rule of Property*, p. 136.
48. Hameeda Hossain, 'The Company's Controls over Textile Production', *Journal of the Asiatic Society of Bangladesh*, June 1983, offprint, p. 13.
49. Bolts, *Considerations*, p. 193.
50. Ibid., p. 74.
51. Ibid., p. 194.
52. Shahid Ali, from the 'Dacca Gauzes', in *The Half-Inch Himalayas*, Middletown: Wesleyan University Press, 1987.

53. Quoted in Harvey, *Clive*, p. 309.
54. Furber, 'Rival Empires of Trade', p. 177.

5: THE GREAT EAST INDIAN CRASH

1. Quoted in Jeremy Bernstein, *Dawning of the Raj: The Life and Trials of Warren Hastings*, London: Aurum Press, 2000, p. 66.
2. Quoted in Penelope Hunting, *Cutlers Gardens*, London: Standard Life, 1984.
3. Sutherland, *The East India Company*, p. 47.
4. Macaulay, 'Essay on Clive', 1840.
5. Quoted in Keay, *The Honourable Company*, p. 324.
6. Quoted in Dutt, *The Economic History of India*, p. 37.
7. Quoted in Huw Bowen, 'Lord Clive and Speculation in East India Company Stock, 1776', *Historical Journal*, 1987, p. 910.
8. Quoted in James Mill, *History of British India*, vol. III, book IV, chap. VII, p. 300.
9. Baron, *An Indian Affair*, p. 80.
10. Mill, *History of British India*, III, IV, chap. VII, p. 307.
11. *Gentleman's Magazine*, December 1769, p. 618.
12. *Gentleman's Magazine*, April 1769, p. 211.
13. Quoted in Sutherland, *The East India Company*, p. 192.
14. Cornelius Walford, 'Famines in History', *Journal of the Statistical Society*, vol. 41, 1878, pp. 442–3.
15. Walford, quoted in Davis, *Late Victorian Holocausts*, p. 287.
16. Davis, *Late Victorian Holocausts*, p. 286.
17. Quoted in Palme Dutt, *India Today*, p. 115.
18. *Gentleman's Magazine*, 1771, p. 402.
19. Ibid., p. 403.
20. Quoted in Sen, *Empire of Free Trade*, p. 147.
21. Dutt, *The Economic History of India*, p. 52.
22. George Chesney, quoted in Walford, 'Famines in History', p. 519.
23. Quoted in Chandra Prakash N. Sinha, *From Decline to Destruction: Agriculture in Bihar during Early British Rule*, New Delhi: Manohar, 1997, p. 25.
24. Rajat Datta, *Society, Economy and the Market: Commercialisation in Rural Bengal c.1760–1800*, New Delhi: Manohar, 2000, p. 264.
25. Cornwallis, quoted in Datta, ibid., p. 264
26. Quoted in Mukherjee, *The Rise and Fall of the East India Company*, p. 353.
27. Dean Mahomet, *The Travels of Dean Mahomet*, Berkeley: University of California Press, 1997, pp. 35–6.
28. Ibid., p. 54.
29. See Sugata Bose, *Peasant Labour and Colonial Capital: Rural Bengal since 1770*, Cambridge, New York: Cambridge University Press, 1993.
30. Bolts, *Considerations*, p. x.
31. Derived from Marshall, *East Indian Fortunes*, Table VI, p. 232, Table VII, p. 241 and Table VIII, p. 250.

32. 'In 2002, £1,086,255 from 1770 is worth £98,490,650 using the retail price index.' See <www.eh.net> [last consulted 30/10/2005].
33. *Gentleman's Magazine*, April 1769, p. 197.
34. Quoted in Marshall, *East Indian Fortunes*, p. 200.
35. Quoted in Sutherland, *The East India Company*, p. 137.
36. Quoted in Harry Verelst, *A View on the Rise, Progress and Present State of the English Government in Bengal*, London [1772], in *The East India Company: 1600–1858*, ed. Tuck, p. 123.
37. Quoted in Bolts, *Considerations*, p. 53.
38. *Gentleman's Magazine*, December 1770, p. 587.
39. Baron, *An Indian Affair*, p. 79.
40. *Gentleman's Magazine*, 30 March 1771, p. 141.
41. Bolts, *Considerations*, p. 216.
42. Francis Sykes to Warren Hastings, 14 September 1773, quoted in Willem Kuiters, *The British in Bengal 1756–1773*, Paris: Les Indes Savantes, 2002, p. 68.
43. *Gentleman's Magazine*, December 1769, p. 618.
44. Quoted in Charles Kindleberger, *Manias, Panics and Crashes – A History of Financial Crises*, New York: John Wiley & Sons, 2000, p. 91.

6: REGULATING THE COMPANY

1. Quoted in Ian Simpson Ross, *The Life of Adam Smith*, Oxford: Clarendon Press, 1995, p. 241.
2. Quoted in Robert Heilbroner, *The Worldly Philosophers*, New York: Touchstone, 1999, p. 55.
3. Smith, *The Wealth of Nations* [1998 edn], book IV, chap. IX, p. 745.
4. Ibid., IV, chap. II, p. 485.
5. Ibid., I, chap. XI, p. 288.
6. Ibid., I, chap. XI, p. 287.
7. Ibid., IV, chap. VII, p. 675.
8. Ibid., IV, chap. VII, p. 693.
9. Ibid., I, chap. XI, p. 288.
10. Ibid., I, chap. X, part 2, p. 148.
11. See Sutherland, *The East India Company*, p. 38.
12. Quoted in David Korten, *When Corporations Rule the World*, London: Earthscan, 1996, p. 56.
13. Smith, *Wealth of Nations*, IV, chap. VII, pp. 681–2.
14. Ibid., I, chap. XI, part 1, p. 170.
15. Ibid., IV, chap. VII, p. 692.
16. *Gentleman's Magazine*, 1767, p. 151.
17. See Jack Greene, *Arenas of Asiatic Plunder*, p. 5.
18. Quoted in Lawrence James, *Raj – The Making and Unmaking of British India*, London: Little, Brown and Company, 1999, p. 47.
19. Quoted in *Gentleman's Magazine*, 13 April 1772, p. 303.
20. Quoted by Harvey, *Clive*, p. 343.
21. Sutherland, *The East India Company*, p. 251.
22. *Annual Register*, April 1773.
23. Harvey, *Clive*, p. 358.

24. Quoted in ibid., p. 372.
25. Quoted from the Ninth Report of the Select Committee, in Marshall, *Writings and Speeches of Burke*, V, p. 200.
26. *Gentleman's Magazine*, 1773, p. 637.
27. Boston handbill, 28 November 1773, quoted in Thom Hartmann, *Unequal Protection: The Rise of Corporate Dominance and the Theft of Human Rights*, Emmaus, PA: Rodale, 2004, p. 58.
28. Benjamin Woods Labaree, *The Boston Tea Party*, New York: Oxford University Press, 1964, p. 73.
29. Hartmann, *Unequal Protection*, p. 56.
30. *Pennsylvania Chronicle*, 15 November 1773, quoted in Leo Huberman, *We, the People*, London: Victor Gollancz, 1940.
31. Hartmann, *Unequal Protection*, pp. 56–7.
32. Jane Anne Morris, 'Corporations for the Seventh Generation', in *Defying Corporations, Defining Democracy*, ed. Dean Ruiz, New York: The Apex Press, 2001, p. 82.
33. Bolts, *Considerations*, p. 213.
34. Petition of Gregore Cojamaul and Johannes Padre Rafael, quoted in Bolts, *Considerations*, p. 109.
35. 'In 2002, £9,700 from 1777 is worth £826,603 using the retail price index.' See <www.eh.net> [last consulted 30/10/05].
36. *Annual Register*, December 1774, pp.170–1; see also *Annual Register*, February 1776, p. 120.
37. Chapter XVI, 'The Armenians in London', in Kuiters, *The British in Bengal*, provides a detailed analysis of these cases.
38. Smith, *Wealth of Nations*, IV, chap. VII, p. 666.
39. Quoted in Ross, *Life of Adam Smith*, p. 353.
40. Smith, *Wealth of Nations*, V, chap. 1, p. 812.
41. Ibid., p. 800.
42. Ibid., art. 1, p. 814.
43. See Richard L. Grossman and Frank T. Adams, *Taking Care of Business* [1993], POCLAD, 2002.
44. John Kenneth Galbraith, *A History of Economics*, London: Hamish Hamilton, 1987, p. 71.
45. Karl Polanyi, *Origins of Our Times – The Great Transformation*, London: Victor Gollancz, 1945, p. 13.
46. Smith, *Wealth of Nations*, IV, chap. V, p. 563.
47. Ibid., p. 564.

7: JUSTICE WILL BE DONE

1. Dutt, *The Economic History of India*, p. 29.
2. Joseph Parkes and Herman Merivale, *Memoirs of Sir Philip Francis*, London: Longman, Green & Co., 1867, II, p. 18.
3. Dutt, *The Economic History of India*, p. 69.
4. Sinha, *From Decline to Destruction*, p. 2.
5. See Inglis, *The Opium War*, p. 26.

6. See Roy Moxham, *The Great Hedge of India*, London: Constable, 2001, p. 45.
7. Thomas Babington Macaulay, *Hastings*, New York: Chautauqua Press, 1886, p. 39.
8. Ibid., p. 40.
9. Bernstein, *Dawning of the Raj*, p. 83.
10. Quoted in Guha, *A Rule of Property for Bengal*, p. 148.
11. Marshall, *The Impeachment of Warren Hastings*, p. 169.
12. Inglis, *The Opium War*, p. 30.
13. See Narahari Kaviraj, *A Peasant Uprising in Bengal – 1783*, New Delhi: People's Publishing House, 1972.
14. Bankim Chandra Chatterji, *Anandamath*, New Delhi: Orient Paperbacks, 2000, p. 40.
15. William Cowper, 'Expostulation', in *The Poetical Works of William Cowper*, Oxford: Oxford University Press, 1913, p. 51.
16. Quoted in *Gentleman's Magazine*, 1782, p. 469.
17. Quoted in Michael Fry, *The Dundas Despotism*, Edinburgh: Edinburgh University Press, 1992, p. 114.
18. Johnstone, November 1782, quoted in *Gentleman's Magazine*, 1782, p. 548.
19. Ninth Report, quoted in Marshall, *Writings and Speeches of Burke*, V, p. 222.
20. Ibid., p. 236.
21. Ibid., p. 269.
22. Ibid., p. 291.
23. Edmund Burke, Speech to Parliament, 1 December 1783.
24. See *History Today*, June 2001, p. 26.
25. *Gentleman's Magazine*, August 1784, p. 702.
26. C.H. Philips, *The East India Company 1784–1834*, Manchester: Manchester University Press, 1940, p. 34.
27. William Atkinson, quoted in Philips, ibid., p. 34, n. 1.
28. Letter to William Eden, 17 May 1784, quoted in Stanley Ayling, *Edmund Burke*, London: Cassell, 1988, p. 162.
29. William Burke, quoted in Ayling, ibid., p. 168.
30. Thomas Babington Macaulay, 'Essay on Clive', 1840.
31. Hastings Evidence, quoted in Marshall, *The Impeachment of Warren Hastings*, p. 108.
32. Quoted in Ayling, *Edmund Burke*, p. 170.
33. Quoted in Fry, *The Dundas Despotism*, p. 122.
34. Richard Brinsley Sheridan, Speech on the Impeachment of Warren Hastings, 7 February 1787.
35. Edmund Burke, Speech on the Impeachment of Warren Hastings, 15–19 February 1788.
36. See Ninth Report, in Marshall, *Writings and Speeches of Edmund Burke*, V, p. 425.
37. John Morley, *Burke*, London: Macmillan, 1892, p. 191.
38. See 'Edmund Burke on the Perils of Empire', in Uday Singh Mehta, *Liberalism and Empire*, Chicago: University of Chicago Press, 1999, pp. 153–89.

39. Quoted in ibid., p. 186.
40. Morley, *Burke*, p. 197.
41. Richard Brinsley Sheridan, *The Rivals*, London: Samuel French, Act V, Scene III, p. 68.
42. See Marshall, *The Impeachment of Warren Hastings*, p. 170.
43. Spear, *A History of India*, vol. 2, p. 95.
44. Ibid.
45. Dutt, *The Economic History of India*, p. 92.
46. Ibid., p. 91.
47. See E.P. Thompson, *Customs in Common*, Harmondsworth: Penguin, 1993.
48. See Guha, *A Rule of Property for Bengal.*
49. John Capper, *The Three Presidencies of India* [1853], New Delhi: Asian Educational Services, 1997, p. 281.
50. Fry, *The Dundas Despotism*, p. 197.
51. Quoted in Philips, *The East India Company*, p. 78.
52. John Evans, *The Gentleman Usher: The Life & Times of George Dempster, 1732–1818*, Barnsley: Pen & Sword, 2005, p. 130.

8: A MERCANTILE SOVEREIGN

1. Inglis, *The Opium War*, p. 89.
2. Quoted in Robert Blake, *Jardine Matheson – Traders of the Far East*, London: Weidenfeld & Nicolson, 1999, p. 46.
3. Quoted in Inglis, *The Opium War*, p. 103.
4. Quoted in Blake, *Jardine Matheson*, p. 96.
5. Hobhouse, *Seeds of Change*, p. xvi.
6. See *The Sunday Times*'s Rich List, 2004.
7. Irfan Habib, *Resistance and Modernisation under Haidar Ali & Tipu Sultan*, New Delhi: Tulika, 1999, p. xl.
8. K.N. Panikkar, *Against Lord and State: Religion and Peasant Uprisings in Malabar, 1836–1921*, New Delhi: Oxford University Press, 1992.
9. K. Ravi Raman, *Bondage in Freedom: Colonial Plantations in Southern India 1797–1947*, Centre for Development Studies, Trivandrum, Working Paper no. 327, March 2002, pp. 8, 32.
10. Wellington's Supplementary Dispatches, quoted in Lawrence James, *The Iron Duke*, London: Weidenfeld & Nicolson, 1992, p. 77.
11. Panikkar, *Against Lord and State*, p. 1.
12. Jac Weller, *Wellington in India*, London: Greenhill Books, 1993, p. 110.
13. Simon Schama, *A History of Britain*, vol. 2: *The British Wars 1603–1776*, London: BBC Books, 2001, p. 496.
14. Quoted in Philips, *The East India Company*, p. 219.
15. Henry Wilson's continuation of Mill's *History of India*, vol. VII, 1858, quoted in Mukherjee, *The Rise and Fall of the East India Company*, p. 404.
16. Syed Muhammed Taifoor, *Glimpses of Old Dhaka*, Dacca: S.M. Perwej, 1956, p. 53.
17. Karl Marx, 'The East India Company – Its History and Results', *New York Daily Tribune*, 11 July 1853.

18. Quoted in Karl Marx, *Capital*, vol. 1, chap, 15, sect. V, 'The Strife Between Workman and Machine'.
19. See Dutt, *The Economic History of India*, pp. 300–1.
20. Huw Bowen, *The Business of Empire*, Cambridge: Cambridge University Press, 2005, p. 235.
21. Hoh-cheung Mui and Lorna H. Mui, *The Management of Monopoly: a Study of the English East India Company's Conduct of its Tea Trade, 1784–1833*, Vancouver: University of British Columbia Press, 1984, p. 127.
22. Quoted in Inglis, *The Opium War*, p. 49.
23. Quoted in ibid., p. 62.
24. Ibid., p. 65.
25. Ibid., p. 92.
26. Quoted in Denys Forrest, *Tea for the British*, London: Chatto & Windus, 1975, p. 96.
27. Quoted in Philips, *The East India Company*, p. 294.
28. James Mill, *History of British India*, II, p. 132.
29. James Mill, 'Affairs of India', *Edinburgh Review*, 16, 1810, quoted in Man To Leung, *James Mill's Utilitarianism and British Imperialism in India*.
30. James Mill, *History of British India*, VI, p. 14.
31. Quoted in Foster, *East India House*, pp. 205, 202.
32. Quoted in Michael Edwardes, *History of India*, London: Thames & Hudson, London, 1961, p. 258.
33. Quoted in ibid., p. 261.
34. Quoted in James Mill, *History of British India*, I, p. xxx.
35. Tirthankar Roy, *The Economic History of India, 1857–1947*, New Delhi: Oxford University Press, 2000, pp. 33–4.
36. Inglis, *The Opium War*, p. 156.
37. W. Travis Hanes and Frank Sanello, *The Opium Wars*, London: Robson Books, London, 2003, p. 157.
38. James, *Raj*, p. 105.
39. Quoted in Karl Marx, 'The Charter of the East India Company', *New York Daily Tribune*, 9 June 1853.
40. Karl Marx, 'The Government of India', *New York Daily Tribune*, 20 July 1853.
41. Ibid.
42. Karl Marx, 'The Future Results of British Rule in India', *New York Daily Tribune*, 8 August 1853.
43. Karl Marx, 'The British Rule in India', *New York Daily Tribune*, 25 June 1853.
44. Marx, 'Future Results of British Rule'.
45. Sir George Birdwood, *Report on the Old Records of the India Office*, London, 1891.
46. Quoted in M. Moir, D. Peers and Lynn Zastoupil, *John Stuart Mill's Encounter with India*, Toronto: University of Toronto Press, 1999, p. 4.
47. John Stuart Mill, *Representative Government*, Oxford: Oxford University Press, 1940 [1861], p. 175.
48. See Francis Wheen, *Marx*, London: Fourth Estate, 2000, p. 188.
49. Edward Said, *Culture and Imperialism*, London: Chatto & Windus, 1993, p. 97.

50. See, for example, Stanley Kurtz, 'Democratic Imperialism: A Blueprint', *Policy Review*, no. 118, April/May 2003.
51. Karl Marx, 'Revolution in China and in Europe', *New York Daily Tribune*, 14 June 1853.
52. Karl Marx, 'Trade or Opium?', *New York Daily Tribune*, 20 September 1858.
53. Karl Marx, 'Free Trade and Monopoly', *New York Daily Tribune*, 25 September 1858.
54. *Gentleman's Magazine*, 30 March 1813, p. 569.
55. Quoted in Karl Marx, 'The Indian Revolt', *New York Daily Tribune*, 16 September 1857.
56. Charles Dickens, quoted in James, *Raj*, p. 283.
57. Karl Marx, 'The Indian Bill', *New York Daily Tribune*, 24 July 1858.
58. 'In 2002, £12,000,000 from 1873 is worth £650,143,844 using the retail price index.' See <www.eh.net> [last consulted 30/10/05].
59. Francois Crouzet, *The Victorian Economy*, London: Methuen, 1982, p. 353.
60. Dutt, *The Economic History of India*, p. 399.

9: UNFINISHED BUSINESS

1. Harvey, *Clive*, p. 368.
2. Jeremy Bentham, *An Introduction to the Principles of Morals and Legislation*, in *Utilitarianism*, London: Fount Paperbacks, 1979, p. 46.
3. *Annual Register*, 10 May 1773.
4. See Russell Sparkes, *From Mortmain to Adam Smith: Historical Insights on the Problem of Corporate Social Responsibility*, London, 2005.
5. See P.B. Buchan, 'Origins of the Knowledge Based Corporation', EBHA Conference, July 2001.
6. Philip Francis, letter to William Ellis, January 1777, quoted in Ranajit Guha, *A Rule of Property for Bengal*, p. 93.
7. Court of Directors, 8 December 1732, quoted in Chaudhury, *From Prosperity to Decline*, p. 37.
8. Sinha, quoted in Furber, 'Rival Empires of Trade', p. 177; and Datta, *Society, Economy and the Market*, p. 357.
9. Dutt, *The Economic History of India*, p. 400.
10. 'In 2002, £723,997,917 0s 0d from 1838 is worth £43,231,809,693.82 using the retail price index.' See <www.eh.net> [last consulted 31/10/05].
11. Alexander Dow, *History of Hindostan*, vol. III, quoted in Guha, *A Rule of Property for Bengal*, pp. 31–2.
12. Brooks Adams, *The Law of Civilisation and Decay* [1895], quoted in Palme Dutt, *India Today*, p. 119.
13. Prakash, *European Commercial Enterprise in Pre-Colonial India*, p. 349.
14. Utsa Patnaik, 'New Estimates of 18th Century British Trade and Their Relation to Transfers from Tropical Colonies', in K.N. Panikkar, Terence J. Byres and Utsa Patnaik, *The Making of History*, London: Anthem South Asian Studies, 2002. See Table B.5, p. 397.
15. Ibid., Table 5, p. 389.

16. Nehru, *The Discovery of India*, p. 247.
17. Maddison, *The World Economy*, p. 112.
18. Quoted in Cornelius Walford, 'Famine through History', p. 519.
19. Edmund Burke, Speech on the Impeachment of Warren Hastings, February 1788.
20. Marjorie Kelly, *The Divine Right of Capital*, San Francisco: Berrett-Koelher, 2001, p. 4.
21. Russell Sparkes, 'Through a Glass Darkly – Some Thoughts on the Ethics of Investment', The Beckley Lecture, 1998.
22. See <www.corporate-responsibility.org>.
23. See Nick Robins, 'Downsizing the Corporation', in *Return to Scale*, London: New Economics Foundation, 2003.
24. Quoted in Ian Hargreaves, 'The threat to democracy', *Financial Times*, 21 May 2002.
25. Oko-Institut e.V., 'Power Generation Market Concentration in Europe 1996–2000. An empirical analysis', Freiburg, May 2002, <www.oeko.de>.
26. Bill Vorley, *Food Inc.– Corporate concentration from farm to consumer,* London: UK Food Group, 2003.
27. Jean Ziegler, 'The Right to Food', Report submitted by the Special Rapporteur, Commission on Human Rights, UN Economic and Social Council, 9 February 2004.
28. Mark Townsend, 'Tesco in row over foreign workers', *Observer*, 10 April 2005.
29. Quoted in John Christensen and Richard Murphy, 'The Social Irresponsibility of Corporate Tax Avoidance', *Development Journal*, vol. 47, no. 3, 2004.
30. Galbraith, *A History of Economics*, p. 163.
31. John Kenneth Galbraith and Nicole Salinger, *Almost Everyone's Guide to Economics*, Harmondsworth: Penguin, 1981, p. 53.
32. ATCA specified that 'district courts shall have original jurisdiction of any civil action made by an alien, for a tort only, committed in violation of the law of nations or a treaty of the United States'.
33. See <www.earthrights.org>.
34. Nehru, *The Discovery of India*, p. 452.
35. Edward Thompson, *The Other Side of the Medal*, London: The Hogarth Press, 1925, p. 131.
36. See <www.museumofthecorporation.org/homePage.htm>.
37. Ben Okri, quoted in Bhiku Parekh, *The Future of Multi-Ethnic Britain*, London: The Runnymede Trust, 2000, p. 103.
38. Edmund Burke, *Correspondence*, quoted in Uday Singh Mehta, *Liberalisation and Empire*, p. 169.

Select Bibliography

Albom, Timothy, *Conceiving Companies*, London: Routledge, 1998

Ali, Shahid, *The Half-Inch Himalayas*, Middletown: Wesleyan University Press, 1987.

Allen, Robert J. Allen, ed., *Addison and Steele*, Orlando: Rinehart, 1974

Amnesty International, *Clouds of Injustice – Bhopal disaster 20 years on*, London: Amnesty International Publications, 2004

Baron, Archie, *An Indian Affair*, London: Channel 4 Books, 2001

Bentham, Jeremy, *An Introduction to the Principles of Morals and Legislation*, in *Utilitarianism*, London: Fount Paperbacks, 1979

Bernstein, Jeremy, *Dawning of the Raj: The Life and Trials of Warren Hastings*, London: Aurum Press, 2000

Blake, Robert, *Jardine Matheson – Traders of the Far East*, London: Weidenfeld & Nicolson, 1999

Bolts, William, *Considerations on Indian Affairs*, London [1772], in *The East India Company: 1600–1858*, ed. Patrick Tuck, London: Routledge, 1998

Bowen, Huw, *Revenue and Reform*, Cambridge: Cambridge University Press, 1991

—— *The Business of Empire*, Cambridge: Cambridge University Press, 2005

Bowen, Huw, Margarette Lincoln and Nigel Rigby (eds), *The Worlds of the East India Company*, Woodbridge: Boydell, 2002

Braudel, Fernand, *Civilization and Capitalism*, vol. 2: *The Wheels of Commerce*, London: Collins, 1982

—— *Civilization and Capitalism*, vol. 3: *The Perspective of the World*, London: Collins, 1984

Campbell, Olwen, *Thomas Love Peacock*, London: Arthur Barker, 1953

Capper, John, *The Three Presidencies of India*, New Delhi: Asian Educational Services, 1997 [1853]

Chancellor, Edward, *Devil Take the Hindmost*, London: Macmillan, 1999

Chatterji, Bankim Chandra, *Anandamath*, New Delhi: Orient Paperbacks, 2000 [1882]

Chaudhuri, Kirti N., *The Trading World of Asia and the East India Company 1660–1760*, Cambridge: Cambridge University Press, 1978

Chaudhury, Sushil, *From Prosperity to Decline: 18th Century Bengal*, New Delhi: Manohar, 1999

—— *The Prelude to Empire: Plassey Revolution of 1757*, New Delhi: Manohar, 2000

Crouzet, François, *The Victorian Economy*, London: Methuen, 1982

Dalrymple, William, *White Mughals*, London: HarperCollins, 2003

Das, Gurcharan, *India Unbound*, New Delhi: Penguin India, 2002

Datta, Rajat, *Society, Economy and the Market: Commercialisation in Rural Bengal c.1760–1800*, New Delhi: Manohar, 2000

Davis, Mike, *Late Victorian Holocausts*, London: Verso, 2002

Dutt, Romesh Chunder, *The Economic History of India under Early British Rule (1757–1837)*, London: Kegan Paul, Trench, Trubner & Co, 1908

Dutta, Krishna, *Calcutta*, Northampton: Interlink Books, 2003
Evans, John, *The Gentleman Usher: the Life & Times of George Dempster, 17321818*, Barnsley: Pen & Sword, 2005
Farrington, Antony, *Trading Places*, London: The British Library, 2002
Forrest, Denys, *Tea for the British*, London: Chatto & Windus, 1975
Foster, William, *Catalogue of Paintings, Statues etc. in the India Office*, London, 1921
—— *The East India House*, London, 1924
Fry, Michael, *The Dundas Despotism*, Edinburgh: Edinburgh University Press, 1992
Furber, Holden, *John Company at Work: a Study of European Expansion in the Late Eighteenth Century*, New York: Octagon, 1970
—— 'Rival Empires of Trade 1600–1800', in *Maritime India*, New Delhi: Oxford University Press, 2004 [1976]
Galbraith, John Kenneth, *A History of Economics*, London: Hamish Hamilton, 1987
Galbraith, John Kenneth and Nicole Salinger, *Almost Everyone's Guide to Economics*, Harmondsworth: Penguin, 1981
Gardner, Brian, *East India Company*, London: Rupert Hart-Davis, 1971
Griffiths, Percival, *A Licence to Trade*, London: Ernest Benn, 1974
Guha, Ranajit, *A Rule of Property for Bengal*, New Delhi: Orient Longman, 1981
Habib, Irfan, *Resistance and Modernisation under Haidar Ali & Tipu Sultan*, New Delhi: Tulika, 1999
Hall, Richard, *Empires of the Monsoon*, London: HarperCollins, 1996
Hanes, W. Travis and Frank Sanello, *The Opium Wars*, London: Robson Books, 2003
Harvey, Harvey, *Clive: Life and Death of a British Emperor*, London: Hodder & Stoughton, 1998
Heilbroner, Robert, *The Worldly Philosophers*, New York: Touchstone, 1999
Hobhouse, Henry, *Seeds of Change: Six Plants that Transformed Mankind*, London: Papermac, 1999
Huberman, Leo, *We, the People*, London: Victor Gollancz, 1940
Hunting, Penelope, *Cutlers Gardens*, London: Standard Life, 1984
Inglis, Brian, *The Opium War*, London: Hodder & Stoughton, 1976
Jacobs, Els M., *In Pursuit of Pepper and Tea, The Story of the Dutch East India Company*, Amsterdam: Netherlands Maritime Museum, 1991
James, Lawrence, *The Iron Duke*, London: Weidenfeld & Nicolson, 1992
—— *Raj – The Making and Unmaking of British India*, London: Little, Brown & Company, 1999
Jeeninga, Willke, *The East Indies House and St Jorishof*, Utrecht: Wanders Uitgevers, 1995
Kaviraj, Narahari, *A Peasant Uprising in Bengal – 1783*, New Delhi: People's Publishing House, 1972
Keay, John, *The Honourable Company*, London: HarperCollins, 1993
Kelly, Marjorie, *The Divine Right of Capital*, San Francisco: Berrett-Koelher, 2001
Kindleberger, Charles, *Manias, Panics and Crashes – A History of Financial Crises*, New York: John Wiley & Sons, 2000

Korten, David, *When Corporations Rule the World*, London: Earthscan, 1996
Kuiters, Willem, *The British in Bengal 1756–1773*, Paris: Les Indes Savantes, 2002
Landes, David, *The Wealth and Poverty of Nations*, London: Little, Brown & Company, 1998
Lawson, Philip, *The East India Company*, London: Longman, 1993
Litvin, Daniel, *Empires of Profit: Commerce, Conquest and Corporate Responsibility*, London: Texere, 2003
Logan, William, *Malabar Manual*, New Delhi: Asian Educational Services, 2000 [1887]
Macaulay, Thomas Babington, 'Essay on Lord Clive', January 1840
—— *Hastings*, New York: Chautauqua Press, 1886 [1841]
—— *History of England from the Accession of James II*, London, 1848–60
—— *A History of England in the 18th Century* [1849], London: Folio Society, 1980
Maddison, Angus, *The World Economy – A Millennial Perspective*, Paris: OECD, 2001
Mahomet, Dean, *The Travels of Dean Mahomet* [1794], ed. Michael H. Fraser, Berkeley: University of California Press, 1997
Marshall, P.J., *The Impeachment of Warren Hastings*, Oxford: Oxford University Press, 1965
—— *Problems of Empire: Britain and India 1757–1813*, London: George Allen & Unwin, 1968
—— *East Indian Fortunes: the British in Bengal in the Eighteenth Century*, Oxford: Clarendon Press, 1976
—— ed., *Writings and Speeches of Edmund Burke*, vol. V, Oxford: Clarendon Press, 1981
—— *Bengal: the British Bridgehead: Eastern India 1740–1828*, Cambridge: Cambridge University Press, 1987
Mason, Philip, *The Men Who Ruled India*, London: Jonathan Cape, 1985
Mehta, Uday Singh, *Liberalism and Empire*, Chicago: University of Chicago Press, 1999
Mickelthwait, John and Adrian Wooldridge, *The Company: A Short History of a Revolutionary Idea*, London: Weidenfeld & Nicolson, 2003
Mill, James, *History of British India* [1858 edition, with notes and continuation by Horace Hayman-Wilson], 10 vols, London: Routledge/Thoemes Press, 1997
Milton, Giles, *Nathaniel's Nutmeg*, London: Hodder & Stoughton, 1999
Mitra, Debendra, *The Cotton Weavers of Bengal 1757–1833*, Calcutta: Firma KLM, 1978
Moir, M., D. Peers and Lynn Zastoupil, *John Stuart Mill's Encounter with India*, Toronto: University of Toronto Press, 1999
Morley, John, *Burke*, London: Macmillan, 1892
Morris, Jane Anne, 'Corporations for the Seventh Generation', in *Defying Corporations, Defining Democracy*, ed. Dean Ruiz, New York: The Apex Press, 2001
Moxham, Roy, *The Great Hedge of India*, London: Constable, 2001

Mui, Hoh-cheung and Lorna H. Mui, *The Management of Monopoly: a Study of the English East India Company's Conduct of its Tea Trade, 1784–1833*, Vancouver: University of British Columbia Press, 1984

Mukherjee, Ramkrishna, *The Rise and Fall of the East India Company*, New York: Monthly Review Press, 1974

Nehru, Jawaharlal, *The Discovery of India*, London: Meridian Books, 1946

Palme Dutt, R., *India Today*, London: Victor Gollancz, 1940

Panikkar, K.N., *Against Lord and State: Religion and Peasant Uprisings in Malabar, 1836–1921*, New Delhi: Oxford University Press, 1992

Panikkar, K.N., Terence J. Byres and Utsa Patnaik, eds, *The Making of History*, London: Anthem South Asian Studies, 2002

Parkes, Joseph and Herman Merivale, *Memoirs of Sir Philip Francis*, London: Longman, Green & Co., 1867

Parthasarathi, Prasannan, *The Transition to a Colonial Economy: Weavers, Merchants and Kings in South India, 1720–1800*, Cambridge: Cambridge University Press, 2001

Partnoy, Frank, *Infectious Greed, How Deceit and Risk Corrupted the Financial Markets*, London: Profile Books, 2004

Philips, C.H., *The East India Company 1784–1834*, Manchester: Manchester University Press, 1940

Plumb, J.H., *England in the 18th Century*, Harmondsworth: Penguin, 1990

Polanyi, Karl, *Origins of Our Times – The Great Transformation*, London: Victor Gollancz, 1945

Prakash, Om, *European Commercial Enterprise in Pre-Colonial India*, New Delhi: Cambridge University Press, 2000

Ross, Ian Simpson, *The Life of Adam Smith*, Oxford: Clarendon Press, 1995

Roy, Arundhati, *The Algebra of Infinite Justice*, London: Flamingo, 2002

Roy, Tirthankar, *The Economic History of India, 1857–1947*, New Delhi: Oxford University Press, 2000

Said, Edward, *Culture and Imperialism*, London: Chatto & Windus, 1993

—— *Orientalism*, Harmondsworth: Penguin, 2003

Sampson, Anthony, *Company Man: The Rise and Fall of Corporate Life*, London: HarperCollins, London, 1996

Schama, Simon, *A History of Britain*, vol. 2: *The British Wars 1603–1776*, London: BBC Books, 2001

Sen, Amartya, *Poverty and Famines: An Essay on Entitlement and Deprivation*, Oxford: Oxford University Press, 1997

Sen, Sudipta, *Empire of Free Trade: the East India Company and Making of the Colonial Marketplace*, Philadelphia: University of Pennsylvania Press, 1998

Sheridan, Richard Brinsley, *The Rivals*, London: Samuel French

Sinha, Chandra Prakash N., *From Decline to Destruction: Agriculture in Bihar during Early British Rule*, New Delhi: Manohar, 1997

Smith, Adam, *Inquiry into the Wealth of Nations*, New York: The Modern Library, 1994 [1776]

Spear, Percival, *A History of India*, vol. 2, Harmondsworth: Penguin, 1968

Sutherland, Lucy, *The East India Company in Eighteenth-Century Politics*, Oxford: Clarendon Press, 1952

Taifoor, Syed Muhammed, *Glimpses of Old Dhaka*, Dacca: S.M. Perwej, 1956

Thompson, Edward, *The Other Side of the Medal*, London: The Hogarth Press, 1925

Thompson, E.P., *Customs in Common*, Harmondsworth: Penguin, 1993

Verelst, Harry, *A View on the Rise, Progress and Present State of the English Government in Bengal*, London [1772], in *The East India Company: 1600–1858*, ed. Patrick Tuck, London: Routledge, 1998

Visram, Rozina, *Asians in Britain: 400 Years of History*, London: Pluto Press, 2002

Waller, Maureen, *1700: Scenes from London Life*, London: Hodder & Stoughton, 2000

Weller, Jac, *Wellington in India*, London: Greenhill Books, 1993

Weitzman, Sophia, *Warren Hastings & Philip Francis*, Manchester: Manchester University Press, 1929

Wheen, Francis , *Marx*, London: Fourth Estate, 2000

Wild, Antony, *The East India Company: Trade and Conquest from 1600*, London: HarperCollins, 1999

Wills, John E., *1688 – A Global History*, London: Granta, 2002

Zandvliet, Kees, *The Dutch Encounter with Asia, 1600–1650*, Amsterdam: Rijksmuseum, 2002

Index

Compiled by Sue Carlton

Adams, Brooks 178
Addison, Joseph 56
Agra 44, 146
Ahmadnagar Fort 12, 187
Ahmedabad 44, 54
Aldrich, William 43
Ali, Karim 92
Ali, Shahid 78
Alien Tort Claims Act (ACTA) (1789) 186–7
Alinagar, Treaty of (1757) 70
Alipur 117
Alivardi Khan 64, 67, 68, 84
Allahabad 120
Allborn, Timothy 34
Ambon (Amboina) 44
America
  Declaration of Independence 113
  and import duties 109–11
  see also United States
American War of Independence (1775–83) 5, 120, 139
Amir Chand 65, 70–1, 71, 72, 75, 122, 170
Anjarakandi spice plantation 144–5
antitrust laws 185
Arcot
  debt 130, 132
  siege 168, 170
Armenian merchants 112
  see also Cojamaul; Estephan; Philip; Rafael
atonement 188
Aungier, Gerald 29
Aurangzeb (Mughal emperor) 49–50, 54, 61, 66
Aurora 105
Awadh 120, 123, 133, 134, 157, 163
Ayr Bank (Douglas, Heron & Co) 97, 99

Bagehot, Walter 98
Bahadur Shah (Mughal emperor) 163
Baiganbari 73
banians 58
Bank of England 8
Bantam 32, 43, 44
Barre, Israel 89
Basra 6
Batavia (Jakarta) 40
BBC, chartered company 27
Becher, Richard 68, 91
Beckford, William 103
Bell, Robert 44–5
Belvedere House 117, 121, 140
Benfield, Paul 132
Bengal 7, 49, 54, 57, 58–80, 175–6
  breakdown of Mughal authority 66, 176
  commercial plunder of 74, 75–6, 94–5, 127, 178
  famine 4, 90–4, 95, 96, 102, 116, 180
  textiles 11, 55–6, 61–3, 81
  treasury looted 3, 13, 75
  wealth 61–6
  weavers 76–8, 148–9
Bengal Bubble 87–90, 175
Bengal Warehouse 81–2
Benn, John 122
Bentham, Jeremy 172
Bentinck, William 149, 156
Bernstein, Jeremy 122
Betsy 122, 151
Bhagavad Gita 17
Bhopal disaster 37–8
Bihar 142, 150, 167, 176
Bijapur 49
Birbhum 93
'black hole' incident 69, 72, 106
Blackwall docks 4, 19–20, 154
Boger, Deeble 166
Bohun, Thomas 53

Bolts, William 58, 78, 94, 96, 111–12
Bombay (Mumbai) 6, 32, 45, 46, 50
Boston Evening Post 110–11
Boston Tea Party 5, 111
Bourke, John 118
Bowen, Huw 85, 177
Braudel, Fernand 60
British civil wars (1640–47) 46
British Library 166
British Raj 6, 12, 165, 167
Brown, Murdoch 145
Brunswick Basin 20
Bubble Act (1720) 29, 56, 114
  repeal of 174
Buckingham, James Silk 153
Budhmal, Rajah 93
Burgoyne, John 105–6, 132
Burke, Edmund 89–90, 116, 125, 126–30, 132, 159, 176–7, 190
  and drain of wealth 5, 177, 178
  impeachment of Hastings 119, 132–6, 139, 179–80, 186
Burke, Richard 89–90
Burke, William 90, 127
Burma 187
Bush Administration 187
Buxar, battle of (1764) 74

Calcutta (Kolkata) 3, 6, 10–12, 32, 50, 55
  capture of (1756) 59, 68–70
  statue of Clive 170
calico 55–6, 62, 146–7
Calicut (Kozikhode) 41, 42
Canton (Guangzhou) 3, 6, 150, 151, 157
Capper, John 138
Carey, Maria 162
Carnatic, Haidar Ali's invasion of 123, 125
Catherine of Braganza 45
Chandernagore 70, 74
Charles II 45, 46, 48
Charnock, Job 11, 12, 49–50
Charter Act (1793) 138
Charter Act (1813) 147
Charter Act (1833) 154, 166
chartered companies 23, 27, 29, 50–1, 173–4
  see also East India Company, as chartered company; Hudson Bay Company; Levant Company; Muscovy Company; Virginia Company
Chattopadhyaya, Bankim Chandra 123
Chaudhuri, K.N. 22
Chesney, George 180
Chevron 186
Child, Sir Josiah 47–50, 51–2, 54–5, 177
China
  and opium imports 6, 7, 16, 17, 141–3, 150–3, 157–8, 161–2, 167, 176
  and tea trade 150
Christianity, forced conversion to 162, 163
Churchill, Caryl 103
Clarke, Richard 18
Clavering, General John 121, 122
Clive, Robert 34, 66, 67–8, 79–80, 103, 176–7, 179, 180
  and corruption 4, 72–3, 106–7, 168
  and *diwani* rights 75–6, 80, 85–6, 102, 170
  insider trading 85–6
  jagir 84–5
  and Nabakrishna 59
  and private trade 74, 86, 95
  properties of 67, 170
  rehabilitating memory of 168–72
  self-interest 86–7
  statues of 8, 168–71, 188
  takeover of Bengal 2–3, 13, 60, 69–72, 170, 176
  treaty with Amir Chand 71, 72, 122, 170
Co-Hong 150
Coen, Jan Pieterszoon 40, 48
Cojamaul, Gregore 112, 186, 187
Coleridge, Samuel Taylor 9
Columbus, Christopher 41
Commutation Act (1784) 149
Compagnie des Indes 2, 65, 74

Compagnie van Verre 39
Company Act (1862) 174
Company of Royal Adventurers 23
competition 39, 56, 65, 101, 153, 184
Conrad, Joseph 164
Cooke, Sir Thomas 51–2
Coote, Eyre 172
Cornwallis, Charles, 1st Marquis 9, 136–8, 143
Coromandel 44, 46, 54, 63
Corporate Responsibility (CORE) coalition 183
corporations
  accountability 129, 133–4, 179–81, 186–7
  corporate abuse 37–8, 186–7
  corporate design 34–8, 182, 190
  corporate over-stretch 38, 115
  corporate responsibility 182–3
  duty to shareholders 182
  and ethics 181–3
  mergers and acquisitions 184
  and monopoly powers 101–2, 114, 184
  Smith's opposition to 100–1, 114–16, 174–5, 185
Corpus Christi College 166
cotton 46, 61–3, 156
  exports from Britain to India 147, 148–9, 156
Courteen Association 45–6
Cowper, William 124
Cromwell, Oliver 46
Crosby Hall 8
Curzon, George, 1st Marquess of Kedleston 168–70

Dabhol power project 13
Dalrymple, William 15
Das, Gurcharan 13
dastaks (duty-free passes) 64, 68, 69, 70, 73, 74
Datta, Rajat 93, 178
Daud, Justice 13
Debates in the Asiatic Assembly 103
Defoe, Daniel 48, 55–6
Delhi (Shahjahanabad) 57, 146, 163
Dempster, George 139–40
Dhaka 62–3, 66
  earthquake (1812) 148
Dickens, Charles 164
Dinajpur 123
Disraeli, Benjamin 142
Dividend Bill (1767) 104
diwani rights 17, 81, 91, 104, 137, 176
  and Clive's acquisition of 75–6, 80, 102, 170
  and East India Company share prices 85–6, 87
Dobree, Joseph 166
Dow, Alexander 178
Drake, Roger 68
Dundas, Henry 125–6, 131, 133, 136, 138–9, 154
Dupleix, Joseph François 65, 67
Dutch United East India Company (VOC) 1–2, 30, 32, 39–40, 46, 55, 56–7, 74–5, 175
Dutt, Romesh Chunder 12, 167

Earl of Abergavenny 9
East India Company
  and armed force 4, 28–9, 45, 49–50, 66, 125–6, 143–6, 157, 170
  as chartered company 5, 23, 27–9, 43, 104, 127, 128, 180
    charter renewal 48, 51, 103, 125, 147, 158–62
  Company archives 166
  and corporate rule 175–7
  corruption 4, 25, 55, 94, 123, 164
    bribery 50, 51–2, 59–60, 83–5, 151, 180
  Council in-fighting 117–19, 121–2, 124
  Court of Directors 30–2
  differences from modern corporations 27–9
  dissolution of 6, 166–7
  and financial crisis 4, 97, 100, 175
  governance structure 23–4, 30–3
  and government loans 106, 107, 124, 130–1, 147

historical significance of 5–6, 7, 10, 18
joint stock model 23–5, 29, 43, 46, 57, 174–5
lack of monuments to 10
and local Asian merchants 64–5
London warehouses 81–3, 147, 189
management failure 94–5, 96, 101, 105, 107, 128–9
merger of Old and New companies 54
as model for multinational companies 5, 22, 25, 29–33, 34, 35, 174, 185, 188
monopoly powers 28, 35–6, 57, 101–2, 114, 138, 146–8, 151, 154, 174, 180
nationalisation of 6, 164–5, 167
need to re-examine 188–90
New Company 50–1, 53–4, 56–7
parliamentary investigation of 105–6
perceptions of 16–18, 172–3
and private trade 33, 74, 83, 86, 95, 119, 176, 177
romantic reinterpretations of 14–16
semi-sovereign rights 28–9
share prices 4, 5, 24–5, 26, 56, 65, 82–3, 87–90, 96, 97–8, 153
shareholders
in conflict 84–5
disenfranchised 107
role of 30–1, 47
shift in strategy 47–50
size of operations 5–6
and speculation 4, 36–7, 82, 87–90, 96
and spice trade 42–4, 144–5
and state intervention 25, 103–5, 107–8, 154
tax collection 137–8, 144, 159, 167
see also diwani rights
East India Company Syndrome 13–14
East India Docks 19–22
East India House, Leadenhall Street 4, 7–10, 172
attacked by weavers 53
and bailiffs 130
demolition of 174
painting and sculpture 1–2, 8–9
sold off 166
East India Stock Redemption Act (1874) 166
'East Indiamen' ships 19, 20, 27
see also Aurora; *Betsy*; *Earl of Abergavenny*; *Nonsuch*; *Valentine*
The East Offering Her Riches to Britannia (Spiridione Roma) 1, 4, 5, 10
Eddington, Rod 14–15
Elizabeth I 8, 42–3
Ellenborough, Edward Law, 1st earl of 158
Encounters exhibition, Victoria and Albert Museum 189
Enron 13, 37
Estado do India 42
Estephan, Wuscan 112
Evelyn, John 54–5
Exxon 186

famine 4, 90–4, 95, 96, 102, 116, 180
Farrukhsiyar (Mughal emperor) 54, 64
Firebrace, Sir Basil 52, 54
firmans (imperial decrees) 54, 64, 175–6
Foote, Samuel 103
Fordyce, Alexander 96–7
Fort St David 68
Fort St George 45
Fort William 11, 68, 69
Fox, Charles James 126, 128, 129–30, 139, 140
France
Anglo-French rivalry 67–8, 139, 143–4
Compagnie des Indes 2, 65, 74
Francis, Philip ('Junius') 77, 133, 137, 138–9, 139, 174
feud with Hastings 117–19, 121–2
portrait 140

free trade 35, 45, 51, 53–4, 114, 115–16, 142, 153, 154
Freeport 186
Friedman, Thomas 29
Fry, William Storr 157

Galbraith, John Kenneth 115, 185
Gama, Vasco da 41–2
Gent, Christopher 73
Gentleman's Magazine 17, 38, 91–2, 96, 102, 108
George III 9, 117, 124, 129–30, 135, 168
Ghalib, Asadullah Khan 18
Girdler's Carpet 44–5
Gladstone, William 158
globalisation 37, 56, 172, 174, 184, 185
Glorious Revolution 1688 24–5, 50, 54, 67, 126
Goa 42, 45
Gombroon (Bandar Abbas) 6
Government House, Calcutta 11
The Governor and Company of Merchants of London Trading to the East Indies 8
  see also East India Company
Great Rebellion (Indian Mutiny) (1857–58) 6, 162–5
Greeley, Horace 159
Guha, Ranajit 138
Gujarat 44, 46, 50, 54, 63, 146
Gulbenkian, Calouste 71

Harvey, Robert 72
Hastings, Warren 5, 17–18, 89, 94, 105, 108, 163
  and Bengal famine 92–3
  and bribery 59–60
  feud with Francis 117–19, 121–2
  financial management 119–21, 122–4, 128
  impeachment 18, 59, 120, 124, 132–6, 139, 179–80
  monument to 172
  and opium trade 122, 151, 167
  portrait 140
Havel, Vaclav 184
Hawkins, William 44
Hickey, Thomas 58
Hindu civilisation 155, 156, 159–60
Hong Kong 158
Hormuz 45
Hornby, William 126
Hossain, Hameeda 77
Hudson Bay Company 23, 174
Hume, David 99
Hume, Joseph 146
Hunet, Leigh 9
Hyder Ali 82, 123, 124, 125, 126, 144
Hyderabad 49, 54, 57, 68, 157

Impey, Elijah 122
India
  British attitudes to 156, 160, 161
  drain of wealth 5, 177–9
  and French-British rivalry 67–8, 139, 143–4
  impact of East India Company 6, 10–14, 17
  independence 12, 187–8
  and multinational companies 13–14
  and textiles 46–7, 55–6, 61–3, 81, 146–9, 156, 160
India Act (1784) 136, 143, 146, 157, 177
India Act (1858) 6
India Bill (1783) 129–30, 140, 180
India Office 168
An Indian Affair (TV documentary series) 15
Indian Mutiny *see* Great Rebellion (1857–58)
Indian sailors 20
Indonesia 28, 32, 39, 43
Industrial Revolution, financing of 178
Inglis, Brian 151
international law 37–8, 186–7
investment, socially responsible 182–3
invisible hand 99, 115
Iraq, invasion of (2003) 181
Isaacz, Pieter 1–2

Jackson, Randle 146

Jagat Seths 65, 70, 73
Jahangir (Mughal emperor) 28, 44
James II 49, 50
James, Robert 38
James, Sir William 129
Japan 6
Jardine Matheson 141–4, 157, 167
Jardine, William 141–2
Jefferson, Thomas 115
Jenkinson, Charles 95
Jhansi 157, 163
Johnson, Dr Samuel 107
Joint Stock Act (1844) 174
joint stock companies 114
  ban on 29
  and collective interest 83
  see also East India Company, joint stock model
Jones, William 17, 155
'Junius' 102, 117–18
  see also Francis, Philip

Kanpur (Cawnpore) 163
Karadzic, Radovan 186
Kelly, Marjorie 181
Keswick family 143
Kora 120
Kurichiar tribals 145

Lamb, Charles 9, 20
lascars (Indian sailors) 20
laudanum 150
Lawrence, Stringer 8–9
Legal Quays 19
Lemon, John and Elizabeth 20
Levant Company 23, 43, 174
Lewis, George Cornewall 164
Lin Tse-hsu 157, 188
List, Friedrich 149
London Stock Exchange 24
Lonsdale, James 140

Macaulay, Thomas Babington 22, 50, 87, 153–4
  on Child 47
  on Clive 72, 73, 74, 168
  contempt for India 156, 190
  on impeachment of Hastings 120–1, 132
Mackenzie, John 120
Macrabie, Alexander 121
Madras (Chennai) 6, 32, 45, 46, 47, 68, 79
Mahomet, Dean 93–4
Malabar 144, 145
Malabar itch 145
Malaysia 15
Malda 93
Malthus, Thomas 116
Mannesmann 73
Maratha raids 67, 68, 79
Marathas 146, 151
Marcos, Ferdinand 186
Martin, Montgomery 178
Marx, Karl 38, 134, 159–60, 161, 165, 176–7
Mary II 50
Masefield, John 82, 98
Masulipatam 44
Matheson, James 141, 142, 158
Meerut 163
Meredith, William 106
Metrojava department store 15
Mill, James 9, 76, 134, 154–6, 160, 161
Mill, James Bentham 9
Mill, John Grote 9
Mill, John Stuart 9, 20, 134, 160–1, 164, 166
Mir Jafar 3, 12, 70, 71, 73, 74, 75, 84, 117
Mir Kasim 73, 74, 75, 137
Moluccas 44
Monson, George 121
Morley, John 134, 168
Morris, Jane Anne 111
Mowbray, John 58
Mughal system
  breakdown of 66, 176
  and famines 90–2
multinational companies 13–14
  and East India Company model 5, 22, 25, 29–33, 34, 35, 174, 185, 188
Munro, Thomas 156
Murhid Quli 66
Murshidabad 59, 66, 71
Muscovy Company 23

Museum of the Corporation 188–9
muslin 3, 62
Mysore 9, 79

Nabakrishna Deb, Rajah 58–61
Nadir Shah 57
Nagpur 157
Najim-ud-Daula 74, 85
Nandakumar, Rajah 121–2, 124, 136
Nanking, Treaty of (1842) 158, 162
Napier, Sir Charles 158
Napoleonic War 1815 25
National Portrait Gallery 140
Nehru, Jawaharlal 12–13, 17, 179, 187
New York Daily Tribune 159
Nonsuch 122, 151
Noorthouck, James 9
Norfolk, Lawrence 7–8
North, Frederick, Lord 106, 122, 127
  coalition with Fox 126, 128, 129–30
  Regulating Act 107–8
  and renewal of East India Company charter 125
  Tea Act 108, 110–11

Okri, Ben 189
Oostindisch Huis 39
Opium Society 75
opium trade 122, 156
  and China 6, 7, 16, 17, 141–3, 150–3, 157–8, 161–2, 167, 176
  East India Company monopoly 119–20, 155
  Malwa opium 151–2
  Patna Group 6, 75, 119
  VOC and 75
Opium Wars 157–8, 161–2, 174
Orme, Robert 66
Osborne, Thomas 52
Overend & Gurney 174

Pahareas 93–4
Paine, Tom 134
Papillon, Thomas 47, 49, 51
Parthasarathi, Prasannan 77
Patna Group of English Traders 75
Patnaik, Utsa 179
Pazhassi Rajah 145
Peacock, Thomas Love 9
Peking, Convention of 167
Penang 6
pepper 41, 42–3
Philip, Melcomb 112
piracy 43
Pitt, William, the Elder 31, 75, 102, 104, 168
Pitt, William, the Younger 125, 130–3, 136, 139, 149
Plassey (Palashi), battle of 3, 11, 12, 13, 59, 66, 71–2, 103, 168
  250th anniversary of 18
  and Bengal's weavers 77
  as colonial conquest 3, 60
  effect on share prices 82, 87
  and intensification of corruption 83–4
Platform 188
Pliny 61
Polanyi, Karl 115
Polilur 123
Pollexfen, John 52
Poonamallee 68
Poplar 19
Portugal 45
  and Protestant Dutch revolt 42
  and spice trade 41–2
primitive accumulation 160
Pultenay, William 99
Punch 158, 164
Purnea 93

Qing dynasty 161, 176

racism 162
Rafael, Johannes Padre 112–13, 186, 187
Raj Bhavan 11
Rajshahi 93
Rangpur 123
Red Sea Telegraph Company 166
Reform Bill (1832) 153
Regulating Act (1773) 107–8, 119, 120, 124, 127, 128
Reynolds, Joshua 140
rice 91–2

Roe, Sir Thomas 44
Rohilkhand 120
Rohilla war 136
Roy, Arundhati 13
Roy, Ram Mohun 156
Royal African Company 23, 47, 174
royal charter 5, 23, 27, 43, 51
  see also chartered companies; East India Company, as chartered company
Royal Exchange 24
Royal Navy 174
Rumbold, Thomas 126
Run island 44
Russell, John 158
'Rusticus' 111
Rysbrack, Michael 2

Said, Edward 161
St Helena 6
St Matthias Church 19
Salim, Gulam Husain 55
salt trade 17, 64–5, 86, 119, 120
  tax 167
saltpetre 65, 75, 119
San Thome 68
Sandys, Sir Edwyn 45
sannyasin rebellion 73, 94, 123
Savarkar, Veer 163
Sayers, James 129
Scottish East India Company 45, 51
Scrafton, Luke 74
Seringapatam 144
Seven Years War (1756–63) 87, 104, 109, 168
Shah Alam II (Mughal emperor) 3, 73, 76
Shah Munju 94, 123
Shah Musa 123
Shelburne, William Petty, earl of 89, 126
Shell 186
Sheridan, Richard Brinsley 133, 135
Shujauddin 66
silk 46, 62, 156
silver 6, 63, 150
Sind, conquest of (1843) 158
Singapore 6, 162
Singh, Debi 123
Singh, Narayan 69
Sinha, Chandra Prakash 119
Sinha, N.K. 178
Siraj-ud-Daula 59, 64, 67, 68–9, 70–2, 117
slave trade 23, 47, 56, 174
Smith, Adam 4
  and colonialism 113, 139
  and corporate design 35, 61, 100–2, 113–14, 174–5, 182
  and free trade 35, 53, 99, 147, 149
  and monopoly power 35, 57, 101, 114, 180, 184, 185
Smith, Nathaniel 130–1
Smythe, Sir Thomas 8
Society of Trade 86, 119
South Sea Bubble 25, 29, 48, 56, 60, 89, 175
South Sea Company 8, 29, 56, 174
Sovabazar 58, 59
Spain, and spice trade 41
spice plantation 144–5
spice trade
  competing companies 39, 40–1
  East India Company and 42–4
  and violence 41–2
Spiridione Roma 1, 3, 4, 10, 38, 87, 172
Standard Chartered Bank 14
states, and accountability 181
Steengaard, Niels 42
Stepney Green 4
Strahan, William 113
Styche Hall, Shropshire 67
Sulivan, Lawrence 80, 84–5, 89, 96, 105, 180
Sulivan, Stephen 122, 180
supermarkets 184–5
Surat 32, 44, 46, 50

Taifoor, Syed Muhammed 148
Taiping rebellion 161
Tanjore, Rajah of 127
Tea Act (1773) 108, 110, 130
tea trade 3–5, 6, 98, 108–11, 149–50, 151, 152
  removal of tax 130

textiles 3, 11, 55–6, 61–3, 81, 146–9, 156, 160
  British protectionism 146–7, 148–9
Thompson, Edward 187–8
Thurlow, Edward 173
Tipu Sahib 144, 163
  clockwork tiger 10, 144
Townsend, Charles 109–10
Trading Places exhibition, British Library 14, 15–16
Trichinopoly 68

UN Commission on Human Rights 184
Union Carbide 37–8
United Company of Merchants Trading to the East Indies 54, 173
  see also East India Company
United Joint Stock 46
United States
  and corporations 115
  and international law 187
  see also America
Unocal 186, 187
unrequited trade 75–6, 177, 179

Valentine 89
Varanasi (Benares) 120, 133, 136
Verelst, Harry 112–13, 186
Victoria and Albert Museum 10, 14, 189
  Encounters exhibition 189
Victoria, Queen 157
Virginia Company 23
Virmanji, Arvind 13–14
Vodafone 73
Vondel, Joost van der 40

Wajid, Khwaja 64–5
Wal-Mart 36
Walford, Cornelius 90
Walpole, Horace 95
Walsh, John 85
War of the Austrian Succession (1740–48) 67
War of the Spanish Succession (1701–14) 67
Waterloo, Battle of (1815) 67, 146
Watson, Admiral Charles 69, 71, 172
weavers
  Bengal 76–8, 148–9
  England 52–3
  protest marches (London) 53
Wedderburn, General Alexander 173
Wellesley, Arthur (later Duke of Wellington) 9, 145
Wellesley, Richard 11, 144, 146, 151
Wilberforce, William 147
Wilkes, John 102
William III 50
Wilson, Henry 148
Window Tax 130
Wood, Charles 158–9
Wordsworth, William 9
World Trade Organisation (WTO) 185
Writer's Building, Calcutta 11

Yadana gas pipeline 187
Young, William 122

Ziegler, Jean 184